THE BOY AT THE GATE

THE BOY AT THE GATE

A Memoir

DANNY ELLIS

Arcade Publishing • New York

Arcade Publishing books may be purchased in bulk at special discounts for sales promotion, corporate gifts, fund-raising, or educational purposes. Special editions can also be created to specifications. For details, contact the Special Sales Department, Arcade Publishing, 307 West 36th Street, 11th Floor, New York, NY 10018 or arcade@skyhorsepublishing.com.

Arcade Publishing® is a registered trademark of Skyhorse Publishing, Inc.®, a Delaware corporation.

Visit our website at www.arcadepub.com.

10 9 8 7 6 5 4 3 2 1

Library of Congress Cataloging-in-Publication Data

Ellis, Danny, author.
The boy at the gate : a memoir / Danny Ellis.
    pages cm
Originally published: Dublin : Transworld Ireland, 2012.
ISBN 978-1-61145-892-3 (hardcover : alk. paper) 1. Ellis, Danny.
2. Singers—Ireland—Biography. I. Title.
ML420.E437A3 2013
780.92—dc23
[B]
                        2013012320

Printed in the United States of America.

This book is dedicated to institutionalized children everywhere.

PROLOGUE

I was born in the heart of Dublin City. In the same old one-bedroom tenement flat where my granny, eighteen years before, gave birth to my ma. Where the rats, emboldened by my poor marksmanship, would saunter over to the rug beneath the dining table and, finding no crumbs again, would dine where they left off last time: on the rug itself. Where the wooden shelves from cupboards and scullery, relegated like that rug to a station never intended by their makers, were chopped up for kindling with bread knife and rolling pin. Where Ma, at night, with Guinness and without Da, would sing for my two younger sisters and I by that little fire, her dark, beautiful voice so filled with emotion that she'd almost scare us. With eyes darting nervously around the room, following the shadows cast by the flames, we'd forget the hunger and the cold as the deep river of her voice held us like boats in the night.

Life was hard, turbulent, often violent, but always colorful.

Later, there was the drab corporation housing estate in Rathfarnham, where events too terrible for words spun our already unstable world completely out of control. Later still, there was the orphanage, the now infamous Artane Industrial School, where the laser malice of the Christian Brothers would imbue those earlier memories of Green Street with a haunted nostalgia they really shouldn't hold.

In Artane, the blessing of music captured my soul. Running like a mountain stream through the dark, ancient corridors of that harsh institution, it fought for my heart even as events hardened it; *where are you, my friend?* Even after I left the orphanage, as I fought desperately not to be defined by my past, as I buried it beneath my career and my quest for musical excellence, I felt music herself plead with me to slow down, to feel what was truly going on inside me.

And that's where this story begins: on the night music finally took me across half a century of avoidance, to face the lost child within me. In an ancient log cabin in the mountains of North Carolina, I found him, that cold December night, in a song.

The Boy at the Gate

CHAPTER 1

I am the shadow of the eagle hiding the coalfields
   from the sky
I am the water that's undrinkable, I am the tears you
   never cry
I am the sigh of endless yearning behind the burning
   of the day
I am the warrior remembering that I am the child
   who came to play.

   —DANNY ELLIS, "I CAME TO PLAY"

Liz and I call it Cooper's Cabin, after our landlord and friend Cooper Cartwright. I'm just back from my gig at the Mountain Air Country Club in Burnsville, where I sing during dinner. My wife is asleep in our tiny bedroom, where the wind sneaks through the chinking between the logs as easily as the ants. Her thirteen-year-old daughter, Irene, is also asleep upstairs. After I've checked on Irene, I creep into the bedroom for a sleepy kiss from Liz.

"How was the gig, sweetie?" She reaches out a hand to touch my cheek and is back asleep before I can answer.

I load up the firebox in the living room to the brim—enough wood, I hope, to last till morning. It's our only source of heat, our first departure from central heating. With the heat from the log fire wafting up over the open balcony, the loft is ten degrees warmer.

I catch my reflection in the picture of Liz and Irene on the wall behind the fire. I look very tired. My focus changes to look at the girls. I took this photo—Siesta Key Beach in Sarasota, Florida—a couple of years ago. It's my favorite picture of my girls. The palm trees in the background and the sugar-white sand in the foreground are exotic and evocative, but it's the look between Liz and Irene that gives the scene its strength; it fills the whole frame. That gaze characterizes their relationship. That deep, mother–child knowing never ceases to surprise and fascinate me. My focus changes once more and I'm looking at my own reflection again. I shrug off my vague dissatisfaction with the image. I step outside to fetch my keyboard from the Ford, and set it up in my studio: a tiny, separate building, five yards from the cabin.

Though I'm tired after the four-hour gig and the long drive home, I'm soon tinkling away on the keys as I let myself relax into the music. This is how I unwind: the hair of the dog. It works for me. Tonight, I'm a little fed up. I don't know why.

Maybe it's because Christmas is coming.

Usually, when I'm taken by this mood I'll start a new song. Something nice and sad that no one will ever hear. Thirty years of meditation have taught me to embrace emptiness as a friend. I'm always up for a little downward mobility. I've been here a thousand times. Down I go, playing the keys: lonely chords, seeped in the melancholy maybe only a certain type of Celtic music or Indian ragas are comfortable plumbing. Melodies rise, feelings fall; the sad notes are unashamed of their nakedness, proud of their vulnerability. I hum the cadence, letting it take me. The music articulates what words cannot. I let myself float, then sink more deeply. Words are taking form now, vowels and consonants springing freely from this primal surrender. I let them come up unedited—as I always do with a new song—without knowing their meaning. I barely comprehend them:

> 800 voices echo 'cross the grey playground
> Shouts of fights and God knows what
> I still can hear that sound.

Christ! It's him. The kids are playing in the orphanage school-yard! He's standing by the gate, watching them, petrified with fear. The song continues to unfold the playground tapestry within my body and soul. I'm transfixed, leaning over my keyboard, aghast that I've allowed this, but unable to stop:

> *With their hobnail boots and rough tweed*
> *Angry seas of brown and green*
> *The toughest godforsaken bunch that I had ever seen.*

Outside, the cold winter air falls heavily over Tanbark Ridge. It makes its way down through Bull Creek Valley to moan in the pine and poplar that grace the 150 acres of the Cartwright Farm. The wailing wind encourages the reverie. From a well deeper than I've ever drawn from, the song continues to write itself, the words springing up in phrases—as if already written:

> *I was taken 'cross the schoolyard*
> *In the cold December morn*
> *Through the games of ball and the wrestling kids*
> *All fighting to stay warm*
> *There I handed in my trousers and my khaki gabardine*
> *Farewell to the last reminders of a home in smithereens.*

Silent tears run down my cheeks. I can't stop this headlong descent into the memories of that first dreadful day in Artane. I'm not sure I want to stop it. My quivering lips can barely form the words:

> *I'll be back for you this Christmas*
> *I can hear my mammy say*
> *And the bitter truth within that lie*
> *I've yet to face today.*

Now I'm shaking, and the quiet tears have turned to heaving sobs, each one a wave surging up from my stomach to my chest. I can't believe I'm letting myself feel this. I'm thoroughly ashamed of myself. This isn't supposed to happen! It's the kind of indulgence I've avoided for nearly five decades. I've meditated my way past it, transcended it, shouted my way beyond it in rock 'n' roll songs in smoky pubs halfway around the world.

Now, here I am letting that whiny little eejit of an eight-year-old boy come through unbridled in a damn song, for God's sake. *Get a grip on yerself, yer falling apart here.* That's better. There ya go. Sorry 'bout that. Went a little bit mad there for a bit, didn't I? *Tighten up, man! Get above it.*

But another wave of sympathy for the boy breaks across my rationale, catching me between compassion and abhorrence. For a moment, compassion wins. Okay. Let's sing the damn song again and see what happens:

> *I'll be back for you this Christmas*
> *I can hear my mammy say*
> *And the bitter truth within that lie*
> *I've yet to face today.*

Surrendering to the feelings, I allow new words to spring up without conscious direction:

> *When it gets too much for feeling*
> *You just bury it somehow*
> *And that eight-year-old abandoned lad*
> *Still waits for her right now.*

That's it. It's all over. Those words, they'll never go back in again—ever. Under the cover of the melodies and the feelings, he slipped out past me when I wasn't looking. But I'm looking now and

I can see him. Feel him, too, and smell that rough orphanage tweed that chafes his thighs and wrists till they're blood raw. I hear him; *Mammy, Daddy, Mammy, Daddy, Mammy, Daddy, Mammy, Daddy.* There's a fire in the center of my chest, and again I give in to the heaving sobs. Thank God Liz can't hear them. I'll never play this song for her—or anybody else. This stuff is mad and I'm lost in it. But I'm breathing more deeply and freely than I've ever done. Why does it feel so bloody good to be so bloody lost?

I've been lost before, God knows. Meditation and contemplation have shown me some home truths about myself that shattered me to the . . . well, almost to the core. My personality is a fake, it's all made up, isn't it? Bits and pieces of stuff I've gathered from everyone, all held together by glue, Scotch tape, and hope-nobody-notices. It's been broken and rebuilt, challenged and found wanting so many times that I'm almost happy to have it fall apart every now and then so I can start over. But this is different. Till now, I always felt sure some angel of light would fix it from above; through meditation, the wisdom of the soul would trickle down and put everything right. Well, whatever is underneath my transcendence isn't getting any trickle-down. It's pissed off, with plenty to say, and I'm not at all sure I'm ready to hear it.

I lock up my studio and shuffle across the yard to the cabin in the cold. I'm a little unsteady on my feet and it's not because of the wind that's shaking the evergreens. As I creep into bed beside Liz, she sighs contentedly. She feels soft and warm—and whole. I snuggle up beside her in the dark, trying to stop processing what just happened.

But my mind is racing. No sleep tonight. After a while, I creep out of bed and tiptoe into the living room. I sit and stare at the fire. It's burning way too fast. *Adjust the damper, quick, for God's sake.* But it's too late. It's blazing far beyond turning down. *He's not going away, is he?*

Then it hits me like a smack in the face: I'm talking about a part of myself in the third person; my childhood self. I'm calling that part of myself *him*. My God! I've abandoned him just like everyone else did. This realization fills me with sadness. Something inside cracks open and I find myself asking softly, *Okay, what do you want to say to me?*

No answer. But at least now I'm calling him *you*. That's about halfway between *him* and *me*. Maybe that's close enough for now.

I stand up from the fire and stretch. I feel a little better. I get a drink of water, grab my old Washburn guitar from the hook on the cabin wall, and start to sing the song again—quietly, so as not to wake Liz or Irene. It feels so different on the guitar, more intimate and personal than the keys. I'm surprised to realize I want to finish the song, surprised to find that I don't want to lose him again.

I take down the old picture of the orphanage band from atop the oak cabinet: *The Artane Boys Band*. I've had that picture for almost four decades and I've barely glanced at it. But there he is now, in the back row, with the trombone section; God, but he's a sorry-looking sod! Lost as Lent, no trace of a smile, no glint in his eye. I look at him for a long while with mixed feelings of rejection, pity, and shame.

But I know what I must do. This is going to take a while—all night maybe. But after fifty years, what's the hurry?

I drape myself around the guitar, my chin resting on its waist. As my fingers strum the chords, deep within my breath something moves to make room.

Here they come: memories, gentle as the breezes that blew over Ireland from the Gulf Stream; sudden warmings in the dead of winter that lifted the drab, sunless mornings to new hope. Then they're cold and gray as the concrete of the orphanage playground where I was forced to hide my sorrow away like a deranged relative. Memories: soft and easy as the light from the old street lamps on Green Street, then hard and cruel as the leather strap across my legs on a cold day.

Right from the beginning, even before I had the words to record why, it was so easy for me to drift away into an inner world. The casual rejection of Ma and Da was surely present even before my first memory of it at the age of two. I had impetigo, my face was red, raw, and covered with sores. Da recoiled like he'd seen a leper as Ma tried to get him to hold me.

"Get that scabby git away from me, before I throw up."

"I've been rocking him for an hour and now it's your bloody turn. If he doesn't stop crying, I'll throw him out the shagging window."

Ah, yes, out the window. That's nice. Out I'll go and fly off like a bird. Pushed away from the harshness of their world into a realm of fantasy, I was already an expert at disengaging. Completely self-absorbed, left alone on the cold floor, hardly even noticing the chill, I'd still be in the exact same position when they turned back to me an hour later with the Guinness breath.

"Come to yer mammy, ya poor unfortunate crature. Yer bloody freezing with the cold."

Ah, that's what that funny feeling is—cold.

Hunger was the same.

"Ya must be starvin', son."

Oh, is that what you call it? I was wondering what that feeling was.

Barely aware of my body, my vacuous look drew more abuse than sympathy. "What's wrong with that bloody child?" relatives asked.

Nothing's wrong with me. I'm grand.

I probably came out of myself a little as my sisters were born—first Patricia, strong and willful, then Kate, sweet-natured and shy. When Da left for other shores to find work, the houseful of girls softened my remoteness a bit. But not too much; I still reserved the right to vanish inside myself at the drop of a hat. That was a skill I wasn't going to give up without a fight, a fight I would win until I was forced to show up by events on the Artane playground.

If I'd had the language then, I might have said I was being shaped by absence; absence of love, warmth, touch.

CHAPTER 2

Yeah, absence. It's all over the bloody place. Now, it's the absence of *Black Bob*, my Christmas present, that's causing all the trouble.

"Where's me *Black Bob* annual?"

My two younger sisters don't even look up from opening their presents, wrapped in yesterday's *Evening Herald*.

"What *Black Bob* annual?" Ma's pretending not to remember her promise.

"The one you said I'd be getting on Christmas morning."

"I never said any such thing." Ma rubs her belly tenderly. She's been doing that a lot lately.

"You did, Ma, didn't she, Patricia?"

"No, she didn't." I wish I had more important enemies than Patricia, but at least she's more than willing to be my first.

Ever since the day I played football with her orange, Patricia has hated me. I kicked that unfortunate orange all the way down Moore Street to Parnell Street and up Little Britain Street to join with the lads, John O and Jemser, on Green Street, booting it all the way to number nine, where we live. Finally, I carried it up the stairs, where Patricia lay sick in bed with the flu, for which the only cure, known to all in Ireland except meself, is an orange.

Ma meets me at the door. Behind her, Kate, my youngest sister, is holding Patricia's hand as she lies in Ma's bed in the living room. Ma's hand is outstretched for the magical cure. I give it to her and she drops it instantly.

"Jesus Christ, what happened to that bloody orange? It's squishy as a squashed fish." Ma groans. "What did you do to it?" A little smack on the head for me.

"It's not just my fault, Ma, I swear. Jemser and John O kicked it too, up the street like a football."

"I'll kick *you* up the street, you dirty-looking eejit. That orange is good for nothing now. You've kicked all God's goodness out the bloody thing. Patricia could have new-monia for all you care."

I wish she had, I thought, and as if she heard me, Patricia started up like she was a banshee trying out for a job on Halloween.

"Oh, me orange! It's all flat and floppy. I'm awful sick, that's what I am and I'll never get better now. Yer just a fecking bowsie, Danny Ellis!"

Ma smacks me across the head again. "Stop cursing, ya Protestant, or I'll banjax ya."

"I'm not cursing, Ma, it's Patricia."

"Don't call me Ma either. Call me Mammy. Only poor people call their mothers Ma."

The orange was months ago, and don't ask me why, but Patricia's still mad at me. Maybe she needs enemies too. No help there then, from her. So with *Black Bob's* absence laying the seeds of a lifelong hatred of Christmas in my six-year-old heart, I do the only decent thing a lad can do at my age. I run away. Later in the evening, as the girls are doing girly things with girly toys, I take off for America.

Patricia couldn't care less if I run away and I'm not sure about Ma. Patricia's full of a wild, quick fire, like the newspapers Ma burns when there's no wood. They flare up real fast and swoosh up the chimney. That's Patricia—blue-red flames quick as lightning. Wish I could give dirty looks like that; she could stop a bus. So she doesn't care less whether I run away to America or China. Kate cares, but she cares for everyone, so that doesn't really count. What's the use of having someone on your side who's also on everyone else's? But Katie is everybody's favorite. Her gorgeous blonde curls fall around her sweet, wide eyes like the golden, spirally Christmas decorations Ma's hung beneath the gas mantles on the walls. I love Katie and she loves me. I love Patricia too, but I wouldn't tell her, she'd probably . . . well, I don't know what she'd do cos I've never told her. Maybe I should tell her. But I'm afraid. I'll practice on Katie first. I give her a kiss. Katie's heart is as open as the gates of Smithfield Market on a Wednesday morning. She cried all day when I first started school at Halston Street. I'm her hero. If I wasn't afraid of me own shadow, I'd fight anyone who upset her. But she's too sweet to ever get upset at anyone, so my cowardice is never revealed.

But she's going to miss me in my absence. I'm off to the docks. I'll cadge a lift across the ocean on a boat and I'll meet Da in New York. He'll buy me a *Black Bob* annual and I'll join him in the American army. Wait, now. I'll need his address. I grab one of his letters from the stack behind the clock on the mantelpiece and stick it in me back pocket.

Da's letters from America—the red and blue borders on the envelopes, the crispy, important feel of the paper—always set my heart pounding, my imagination racing. Ma reads them feverishly, over and over. I watch as the faraway look in her eye slowly hardens and I wander off to play, confused.

Da is a hero when absent and a stranger when home. Heroes don't stay home. Like arrows, they're made to fly, and wherever they land, they don't belong there.

But I'll punch anyone who says I don't have a da—anyone smaller. I suppose I miss him—I'm not sure really. When he was here we didn't see him very much cos he wasn't here very much. He was always off somewhere else looking for work. Work seems very important to everybody, but I never understand why anyone would have to look for it. Ma complains sometimes: "There isn't enough hours in God's long day for all the work I have to do. Every bloody place I look, all I see is work, work, and more work."

So, if work is to be found everywhere, why is everyone always looking for it? I once heard Ma get real mad at Da, when he came home tipsy one Monday afternoon and crawled into bed. "If there was work in that bed, you'd sleep on the floor." I never saw him sleep on the floor so I knew work couldn't be in the bed. Where work was and where it wasn't seemed to decide whether or not we saw Da. But it looks like work is in New York cos Da's been there for a year now. And work must be in the army too—he's a soldier. At first, Ma thought that was all great, cos Da promised to save enough money to bring us all over to America. I thought that was great too.

America is the place in the Technicolor pictures we see at the Maro, the cinema on Mary Street. The English flicks are all in black and white and the American ones are in color. America is beautiful in lovely reds and blues and greens, and England is boring in stupid grays and blacks. No wonder there's work in America; that's where I'd be if I was work. Maybe God is in America. And the way Americans talked, all slow and low and smooth: "Git yore hands up." Not all fast and squeaky like the English: "I say old chap, can you spare a fag?"

There's a troubled look in Ma's eye when she says the word *America* these days. But that's where Da is and that's where I'm headed. I run down Green Street toward the quays. The street is empty. So is the little park by the courthouse. My footsteps echo between the brick of the tall tenement buildings to my left and the park wall to my right. I run past Clark's grocery and the barber's shop in the middle of the flats. I pause at the pub on the corner, to run my shoe over the metal grating of the pub's cellar a couple of times, like I always do. The eight or ten feet of pavement between the buildings and the road is wider than most. Ma says it's to give the men some staggering-room when they fall out of the pub at night, drunk and singing loudly.

As I cross the wet cobblestones into Smithfield Market, here comes the Liffey stench. It's a slow, sly sort of a smell. Like the silent farts me sisters and I let fly beneath the blanket at night, when me Ma is out late with her friends. Ma hates the Liffey smell. On warm days it makes its way north to Green Street. Walking home from school, sometimes I'll make a mark on the ground when I'm not able to smell it any more, then walk backward with my eyes closed till I can smell it again. It's a different spot every day.

"Close that bloody window before we all faint, for Christ's sake," I once heard Ma say to her brother, my Uncle Matty. "Why don't they just dredge the damn thing so we can all breathe again?"

"You can't go dredging the Liffey," Uncle Matt said impatiently. "You'd poison the whole city with the years of shite clumped beneath it. Better leave well enough alone."

Maybe that's a good idea.

—⁂—

"What's that song, Danny? It's beautiful." I spin around from the fire. Flustered, I bang my guitar on the chair. Liz is back from shopping. I didn't hear her come in behind me.

"Nothing really. It's just something I've been working on." It's been three days and I still haven't plucked up the courage to sing her the song. Normally, I bounce every line of every new composition past her. Not this one—not yet.

But she's caught me. I'm strumming idly, avoiding her eyes. She stays quiet. After an awkward minute, I say nervously, "This is something . . . I mean, it's not really anything . . . Anyway, don't worry about it. It'll never see the light of day."

I try to grin but it's a grimace. She doesn't respond.

"Look, it's not anything I'll ever sing to anyone else. It's just something from my past that sprung up from I don't know where . . . I'm still working on it, I may not even finish it . . . Oh, for God's sake, listen."

She sits down opposite me, mildly concerned with my manner. I start the song"

800 voices echo 'cross the grey playground . . .

I'm barely able to keep my voice from breaking and I'm ashamed of where the song is taking me. Halfway through, I force myself to look over at Liz. Her eyes are swimming in tears. When I finish, there's a long silence.

"You have to finish that song, sweetheart." Her voice is very soft. "That child has something very important to tell you."

—⁂—

Yeah, listen. I'm running away to America. The Liffey smell's getting stronger and stronger. I run down Arran Street and turn left on to Ormond Quay toward the lights on Capel Street Bridge. Its real name is Grattan Bridge, but nobody in Dublin calls it by that stupid name. I cross the wet road and climb the iron ladder that curves over the river wall and look down into the dirty-green water below and breathe it all in slow and deep.

A seagull squawks above. Below, the cigarette packs—Players, Sweet Afton, and Woodbines—the Guinness bottles and banana peels, the bits and pieces of Dublin's shame, all float lazily by. *Anna Liffey, you're not the lass you used to be*, they say. *Your body holds the sins you never committed.* Below and above, Dublin City speaks through you as much as through its songs.

But Black Bob! He'd jump in there now in a flash. So would I if it was summer and I could swim. It's not and I can't, so I don't. But I do the next best, stupidest thing. I climb down the ladder holding on to the freezing iron rungs. When I get to the bottom, eight feet below, I hang on tight to the ladder and imagine I'm on the boat to New York.

Then I see it, downriver a bit—a comic! Gone are thoughts of sailing to Da and here comes . . . wait, it's *Steve Canyon*, in full American color. I'm down on the last rung as the comic comes on the slow promise of the incoming tide. My arse is an inch from the water as the comic floats toward me and with one hand on the ladder I stretch to grab it greedily.

Aargh!! I'm spitting filthy water out of me mouth and coughing and screaming me head off all at the same time. Down I go again. Now I know why the Liffey smells so bad. Shite! Vomiting and choking and I'm not screaming any more. *I'm sorry, Ma—I don't care about the* Black Bob *annual. Stupid dog! I knew you didn't have the money for it anyway, Ma. Patricia, I love you, and I'm sorry about kicking your orange kicking your orange and jingle bells jingle bells jingle home for Christmas.*

A strong hand grabs me by the scruff of the neck. I'm being lifted up the ladder like a rat, still vomiting. I'm dragged over the wall and on to the pavement, coughing and crying.

"Yer all right son, yer all right now, son. There ya are, now. That was too close for comfort, wasn't it? Christ, what a way to spend Christmas."

Gray-haired and unshaven, his dirty clothes are as black as his toothless grin, and the smell of Guinness on his breath is overpowering the Liffey. Cold eyes look at me from under wild bushy eyebrows. The relief and gratitude I feel are mixed with a feeling in my gut that won't leave, even as he shakes me to keep me warm.

"What in the name of Jaysus were ya trying to do? I saw ya climbing down the ladder and thought to meself, has he dropped something?"

It's then I notice that I'm still holding the *Steve Canyon* comic in me right hand. Just in case it was his comic I blurt quickly, "Yeah, me comic, me comic!! I dropped me comic." It's mine now, he's not getting it back.

"Yer comic was nearly the death of ya, son."

Great! It's not his comic.

"Let's get you and yer comic home to yer mam and dad before we all famish with the cold."

"Me da's in America, it's only me ma," I blurt and immediately regret it. He's stopped breathing, and so have I.

He grins and his eyes half-close for a second. "Yer mother will make us a nice cup of tea then."

That's when my belly did an odd, cold turn and it wasn't from the filthy Liffey water I'd swallowed either. I'm looking up at him through the steam of me breath in the dark of the evening and I'm shaking and it's not from the cold.

"Where do ya live?"

I grit my teeth hard. Slowly, a funny feeling creeps all over me, like another person, only it's me, a harder, darker me. *Black Daniel.* Hot and sure, the feeling moves up from my belly to the top of my head. For the first time in my whole life I see a way to control things. It feels like I'm suddenly six feet tall. I stop trembling. I shake the water out of me shoes with strong kicks.

"Bolton Street. Number forty-five," says I. Massive! How easy it is to make things up! I kick my legs a bit more and go on making up stuff: "Close to the fish and chipper, up past the bookies on the left . . ."

He interrupts me impatiently and the grin is gone. "C'mon then. C'mon."

As we walk along I say, "I have a big brother, Seamus, he's a policeman. He's very strong, y'know. He can lift me up with one hand." I'm enjoying this new make-up-stuff trick and besides, I'm gathering reinforcements in case I need them.

He stops suddenly and grabs me by the collar. "I thought you said it was only yer ma."

Christ! You have to be careful with this trick. You have to remember what you made up earlier. "Yeah, it's only me ma and me sisters and me big strong brother Seamus. He's big as a house and very bad-tempered."

He grins and I know he doesn't believe me. I took it too far. But that's all right; I have another idea.

When we get to Green Street, I know exactly what I'm going to do. The street is empty, but the hall doors of the tenements are all open as usual. No locks on Green Street. Nothing worth stealing. When we get to number seven, I bolt through the front door, down the dark hallway, out into the backyard, and over the wall and into number eight's yard before he can turn and see I'm not beside him any more. I crouch by the wall with my heart bursting out of my ribs and my breath heaving like a train and I'm not a bit cold any more. Trying to tame my breathing, I hear him shuffling and cursing at the backyard door of number seven.

"Shite! He's bloody scanoodled. The lying bastard!"

Ah, that's what making up stuff is called: lying. Always wondered about that.

—⁂—

I follow the gravel driveway down to the path that circles the Cartwright Farm. Up the looped trail I go, through the woods and along by the stream. I'm smiling wryly to myself, remembering the Liffey Man affair: the birth of my alter ego, Black Daniel. God knows, it's happened to every child in history, but for me, as I recognize that first, dizzy adventure in falsehood, I'm amazed at the long, winding road it's led me down. Once I learnt how to lie there was no going back. With the disregard for truth echoing all around me, I never thought about it in terms of right or wrong. It was simply the most sensible way forward in a pinch. I'd lied before, hot little denials to escape blame or punishment. But with the Liffey Man it was very different. This was a calm, calculated attempt to manipulate a scary situation and it changed the way I operated forever. I didn't know what I was doing or why I lied to him, but although I was only six, I knew enough to trust the instinct and it felt good—in fact, it was intoxicating. That man who saved my life may have deserved better, but the sense of danger, real or imagined, was more primal than the gratitude. With his filthy black overcoat and smelly Guinness breath, he was not getting past our door—Black Daniel made sure of that. I saw the Liffey Man again, weeks later, on Capel Street, and the dark look he gave me made me think I'd been right. But with this exciting new power I'd discovered, nothing would ever be certain again: whether he was mad at me for betraying his heroism or because I'd foiled his plan to murder us all, I'll never know. Deception confuses the deceiver more than the deceived.

—w—

Ah, but did I pull the wool over his eyes or what? I can't wait to try it out on Ma. I climb the wall between yards number eight and nine. In a jiffy, I'm up the stairs, in the door home, dripping wet and shivering.

"Jesus, Mary, and Joseph, would ya look at the cut of ya?" Ma is more worried than mad.

I'm trying out my new trick. What did the Liffey Man call it? Lying.

"I was walking down by the Liffey, minding me own business, when this bunch of lads caught me and threw me in the water." I'm warming up to the story, with loads of great add-ons ready, when the look on Ma's face stops me dead. She'd been looking at the dripping comic in my hand and now her eyes, beautiful and full of understanding, rise to meet mine.

"Ah, for Jaysus' sake, you'd swim the Liffey itself for a *Steve Canyon* comic." She winks. "Santy is looking out for you after all, eh? Come in, you saturated heap of misery, before you freeze to death."

You don't get too many hugs around Green Street, but I'm getting plenty tonight and I'm not sure why. *Steve Canyon* is drying by the turf fire, Ma is singing to us in her dark, beautiful voice, and Christmas 1953 is behaving itself at last.

CHAPTER 3

John O'Shea is about my age. He lives near the corner by the pub and we swap comics. *Thanks John O, but I've seen that one already.*

No ya haven't, it's just come out today, ya eejit!

Before we started school, my ma would spend hours talking to his ma and we became friends as the mothers talked in our front room. We don't have a back room. That's the scullery, the kitchen. My sisters and I sleep in the bedroom next to the living room.

While our mothers gossiped, John O and me would escape to my room to watch the American War. It's my life's work. It covers the whole of the wall behind our bed. Most of the paper's been stripped from the wall, exposing the white plaster. I have Ma's permission to make it pretty: millions of soldiers and tanks and planes and artillery, all drawn in crayons. Whenever I need to get away for a while and think, I'll add to it. John O always wants to draw something, but I never let him. That's my war.

One day I learnt a shocking secret: every time she'd gossip with Mrs. O'Shea, Ma would send me and John O to fetch two bottles of milk from Clark's grocery shop, promising a ha'penny each if we got back before she counted to twenty. As we'd come up the stairs with the milk, Ma would hear us coming and we'd hear her start counting: "Nineteen and a quarter, nineteen and a half, nineteen and three-quarters, ah, there yez are, just in time too." After weeks of hearing nineteen's subdivided talents sung daily, John O and I decided to really put it to the test and see just how far nineteen could be stretched. We took our time on the way to the shop, playing and gallivanting there and back. An hour later, milk bottles in hand, we crept silently up the stairs. Of course, there were no nineteens, quartered or halved or otherwise dismembered. All we heard was me ma: ". . . and if she ever looks at me in that tone of voice again I'll kick her fat arse into the middle of next week." The secret was out! Ma can't count past nineteen.

—ᴍ—

"Ma, can I come out and listen?" The girls are fast asleep beside me. I can hear Ma talking in the living room by the fire with her friend, my Aunt Deirdre. She's not related to us, but I like calling her aunt. I need all the help I can get here. They're talking about holy stuff.

"Sure, I know, Deirdre, Jesus died for our sins and if he wants to punish me for mine then I'll have to live with it. How can he blame me for wanting some company? Loneliness is a terrible thing," Ma says.

She's not answering my request to join them so I take a different tack.

"Ma, can I come out and listen to yez talk about Jaysus—I mean Jesus." *Jesus* for praying, stupid, *Jaysus* for cursing.

"Let him come in, Frances, he'll be good, I promise." Aunt Deirdre was always ready to talk about God and Jesus. I'm in the living room before Ma can object. A big kiss for Ma and the same for Deirdre. Ma, caressing her belly again, looks like she's too tired to put up a fight.

"C'mon, son. Sit on me lap an we'll talk about Jesus. God knows I'll be needing his help soon enough."

I jump on Ma's lap.

"That's all Jesus does, Frances. He only wants to help us through our trials and trivialations," Deirdre says softly. We're all quiet for a while. The atmosphere is lovely. Ma starts to sing. It's a song we all know: "The Butcher Boy." It's a bit of a depressing song, but Ma likes depressing songs and I love to hear her sing, no matter what:

In Dublin town where I did dwell
A butcher boy I loved so well
He courted me my life away
But now with me he will not stay.
I wish, I wish, I wish in vain
I wish I was a maid again
But a maid again I ne'er will be
Till apples grow on an ivy tree.
I wish my baby it was born

Tears have been filling her eyes. She often gets like that when she sings, but as she gets to that last line she chokes up completely. She can't go on . . . but me and Deirdre know the song well and we help her out:

I wish my baby it was born
And smiling on his daddy's knee
And me poor girl to be dead and gone
Let the long green grass grow o'er me.

By the end of it, we're all a little teary. Who the hell wants to be dead and gone?

"Honest to God, Deirdre, I don't know what I'm going to do now."

She doesn't know what song to sing next? I do.

"I know a good one, Ma," says I. This'll cheer her up. Before they can stop me I start singing:

I'll tell me ma when I go home
The boys won't leave the girls alone
They pulled my hair, they stole my comb
But that's all right till I go home.
She is handsome, she is pretty

She is the belle of Belfast city
She is a courting one, two, three
Please, won't you tell me, who is she?

"That's just bee-yooti-ful, Danny, so it is." Deirdre reaches over and pats my head kindly. I look around at Ma and she's smiling very sweetly though her tears. There's not a more beautiful face in the whole of Ireland.

We're all quiet again now for a long moment. I can feel the movement of Ma's belly against my back as I sit on her lap. She's breathing slowly and deeply as we sit in the silence. The turf fire is hissing softly.

The little alarm clock on the mantelpiece is tick-tocking away. The gas mantles flicker.

Deirdre ruins it.

"God gives us strength to face whatever He sends us. There's no storm too windy, no sea too watery, and no mountain too hilly." She's getting carried away: "His mercy will guide us, no matter what. Jesus, Mary, and Joseph help us all to find our way."

Her sincerity is lovely, but I wish she'd bloody well kept quiet. Ma nods her head sadly. Why should God's help make everyone so sad? It must be the watery seas and the hilly mountains.

But the holy moment doesn't last long for Ma. "Ah, go on Deirdre, ya shoulda been a bloody nun. Next ya know we'll all be on our knees saying the Rosary."

"And no harm it'd do us at all, at all."

Ma stands up as she puts me on the floor. "Okay, that's enough. Off to bed with ya, young man." The spell's all gone now. What's wrong with people? Why can't they all just stay quiet and leave the storms and the winds out-bloody-side where they belong?

"It's time for me to get on home." Deirdre kisses me and goes to the door with Ma behind her. They're standing whispering by the open door. I'm pretending not to listen.

"I'm off to see the doctor on Friday. Please God it's nothing. I just can't afford another child. It's hard enough as it is." Ma's voice is tense. What's so bad about buying a baby?

There's a real funny feeling in the air that I don't like. I'm looking around the room to get away from it. A picture in a nearby newspaper catches my eye. I know! It's time for a favorite game—the Photo People. It's great fun.

This photo is a man; he's grinning his head off. Let's see if we can change that. I tear the picture out as Ma goes out to the landing to whisper some more to Deirdre. I put the smiling man on the smoldering turf fire carefully, face up. I've done this kind of thing a dozen times before. It always ends the same, but it always amazes me. It's been a bit of a sad evening, so it'll be interesting to see if something different happens. Something sad maybe?

But no.

As the flames creep up his legs and body to his head, his big smiling face doesn't show the slightest bit of pain. Massive! Brutal! If anything, his grin seems even bigger than before. No matter what I do to the Photo People, it doesn't make the slightest difference to the looks on their faces. Burn 'em, stick pins in 'em, drown 'em. They feel nothing. No pain. They are unreachable. It's magic.

—⁂—

Why would we be born with such a capacity to feel, with such a throbbing, vulnerable sentience, into a world that seems hell bent on forcing us to close down those feelings? How I envied the Photo People. How I longed to freeze my feelings. But I succeeded too well, I'm sure of that; maybe I don't even know to what degree. But I know it's time for those frozen parts to breathe again. I've enlisted Liz's help.

"How would you feel about letting me ramble on about my early memories? No big deal, just a conversational type of thing. It might even be fun. If something strikes you, make a note, or ask me to elaborate if you feel it's pertinent," I asked her the other day.

Liz was cautious. "Hmm. I think it may help. But I'm not sure I want to take the role of prodding your pain. Are you sure you won't react negatively?"

"Don't worry, I promise to alert you if you're getting too near the bone." I laughed.

I can barely remember the little flat in Spain where Liz and I first lived together, but after fifty years, I can still recall every tenement house on Green Street and who lived there. Of the dozens of places I've lived on two continents, the street where I was born remains the most vivid in my memory. Like many streets in the poorer areas of Dublin City center, Green Street was a kaleidoscope of characters and events that blazed across the cobblestones: the courthouse, with its constant stream of cops and scoundrels; the judges and solicitors, their posh attire contrasted sharply, almost comically, against that of the residents; the little park where the men played cards all day long; the handball alley and the haunted statue—a man with a dog, which local legend had it crapped on the grass in the night when everyone slept, any stool in the morning damp proof enough. The pub, to which the men would wander down of an evening, one by one, their hands deep in their overcoat pockets, their collars turned up against the cold, eyes looking down at the pavement as if in hope of finding a *tanner*, a sixpence to pay for the *gargle*—the Guinness they'll down by the gallon. The grocery store and the barber's where Ma had accounts, forever rising and seldom falling; the drab, terraced tenements with three flats apiece, each flat more often than not housing three generations at once.

Weekday mornings I'd wake to hear the cheerful *clickety-clack* of larry O'Toole's old horse and cart delivering groceries to the grocer, Mr. Clark.

"Morning, Mr. Clark. How is she cutting?" Larry would ask as he sorted out the grocer's order.

"Ah, sure she's cutting rightly, Larry." The stock reply to an old greeting. "What's the use in complaining? But I'll be needing more spuds than that," Clark would often grunt. "There's not much meat being bought these days. Vegetable stew! That's all they're eating at the minute. If things don't get better soon it'll be potato and point for us all."

Potato and point: a reference to the legend about the hard times back when the starving Irish would hang a hunk of meat over the table on a string and rub the potatoes against it for a bit of flavor. When the meat was gone they'd continue to point the potatoes at the dangling string. Times haven't changed much. *What's for dinner, Ma? Potato and point.*

Larry's horse, Shane, a noble, golden animal who looked like Roy Rogers's Trigger, would eat oats gently from my hand and grace the cobblestones with steaming manure that smelled like the countryside. I always knew what Larry was thinking. He had a way of looking at you that didn't need words to make his point. Larry inspired a trust rare in Smithfield. Sometimes he let me ride with him on his rounds and help him with deliveries. How I loved the lazy amble through the Dublin streets: the bikes, buses, and the cars, the drunks and the newspaper boys. All the traffic policemen knew Larry and saluted as Shane passed by, chewing his oats from his nosebag. Larry sat easily, a cigarette dangling from his lips, his right eye half closed, squinting from the smoke, one hand in the pocket of his brown Carton Bros. overalls and the other loosely holding the reins between his nicotine-stained fingers. The hand in the pocket often fingered sweets that he'd chuck back at me from time to time as I sat in the back on a sack among the eggs, the fruit, and the vegetables.

—⁓—

"Thanks, Larry." It's a gobstopper. The kids are mad jealous of my adventures with Larry and Shane. I keep them quiet with these sweets—my wages. Anything that isn't nailed down is fair game for all of us on Green Street, but for me, Larry's cart is strictly off limits. I wouldn't betray his trust for all the apples in Carton Bros., although with the many hints from Ma, I'm often tempted. Anyway, Shane would kick my arse proper for me. He looks back sometimes, when Larry is inside a shop delivering groceries, as if to say, *Go on, lad, just try it and watch what happens.* He's my guardian angel, that horse. I wish we had a big field in our backyard where he could run, instead of being penned up in the smelly old livery down the road where he sleeps at night.

All this week, Larry's deliveries have taken us south across the Liffey and I'm getting to know the city and all the little shops real well. Dogs are always barking at Shane, who never even bats an eyelid. I get mad though; "Feck off yez mangy old mongrels." But Shane won't even look at them. It's a great thing to be able to do, ignore things.

Larry knows how to ignore stuff too. Earlier today, during a delivery, when I asked him does his mammy cry all the time like mine, he just continued writing in his little notebook, licking his pencil till his lips and tongue were black. Wish I could do that. If I could, maybe next time Ma asks me where I got the tin soldier I stole from someone, I'll just squint my eyes like Larry and keep looking at my soldier like she's not even there. But I couldn't manage that to save my life. When Ma asks me a question, I'm answering even before I know it, and next thing I know, I'm getting my ears boxed. Maybe only grown-ups know how to ignore things. Maybe it takes practice. Okay, then, let's see if I can do it. Now, as the cart crawls up George's Street, I'm sitting waiting for Larry to say something so I can ignore him. But he doesn't say a word—not for ages. When he makes the sign of the cross as we pass by a little chapel on our right, I see my chance. I ask, "Why do people bless themselves when they pass a church, Larry?"

"It's a sign of respect, son, for God—who lives in there." Great! I completely ignore him and look away behind at a bus. But Larry doesn't even notice I'm ignoring him. Shite! It's very frustrating when people ignore the fact that you're ignoring them.

Okay, I get it. People only notice you're ignoring them when you don't answer their question. So *he* has to ask *me* a question, then I can ignore him properly, like a grown-up. So, the question is, how can I get him to ask me a question? After a while I say, "You'll never guess what time me ma got home last night, Larry." Larry sighs wearily, looks at me kindly for a long while, squints through the cigarette smoke, and ignores me. How the hell did he do that? I give up.

When we stop at the next shop, Larry rubs my head roughly and says, "Don't try to grow up too quick, son. There's plenty in your world to keep you busy for a while yet."

The shopkeeper is happy to see us and the pocketful of sweets he gives me keeps me occupied on the jaunt home. I count and sort them into bunches for my own little deliveries later, to the kids on Green Street: John O, Jemser and his sister Shelagh, Gunner-eye, Paddywhack, and if I'm in a really good mood, my sisters.

—ᴧᴧ—

Any strangers passing through Green Street are met with dirty looks till we've seen them a few times. Then we give them nicknames. That makes them all right to us—though most hate their nicknames.

"Here comes ol' Squinty Eye."

"Watch out for the Badger."

"Make way for Birdie."

From a dozen others, Birdie is my favorite, probably because he never yells at me when I call him "Birdie." *There ya are, Birdie.* Apart from his constant, sleepy half-grin, Birdie's walk is the only information you'll ever get from him. He walks as if he isn't going anywhere at all and has all day to get there. He walks like the camel I saw in the desert picture at the Maro back awhile. All gangly and slow, he seems to spend more time in the air than he does on the ground. An invisible string seems to be attached to his head and halfway through his step, some mischievous angel pulls the string gently from above and, for one impossible second, both of Birdie's feet leave the ground at once. When he walks, the whole street goes into slow motion: the lads kicking the tin can; the skipping rope and the kids jumping in and out of it, chanting rhymes; the men, out of work, playing cards on the park bench for cigarettes. When Birdie walks down Green Street, we all surrender like an orchestra to a conductor.

Yeah, but I'd love to walk like that. I've been studying him carefully. I try it out whenever I remember, which is usually when Shelagh Carney comes into view. She's never impressed. My heroes are never anyone else's heroes and my imitations of them make no sense. It's like imitating Roy Rogers's cowboy accent to a country farmer who's never seen a cowboy picture in his life. The result is always the same: a puzzled Shelagh and an embarrassed me.

Shelagh won't let me kiss her. Not for sweets, or even toy soldiers. She says I have ears as big as baking potatoes, a face as long as Leinster, and arms and legs and chest so skinny I could fit through the metal grating over the pub's cellar by the corner. But there's one part of my body I'm happy with: I have a scar on my face from a turnip. Well, not exactly from a turnip, but from a milk bottle thrown at me after I threw the turnip at Jemser, Shelagh's brother.

Jemser lives next door at number eight. We play cards together all the time. He's good at poker and pontoon, but not as good as me. I've learned a few tricks from the men in the park.

One day we were sent shopping by his ma. Walking down Little Britain Street, Jemser was carrying the bag of groceries. We were playing Catch the Turnip, back and forth. I had both hands free while Jemser's left hand held on to the groceries. Just as the turnip was flying through the air toward Jemser, Paddywhack Flynn called him from across the street, waving a hurley stick.

Jemser turned his head and took the turnip full in the stomach. Down he went to the ground, winded. If God should be thanked that the bottle of milk in the bag he was carrying didn't break, it won't be by me.

"Ya dirty, fecking bastard!" Still on the ground, Jemser let fly with the half-pint bottle. It hit me smack in the kisser and my left cheekbone did something the pavement didn't have the decency to do—it broke that bottle in a thousand pieces. The result was Jemser's ma and my ma never spoke again, Jemser and I became best friends, and I have a handsome, two-inch scar that'll forever make lads think twice about picking on me. I hope.

The doctor who stitched me up thought I was a brave man, but Ma wasn't impressed by my bravery or my scar. "Any more of that carry on and it'll be Artane School for you, me bucko. Believe you me, the Christian Brothers will smarten your hump for ya."

—⁓—

"How can a mother threaten her children with abandoning them?" Liz is incredulous.

"I dunno. But even now, nearly forty years after leaving Ireland, I'll occasionally run into someone who was threatened by his parents with Artane Industrial School. It was an old trick in Ireland. Kept the kids in line. But it failed gloriously."

Everybody on Green Street knew about Artane—maybe everybody in Ireland. We all knew about the Christian Brothers too: they were the boogiemen, the Hard Men in Black, the hit men of Catholic Ireland. One day they'll come to take you away to a dark place where, with society's blessing, they'll "make a man of you" or "sort you out" or, more explicitly, "beat some sense into you." The implication was you were bad to your core and only the roughest treatment would save your soul. Those threats, delivered with dreadful looks and tones, felt real enough to fill me with such fear that I simply buried it in the same hole where I buried the fear of death or ghosts.

But I must have sensed there was something strange about this use of terror to enforce good behavior because I pushed back at it, testing its validity and stretching its limits at every opportunity with a rebel zeal that bordered on the heroic. Maybe I sensed that by using such tactics the adults had lost their moral authority. But somehow I felt I had permission from the powers-that-be to wreak havoc. Depending on circumstances, everything was up for grabs: truth, money, property, toys—and, on Wednesdays, vegetables.

—ɯ—

Yeah, I hate vegetables. Hate them all. Except potatoes and soft, boiled cabbage. Maybe carrots if they're real soft and there's a bit of butter. Or a nice turnip if it's mashed, with a shake of pepper, don't forget the butter—and salt. But I'll eat anything when I'm hungry. I'm always hungry. I'm hungry now. I love vegetables. Especially on Wednesdays. That's when vegetables taste the best. Cos on Wednesdays, vegetables are free, in the morning, real early.

That's when Smithfield Market is filled with vegetables. Gallons of them—just lying there, asking for it. The market's in the middle of the big, cobblestone square close to the Liffey, five minutes' walk from our house and two minutes' run back. Ah, the run back—a mad thing it is too, my heart pounding, my hands full of stolen—I mean free—vegetables. And some man chasing after me, puffing too, his belly curling over the twine that keeps his trousers from joining the veggies I'm dropping.

The craziness starts with Ma waking me at some ungodly hour. "Up ya get, it's market day. A nice big head of cabbage first, son, and if they don't see ya, back later for a few spuds."

Half asleep, I barely avoid the vans screaming around corners and across the cobblestones, vegetables flying out of the stacked boxes in the back. Sometimes I just pick some up off the ground and head home for my first delivery. But mostly I'm late, arriving after the vans have been unloaded. Heart pounding, I wander through the market, trying to look like a helper or the son of a vendor. I find the right stall—potatoes or cabbages or carrots or . . . Ugh! Bloody parsnips! No thanks! Wait for the right moment, the right veggie, grab it, and run like blazes.

"That's my big man of the house!" Ma's smile, hard won, makes it all worthwhile and off I go again, back and forth till I'm caught or exhausted. Getting caught is real scary, but it's never more than a clip around the ears or a kick in the arse. I'm used to that stuff. But the whole thing makes me edgy.

For now though, a great big steaming bowl of vegetables in the damp of the evening will keep us all going for a bit. No butter? Ah, well, a bit more salt then.

CHAPTER 4

Ma throws the empty Woodbine packet into the grate in disgust.

"Jaysus, and the price of fags. I'd give anything for a puff."

I'm sitting on the floor, looking up at her as she rummages through her handbag looking for a cigarette butt.

"Why don't you make your own, Ma? Jemser Carney's da does."

She laughs. "You need tobacco and papers and where would I get the money for either?"

Then I have a great idea! Down I go to Capel Street, where there's always more people than anywhere in Smithfield. Eyes glued to the pavement, I walk along slowly, looking for discarded cigarette butts.

There's one there! No, that's too small. That's too squashed. That's a beauty! Too much lipstick on that one. Too wet. Ah, perfect!

With ten minutes' pickings my pocket's full and back home I go to Green Street and into number eight, where I cadge a packet of cigarette papers from Jemser's da, and with half an hour's practice on the bench in the park by the handball alley, breaking the burnt bits off the butts, I soon have a dozen slightly bandy cigs to proudly present to Ma.

Laughing uncontrollably at the wonky-looking fags, she lights one up eagerly. "Danny, sweetheart, where on God's earth did you get these?"

I tell her. She goes very quiet and she walks over to the window, looking out across to the courthouse. But she's still smoking and though she doesn't say another word I'm over the moon. She's proud of me.

Those cigs are soon gone, but a wink from Ma and two fingers to
her lips in a pretend-smoking move are enough to send me haring it
down to Capel Street again like a shot. I'm yer man!

Yes, I'm yer man all right! A man you don't meet every day.
Especially at night. Often in the evenings Ma will call me over when
the girls are pretending not to listen and she'll whisper, "Son, I need
you to be a big man for me again tonight. I'm going to be out late, and
if the girls get scared I'm depending on you to take care of everything
for me. Can you do that for me now, tonight, son?"

Enthusiastic nod from meself.

"That's my big brave man!"

Sometimes, we'll have a babysitter—Mary Durcan or Fran
Black. Mary is lovely. She's got long, red hair and big, soft eyes and
always smiles at me. I like Fran too. She's more serious than Mary.
She lives down the street at number five. Her ma, Maggs, makes great
corned beef. You can smell it all the way to the handball alley. That
smell would draw me through the door, where Maggs, nice flowery
apron around her nice belly, would say, "What took ya so long? Here
ya are. Get on the outside of that before yer ma catches us." Ma
doesn't like me eating anywhere else besides home. Which means
she doesn't like me eating.

But there's no babysitter tonight. I'm going to be in charge again.
Ma keeps winking over at me as she gets ready to go out. "That's my
big strong man."

She's lovely. Long auburn hair and green eyes shining like stars.
I watch her burn a match, blow it out, wet the end of it, and draw the
black across her eyebrows with quick little sideways glances in the
mirror. Then she's gone. I'm the big man of the house again. That's
great. I think.

My big strong man—how good it feels to hear Ma speak to me
like that. The steady look in her eyes as she leaves fills me with
strength and courage; I'm a soldier, a hero defending my family,

fighting off all foes. But the night is a strange enemy and loneliness is hard to fight. After three nights alone with the girls, the thrill of being in charge has dimmed and bravery disappears like the dying flames of the gas mantles. Radio Luxembourg is on and soon the girls are asleep. *I'm scared. No, I'm not. Yes, you bloody well are. Go away, sleep! Can't ya see I need to take care of everything? Tighten up!* There ya are, Black Daniel, that's better. Okay. I'll just sing along with the radio again: *"La, la, la, la, la . . ."*

The radio drifts in and out of the station and my mind tries to follow, but it's drifting too.

Static scratches a hole in the song and a strange foreign voice doesn't know how to speak proper but the Canadians are insisting that the gray misty haze trying to swallow me up is not going to sleep till Ma gets home cos the song is different now.

—⁂—

Ma's home. I'm up to greet her at the door, but the hated smell of Guinness stops me in me tracks. A man's voice curses in the dark behind the half-open door. Ma shuts it with a bigger bang than she intends.

"Sweeeetheaaart! My big brave chap, why aren't ya asleep?"

Kisses, sloppy Guinness kisses, and I'm wiping my mouth in confused rejection of something I can't begin to understand. Why mess up a lovely kiss with Guinness, for Christ's sake? She tucks me into bed beside me sisters and I curl up around them.

I hate that smell more than I hate school. It was there on Da's breath when he boarded the boat for New York. It's there in the stale air of the pub on the corner, where Ma drags us sometimes and sings so beautifully she brings the pub to silence as her voice raises the hairs on the back of your neck. We walk home from the pub with the neighbors all singing arm in arm and the Guinness kisses send us to sleep to dream of America in Technicolor. I hope there's no Guinness in America.

—m—

I can walk right in to any flat on Green Street without knocking. Often someone's old granny will be propped up in bed, smack in the middle of the living room. "Ah, Danny, will ya hand me the newspaper? It fell off the bed when I was asleep."

Because we're all free to come and go as we please, sometimes it takes ages to find a pal; I'll barge into every flat, calling out his name—"Jemser, where are ya?"

"He's not here, Dano, try the Maloney's or the Devlin's. But leave the Duncan's alone—Paddy's working the night-shift this week."

The only flat no one's allowed in is Polly-Polly-Pick-Pick's. Poor mad Polly lives alone in number four. She sits at her window all day, picking her nose and talking gibberish. We're not allowed in number four because Polly walks around all day long with no clothes on—or so they say. I've never seen the sight meself, though I've peeked through her keyhole once or twice, hopefully.

I have uncles who are not uncles and aunts who are not aunts all over Green Street. Grandah lives in the flat below us, in the same tenement building. Another family, the Dunnes, with my not-Uncle Mick, live below him on the ground floor. Grandah's not our grandfather either, of course; me da's da is dead of cancer, and me ma's da is in America, working in an ice-cream factory. But we all love to call him Grandah just the same. Usually twice, cos it feels real good.

"Grandah, Grandah!" If God had given me any choice in the matter, and I don't know why he didn't, I'd have picked Barney Nolan for a real grandah. The lovely, sweet smell of his pipe tobacco wafts up the stairs to our floor, and we know he's awake and we all run down to greet him. "Grandah, Grandah!" Nice big, roundy belly, stretching braces barely clinging to a button here and there on his baggy trousers; a soft, gentle voice with just enough vinegar in it to let you know he won't take any nonsense. He's great at answering all the questions I can't ask Ma.

"Grandah, is Artane School really a bad place?" I'm sitting on the floor, playing with a toy car. Grandah stops reading his paper, looks down at me strangely, and sighs.

"Bad? I suppose it's very, very tough. But you shouldn't worry about that place, son. It's only for really, really bad fellahs."

"Am I a really, really bad fellah, Grandah?"

"Yer a bit of a handful at times, lad. No doubt about that. But bad? No, I don't believe you are, son. There's no real harm at all in ya."

That's right. There's no real harm in me. Well, maybe a little bit. Remembering what Aunt Deirdre said to Ma one day when she was smacking me, I ask Grandah, "Grandah, what's the 'little bit o' harm' that's hanging outa me?"

He laughs cautiously.

"Now what might you mean by that, Danny?"

"I heard Aunt Deirdre say to me ma one day, she said, 'Don't be too hard on him, Frances. The only little bit o' harm in that boy is hanging outa him.'"

Grandah laughed so hard I thought he was going to swallow his pipe.

"That'll be yer mickey, son."

Ah, my prick. My willie.

"What's the harm in that?" I ask.

He stops laughing and goes very quiet all of a sudden. He's ignoring me. Just like Larry O'Toole did. I try again. "What's the harm in a mickey, Grandah?"

He lights his pipe real slow, studying it like he's never seen it before in his whole life. Ah, that's it—when people are ignoring you, they become real interested in things they normally pay no attention to. Must remember that.

"That part of a man's body has caused more misery than anything in God's creation," Grandah says wearily.

I pretend not to hear him. I'm holding up my right hand to my eye and staring at it like it belongs to someone else. It's working.

I stare real hard at my hand, turning it over and over in front of my face. Grandah looks totally confused. Gotcha! That's how to ignore someone.

—⁂—

I'm always welcome in Grandah's neat little flat, but it's so different from ours it feels like another world. No matter how often I visit— almost every day—I never get used to it. Why can't our flat be as nice? There are tablecloths on the tables, curtains on the windows, rugs on the floors, and pillows on the *outside* of the bed covers. And as if to show there's better things to do with plates than eat off them, they're hanging on every wall. There are lamps on little tables with open books on top, and the fireplace has a shiny brass screen with spears on the sides. Grandah's wife is dead, but he rents a room to a lady called Mary, who has a hump. She is a sweet, tiny woman, not much bigger than me, and she wears her thin, wire glasses so far down the end of her long nose that if it wasn't for the wart they'd slide off. She's almost as kind as Grandah, but the kids on the street are a bit scared of her cos she looks like the Wicked Witch of the West from *The Wizard of Oz.*

I'm pretty sure she's not a witch, but Patricia isn't. There goes Mary now. Me and the girls are sitting quietly, peeking though the banisters, as Mary sweeps the stairs below with, of all things, a broom. We gasp in horror and look at one another with wide, scared eyes. "I told ya!" whispers Patricia triumphantly. Katie and I nod slowly.

Then I remember how Mary sometimes brings me bundles of rubber bands from the solicitor's office where she works, and the time she nursed a bird back to health, and the soda bread she bakes on weekends, and the time I watched her looking long and quiet out the window at the kids playing below, and before I can stop meself I say out loud, "Nah, she's no witch!"

Jaysus! Mary's heard me.

"How nice of you to say so, Danny."

I run down the flight of stairs to greet her, ashamed. Katie's close behind, and Patricia's still looking down through the banisters, pouting doubtfully.

"Mary, have you any rubber bands for me?" I'm very good at changing the subject, especially when the subject is my own stupidity.

"Well then, let me see." We follow her into Grandah's front room, where he's sitting smoking his pipe and reading the *Evening Mail.*

"Here we are now." Mary reaches deep into her handbag. "I forgot to give them to ya yesterday. Be careful with them now. No more blackguarding out of ya."

I don't know what they use them for in Mary's office, but rubber bands mean only one thing to me: weapons. I nearly took Jemser Carney's eye out a few weeks back. But I've learnt my lesson, and since then I've promised Mary I'll use them properly. And to me that means rats.

The rats in our house wait till it's quiet to come out to look for grub. Good luck there. They've as much chance of finding money— or Da. Breadcrumbs are much too precious to be allowed to fall on our floor. And the cupboards in the scullery—well, they never have food in them long enough for the scent to let the rats know it's there. Sometimes the grub is gone before I know it's there myself. The cupboards don't even have shelves in them any more, long since gone for firewood.

But the rats still come. And when they do I'm waiting for them with my rubber bands. They're not as cocky as they used to be cos I've been practicing. On my belly on Ma's bed in the living room I lie in wait, with one rubber band on the bed in front of me and another stretched to breaking point over my thumb. Ma's off shopping and the girls are outside playing. I let the rats come out well into the room in the hope of getting off a couple of shots before they make it back into their hole in the skirting board. The bullet flies and the ten-minute ambush is rewarded by a high-pitched squeal. I reload in a jiffy and send the second rubber band after his brother running behind him. You'd think they'd learn. But an empty belly will risk a sore arse— and I know what I'm talking about here—so there's no shortage of targets.

Rats are miles more fun than flies, but flies squelch nicely, so it's a toss-up. But flies are stupid. The only brains they have are splattered in little red spots over the ceiling and the windows. I'll lie on the floor on my back and pick off the bluebottles and their little cousins till Ma or my sisters come home and end the slaughter.

I always wonder why there are no rats in Grandah's place. I know there's plenty of grub cos I'm always offered a slice of bread when I visit, which is mostly when I'm hungry. Come to think of it, whenever I visit a pal's house, more often than not his ma will offer me grub.

"Danny, you look famished, for God's sake. Would ya like a nice slice of bread and butter?"

"Yes please, have ya a little bit a jam?"

I'd drop stone dead if Ma offered the same to any of my pals. Or me.

Today there's no offer of bread from Grandah. He's very serious.

"How's yer mammy doing, Danny?"

"She's grand. Can I play with the soldiers?" Grandah has a treasured collection of old lead soldiers. He often lets me play with them for hours at a time.

But now he ignores me and asks, "Has she been sick again?"

Ma has been getting sick almost every day in the sink in the scullery. They can all hear her downstairs. She's always complaining about the lack of privacy. Not that I know exactly what privacy means, but whatever it is, there's none here on Green Street.

"Well, she was sick again this morning, but sure it was only water so maybe she's getting better. Can I get the soldiers out now?"

After a long pause, Grandah sighs. "Go ahead, son, go ahead."

—⁓—

They say poverty creates characters, and Smithfield in the fifties, with plenty of both, encouraged eccentricity like no other place on God's earth. You'd often hear someone say, "Just be yourself." But the person saying it would have a look on their face as if to say, *don't you bloody well dare!* Everyone in Dublin was a thespian. Nothing was ever what it seemed. Emotions were encouraged as long as they were slightly disguised: you could get as mad as you liked if there was a bit of a charade to it. Crying, too, had to be interspersed with sobbing, affected chatter to show due respect for the listeners, who, playing their part, would stand with arms folded and heads nodding in respect for the show. No one on Green Street—or any other street in the Dublin of the fifties—was ever expected just to be himself. That would be considered a terrible waste of God-given talent. You could be yourself alone in private, if you felt so indulgent. Or if you were a priest—or a doctor.

—⁓—

Yeah, the doctor was here again yesterday. He was very serious. When he left, Ma wouldn't say a word all day. Now it's Sunday morning and she's sick again.

It falls to Aunt Deirdre to take me to Halston Street Church. Patricia and Katie are "too young to commit a mortal sin," so they stay at home. I'm sitting on Aunt D's lap, facing her and the back of the church. I'm wondering how much money is in the Black Babies's box, close to the Holy Water. After a while, Deirdre starts to cry. She's always very cheerful, but now the tears are rolling down her face and there's no sobbing chatter either. At first, I think to meself, *She's just being herself now.* But I'm deeply upset by this display of raw emotion—not brought on by a punch in the nose or bad news or harsh words. Not that anyone in Dublin ever cried a tear over harsh words. Most words are harsh, even funny ones. But Auntie D's tears hit me hard. She opens her eyes, sees my concern, and holds me even closer, then cries some more. Very strange. Nobody ever holds me that tight, and nobody ever cries not doing it. "Are ya sick?"

"No," says she.

"Are you sad?"

"Hush, sweetheart, don't talk during Holy Communion."

Okay, but don't cry like that during it either.

When we get home after Mass, Ma is being herself too. She's sobbing even worse than Aunt D, whose tears soon merge with hers in hugs far too tight to be good manners. And not a word is said between them either. What's happening to everyone? Ma's still in her bed in the living room, and Patricia and Katie are pretending to play in our bedroom. I'm very relieved to see someone not being themselves at last so I join them, keeping my ear open for some clue from the living room as to what the fecking hell's going on. Nothing comes except some whispers, followed by loud, angry sobs. The tone of Ma's voice chills me.

"Would ya mind yer own business, Deirdre? I told ya before, only God and I know who the father is, and while there's breath in my body, that's the way it'll stay."

—∞—

It's not fair. We're eating. My sisters and I with nothing but a small plate of potatoes, and Ma with the spuds and sausages and a couple of eggs.

"Can I have a sausage, Ma?" says Patricia.

"Me too," says Katie. "Or a nice running egg."

Ma keeps eating and not looking at anyone.

"Don't worry, girls," says I. "I'm going to the market tomorrow and we'll all have a nice big stew. Loads of spuds and carrots and turnips and maybe I'll even knock off an apple or two."

"I want a sausage." Patricia is crying now and Katie takes her lead.

Ma explodes and slams her fork down on the table. Her mouth full, she throws herself at the mantelpiece, upends a small statue of St. Joseph, and takes a ten-bob note out of the hollowed bottom. So that's where she keeps it.

"In the name of Jesus, Danny, go down to Clark's and get a pound of sausages and half a dozen eggs. The rent can go to hell, I don't give a shite any more, the whole fecking place can fall apart for all I care."

She flings the rolled-up ten-shilling note at me. I catch it and suddenly she's on the ground screaming with pain and I'm running down the stairs to Grandah's shouting, "Me mammy's dying! Me mammy's dying! Quick, for feck's sake!"

Grandah darts past me in the doorway. His belly is shaking from side to side as he runs up the stairs. He's too slow. I rush pass him, and he almost trips. He smacks me across the back of me head, and I nearly die of shock.

He shouts angrily, "Get out of the bloody way, you stupid eejit!" That's a bigger blow to me than Ma dying. She's on the floor holding her tummy, moaning. That's it. I had it once when I ate too many crabapples.

"I think it's only because she ate too many sausages," says I with relief. Grandah is totally calm and cold as ice as he says, "Get out of here and into your bedroom quick or you'll find my boot up yer arse."

They've all gone mad. The girls are screaming, Ma's joining in now, and I'm thinking about catching another boat to America to Da.

"She's going to be fine, it's only a cramp. First thing in the morning I'm taking yez all over to your Granny Ellis. It's all been arranged. She'll take yez all over to the nice home where you'll stay till yer ma has the baby."

Patricia and Katie are jumping up and down, singing, "We're going to have a baby! We're going to have a baby!"

That's massive! I hope it's a boy! And we're going to Granny
Ellis's. I love it over there in Bishop's Street. At least, I love it at me
granny's. Bishop's Street gives me the shivers. Ma has gone to bed
early and I go down to the park, trying not to think about the last time
I was over playing with the lads on me granny's street. I give a little
shudder. I don't want to think about it.

I'm thinking about it.

We were playing relieve-ee-aye-o, which is my favorite game of
chase and catch. One team runs free while the other tries to catch
them. The catchers put the captured lads in the "den" and the
runners try to set them free by running behind the catchers shouting,
"Relieve-ee-aye-o!" Well, that awful day, I was the last to be caught
cos I was hiding in a hallway. The catchers had just given up on
me so I came running out of my hiding place. That's when it all
happened. The Gas Man had come to collect the money from the
meters in Bishop's Street. While he was counting out the shillings in
one of the houses, he dropped down stone dead of a heart attack right
there and then on the spot without a word to anyone.

The news ran around the street like a cat on fire and we all
gathered outside to see the dead man himself. The ambulance came
and they brought him out the door in a wheelchair. "Mind, now,
mind!"

The gas man was sitting back like he was getting a shave, his
eyes wide open, and holy Jaysus Christ, Sweet Suffering, Mother of
Screaming Sorrows—he was grinning. A grin I'll remember till my
last breath. If he wasn't dead, you'd think he'd just won the Irish
Sweepstakes; and his skin so tight around his face, I thought his
skull would burst out through his mouth. His eyes were wide as
windows and popping out of his forehead. The women screamed and
the men cursed at the awful sight of a man they'd seen a thousand
times. I was filled with a dread I'd never known.

"Why didn't they close his eyes, for God's sake? Have they no
culture?" The ambulance men told them all to go and shite.

The lads and I ran up the street laughing too loud and punching one another too hard. But now there was an invisible playmate running with us that we couldn't punch or laugh away. Death had entered our lives, and nothing would ever be the same.

Yeah, but I said I didn't want to think about it and I don't. The Gas Man can feck off with his stupid grin. *Go to bed and don't think about him any more.* Think about what Grandah said: it's all arranged, Granny's gonna take us all over to the nice children's home where we'll stay till Ma has the baby. What's a "nice children's home" mean? *Don't think of that, think about the baby. There ya are. That's better.*

CHAPTER 5

Well, the "nice children's home" wasn't a home and it wasn't nice. It was awful. After two weeks in that terrible depressing place with loads of crazy kids and without my sisters—seems they went to another terrible depressing place with loads of crazy kids and nuns—me and the girls are at Granny Ellis's house in Bishop's Street. Ma is here too, but she's in bed with the baby, which isn't a baby at all. It's Two Twins.

That's right! They haven't been named yet so we just call them the Two Twins. I thought she said she couldn't afford another kid and now she's bought two of them. Maybe they're cheaper by the pair. Ma always has her eye out for a bargain. She's sleeping all the time now and Granny lets us do whatever we want.

Granny is short and kind, her nice round face always ready to grin slyly, and I'm her favorite. So is Patricia, Katie too, but Granny always winks at me, so I'm her special favorite. Her son, me da's sixteen-year-old brother, Joe, is here. Joe's very brave. You can tell because he's always jumping around like a boxer, throwing punches and ducking his head in and out.

Here he is now, beating the crap out of the air. And he gives great advice too: "Danny, no matter how big the other fellah is, let him know he'll be sorry he picked on you. And the most important thing is, if it looks like there's going to be a fight," he's dancing and ducking again, "just make sure you get the first punch in. Bang!" He punches me in the stomach.

Winded, I tell him to feck off.

"Feck off, is it? I'll give ya feck off. You're not half the man your father is, ya skinny little sparrowfart." Another punch in my belly. "Your poor father's off killing himself in a foreign army and the whole world's falling apart."

Me Da's killing himself in the American army? Must be a war. First I heard. I hope he's as good a shot as Roy Rogers. Is he fighting Indians? I don't say any of this to Uncle Joe, because I don't want him to know I don't know Da's in a war.

But I say it to Granny later when she's making tea on the stove. Ma's still asleep and so are the Two Twins. "How many Indians has Da kilt?"

"What in God's name are ya talking about, child?"

"He's in the American army shooting Indians, right? I hope he doesn't get scalped before he saves enough money to bring us all over there."

"He's in the army all right, but none of yez will be going to America. He'll be home soon and God himself won't be able to stop him from shooting every man on Green Street."

"Jaysus, he won't shoot Birdie, will he? Or Grandah, or Larry?" Now I'm really worried.

Granny sees I'm upset now and says, "Don't worry, son, it's all in God's hands now and it'll all be fine."

God must have huge hands.

—⁂—

We've been back in Green Street for two weeks and it's started again.

"Where's that big man of the house?"

I'm right here playing marbles on the floor and she knows it. But I like this game. "I'm here, Ma."

Ma pretends she's just seen me and gives me a big, beautiful smile. She bends down and holds my shoulders, looking straight into my eyes like I'm the loveliest sight in the whole wide world.

"Danny, son, I'm going to be out late tonight, and who's the brave man who'll look after everything for me?"

"I am, Ma." Of course. I'm the only big brave man around here and with five of us now it's even easier to be brave. *Don't worry Ma, I'll take care of things.*

She's gone.

We love the twins, me and the girls, and we love looking after them. Every day, I can't wait to get home from school—when I can drag myself there—to play with them. Mikey and Timmy, they've been named. They're so much fun I hardly ever see my friends on the street any more. Ma won't let my pals—or anyone, now that I think of it—come into the house anymore.

We play with the twins till they start to fall asleep. In the flickering light from the gas mantles Patricia and Katie and meself take turns singing, "Mammy's coming home soon. Mammy's coming home soon."

The girls are asleep and I'm close to it. Maybe I'm still awake. Maybe these long dark corridors I'm walking are real.

I know he's there before I see him.

I turn around a corner into a huge entrance hall with a big wide staircase, like the ones in the scary movies at the Maro cinema, and there he is: the Gas Man. He's standing at the top of the stairs with his hand on the banisters. He's looking straight at me and he's grinning that mad, skull-bursting grin of his. Waves of horror run up and down my spine till I wake up in a cold sweat.

Ma isn't home yet.

—⁓—

I remember reading somewhere that nightmares are actually very beneficial, the body's way of coming to terms with abstract concepts not easily assimilated in waking states. The Gas Man: my first sight of a corpse. In the dark caverns of my childhood dread, he became the prince of fear, the lord of night. My horror of him became the only constant, overshadowing all other fears. Whatever other nameless terrors may have laid dormant before, in him they united in one unholy alliance, which gathered power till I was afraid to sleep at night, afraid to stop moving by day, afraid to look around in case he was there. Like a grain of sand in an oyster, I coated him with a busy salve of jokes, mischief, and general gallivanting, but he was never far away.

—m—

Da's coming home today. He's coming into town shooting. I've told everyone on the street to leave, but they only laugh. It's a funny, forced kinda laugh, but that's their problem now. I've done my best. If they all want to get shot, that's fine with me.

Ma's been crying all the time. You'd think she'd be happy to see Da after a year and a bit. She's asleep on her bed in the living room. Da's not going to shoot her too, is he? Even though he's probably going to murder everyone, I must admit I'm very excited to see him. But I'm not sure I remember what he looks like. I know he's tall and blond and real handsome, and I remember how he whistles little tunes through his teeth and he eats really huge big egg salads.

Patricia and Katie are playing with their toys in our bedroom. The little noises they make are soft and sweet as they play with their dolls. I lie down on the bed, thinking about Da. I fall asleep and wake up real quick with a jump when I think I feel the Gas Man trespassing in me dreams again. My heart is beating like crazy.

I jump up to run out of my bedroom but I fall on the floor cos me leg's gone asleep. Maybe me leg dreamt of the Gas Man too. I hop into the living room. Where's the Two Twins? Over in their cot by the fireplace. They're awake now too. Big huge hugs. So lovely and happy. That's better. Big smiles and gurgles and my heart's not thumping in my chest any more.

"Jesus, Mary, and Joseph, are ya trying to break the floor, jumping up and down like a bloody jack-in-the-box? Feck it anyway, the twins are awake. I'll murder ya!" Ma's up from the bed now. She whacks me on the top of my head. But it knocks the last clinging dregs of the Gas Man outa me so I'm grateful. She's shaping up to give me some more.

Bang, bang, bang! Knocks on the hall door downstairs!

"Christ! It's yer father. Why would he knock on his own bloody hall door?" She calls down the stairs, "It's open." She looks in the mirror over the mantelpiece; though she's very pretty, she always makes herself look kind of ugly the way she looks at herself in the mirror. *Let your face be, Ma, it's grand.*

Da is at the door now and he looks smashing in his American army uniform and cap. I want to say something, but the air is so thick with the look in his eyes, the words stick in my throat. Ma is standing in a funny way, as if someone erased her middle with an eraser. He's standing there, too, and as he looks at her, Ma seems to get smaller and smaller and she's pale as a nun. She looks like she'll faint in a minute, but she just slowly sinks to the floor.

Patricia and Katie run in from our bedroom shouting, "Da, Da!"

Da doesn't even look at them or me. He's just standing there coldly, looking and looking at Ma.

He says quietly, "Danny, take yer sisters and go and play."

"Yer not going to shoot anyone, are ya, Da?" It's just then that I notice he doesn't have his rifle, unless it's small enough to fit in the case in his left hand. Something softer comes over his face and he shakes his head. He's very sad suddenly, and we're all breathing again.

"No, son, the time for that has long passed me."

Great! I can tell Birdie and everyone it's safe to come back now. Da takes his cap off and puts it on my head. It's falling round my eyes as he bends down and sits on the floor beside Ma, who's sobbing softly. He puts his hand gently on her shoulder and looks back at us. Even the Two Twins are quiet now.

"Out you go now, kids," he says kindly.

Katie skips around Patricia to beat her down the stairs. I'm usually first, but my feet feel like lead. I follow them down and out into the chill of the damp, autumn evening. The Green Street kids—Shelagh and Jemser, John O, and a dozen others—are gathering armfuls of leaves again, piling them around the lamp post and between it and the park wall.

Long before I was old enough to join in these games, I'd sit on the ground among the leaves, arms wrapped around my knees, mesmerized by the dancing shadows of the older kids playing in the soft light of the old street lamp. To and fro they'd leap like dancing fairies. The shouts and cries were music, the little accidents and fights small interruptions in the fun. Standing on the park wall, you have to let go of the railings and fall backward into the high-heaped leaves. It's scary. I've never done it before. But I'm seven now. *Go on, Dano. Let go.*

—〰—

Da's leaving today, but I'm downstairs at Grandah's playing with his soldiers anyway. Everyone's been very quiet since Ma nearly banjaxed herself with the gas the other night.

It had all begun with a trip to the Maro cinema. While Ma stayed home minding the Two Twins, Da took me and the girls to see Gary Cooper in *Distant Drums*. I asked him if that's the kind of Indians he fought in America and he told me, "Shush and let Gary kill the Indians in peace." The screen is full of holes and marks where kids often throw stones and bottles at the bad fellahs.

Afterward, when we got back to Green Street, he sent us on home as he stood outside the pub. Rubbing his hands together, he grinned. "I have a terrible thirst on me. I'm in the mood for a couple of gargles. Tell your mammy I'll be home in a bit. Not that she gives a shite."

The lights were off in Grandah's. He and Mary always go to bed early. As we climbed the stairs there was a strange, strong smell wafting down from our flat. Katie started coughing as we reached our landing and Patricia had her hand over her mouth and nose. I was dizzy and feeling like I was ready to puke up the ice cream Da bought us at the Maro.

The main door was closed, but the scullery door was wide open and there was Ma, lying on the floor, asleep. Her feet were facing us, her head on a pillow close to the oven door, which was open and . . . Shite! That's where the smell is coming from. It's gas. That's a stupid place to go to sleep with the oven open and the gas running. That's dangerous! I turned the gas off and tried to wake her up. *Oh, please Ma, wake up.* Nothing.

"Me ma's dead! Me ma's dead!" In a panic I shoved the girls down the stairs and shouted at the top of my lungs. I knocked on Grandah's door. He was in his pajamas and Mary was behind him in a robe. Grandah took a long sniff and shouted, "Gas! For the love of Jesus, don't tell me." He shuffled up the stairs and dragged Ma out the scullery door, huffing and puffing like his last breath was upon him.

"Mary, get those windows open. Danny, where's yer father?"

"He's at the pub."

"Go and get him, son, and don't tell him anything, mind. Not a word in the pub about the gas, ya hear? There's a good man."

Down the street I run and I'm a good man all right. But I'm not that good though, cos I don't care what Grandah said, I think to meself, *I'm telling me da. Are ya codding me with yer "Don't tell him anything."* Me ma's dead, for the second time in a few months, and I'm bloody well telling *somebody.*

I staggered in the door of the pub, almost stopped by the stench of Guinness. Da was in the corner, playing cards and smoking and laughing. He stopped laughing when he saw me.

"What?"

"Me Ma's dead. It's the gas."

I never saw a sorrier looking face than Da's at that moment. "Someone call an amb'lince, quick."

Everyone in the pub was on their feet and they nearly knocked me down, bursting out the door and running up the street to number nine. I couldn't get up the stairs for the crowd, but I could see Grandah looking down at me, shaking his head like I'd betrayed a friend's secret. He can feck off!

By 'n' by, I got upstairs to Grandah's, where Ma suddenly wasn't dead any more. She was vomiting, on her knees in the toilet.

Ma, yer alive, yer alive! Tanks be ta God! Let me get a cloth and wipe yer face. I couldn't find a cloth in Grandah's kitchen— everything's always hidden away in stupid drawers. I gave up and tried to find some toilet paper to wipe her face, but someone stopped me.

"Leave her be, lad. Leave her be."

Everyone was talking at once—except Da. All he did was shake his head. Someone had given Patricia a lollipop and Katie wanted a lick. Grandah and Mary were holding the Two Twins, who were bawling. One of the men was still carrying a bottle of Guinness from the pub and he took a swig. "God bless all here."

No one was paying any attention to Ma. I suppose it's not good manners to stare at someone when they're puking.

Some of the men looked vaguely disappointed that Ma was okay, but now that they knew she wasn't dead they all made their way back to the pub to drink to her continued good health. Da must've been glad, too, cos he went with them to celebrate. Health is an important thing to have, and to keep it you have to drink to it all the time. *Sláinte!*

—✿—

That was a few days ago and Grandah's not mad at me any more.

"Danny, get on home, son. Go on with ya. You'll miss you father." Grandah is very serious. I've been playing with his soldiers for ages, even though I know Da is leaving soon. Maybe he won't go if I can win this war, but when you play soldiers with yourself, you lose even if you win. But Grandah takes the soldier from my hands and pushes me out the door.

Up the stairs and I'm home. Katie's sitting on Da's lap and Patricia's playing with the Two Twins. I'm not hungry at all, but I hear myself say, "Can I have a slice of bread, Ma?"

"Don't make a mess."

I run into the scullery. "Can I put some sugar on it?" No answer. I'm spreading the margarine on the bread, thinking Ma's silence meant "yes" to the sugar. A soft step behind tells me Da has come in quietly.

"I'm off, son."

I keep spreading the margarine. You have to cover every bit of the bread, right over to the very edge. There's a hole by the crust. Fill that too.

Da puts his arms around me and I try to slip under them like his brother Joe showed me how to do when you're grabbed from behind in a fight. But Da knows that trick, too, and he holds me tighter.

"I can't butter me bread. Let me go." Why do we always call it "butter"? I'm crying now, and I'm kicking and squirming, and I don't know why. But Da's got me tightly and suddenly all the strength leaves my body and I'm limp in his arms, bawling me head off.

"I'm sorry, Da, really I am."

"What are ya sorrying outa ya for, for God's sake?"

"It's my fault you're leaving, right? I told the whole pub Ma was dead and she wasn't. Now the whole street knows."

Da has a funny look on his face. "No, no, no, son. Don't be thinking that at all. I couldn't give a shite what the street thinks. Yer all right there, son. Yer all right."

I realize I don't mind the smell of Guinness from him as much as I do from Ma. It feels different.

Patricia and Katie have come in to see the commotion and next thing I'm laughing hysterically as Katie reaches up to nab my bread and it falls butter side down on her face. It's stuck to her forehead and she's walking around the room pretending to be a ghost or something. Da's smiling now; Patricia grabs the bread, takes a bite, and sticks it on to her own forehead.

"It's the bread-and-butter people. It's the bread-and-butter people." Patricia has a sweet singing voice in her. We're all laughing and Ma's in the scullery doorway watching. She's so quiet that we all stop laughing one by one.

The tap's dripping in the sink. Grandah's radio is playing softly downstairs.

"Why don't ya just go, Tommy? Go on now, please." Ma is awful quiet.

Da looks bashful and nods slowly. We all go into the living room. Da grabs his case from Ma's bed and heads for the stairs. He turns around on the landing and gives me a proper American army salute and a wink before Ma closes the door. "See ya later, kiddo!"

I go into our bedroom and draw a few soldiers for my American War. Some planes. No dead bodies. Americans never get kilt. Then I realize I forgot to show my war to Da.

—◆—

I run into the bathroom and quickly wash my face as I hear the car in the driveway. It's Irene. The mother of one of her friends is dropping her off from a home-school meeting—a creative writing class.

Liz is at work. I give Irene an extra big hug as she comes in the door.

"What's all that about?" She laughs. She looks up at me as she pulls away. "Have you been crying?"

"Not at all," I lie. She's seen me cry before, but these are tears from another world. The realization that Da never saw my

American War was the catalyst. Strange, isn't it, what brings on tears sometimes. The memory of his leaving didn't evoke them. But the sudden flash of how I felt when I realized I'd forgotten to show him my war. . . .

Irene drops her backpack on the dining-room table with a bang.

"Hey, we did some cool things in writing class. You wanna see 'em?"

"Sure."

"Okay." She opens her notebook with a mischievous grin. "Do you know a predicate from a preposition?"

I scratch my head and laugh. "Haven't a clue! I used to at one point, but it's long since gone. What I don't know about grammar could fill a book."

"Pretty boring really, that one . . . but we learned some good stuff." She flips a page. "Here's some tips for when you get stuck and you're not sure what to write. That's the kind of thing I need most."

We look through her notes: *Think of an incident that really impacted you. What about it affected you most? What time of day was it? Who was there? What were your feelings and thoughts?*

"This is my favorite. Listen to this: *What were they wearing?*" She giggles. "That one could fill a page or two right there."

"Not for me. I never ever notice what people are wearing. Or even what I'm wearing myself sometimes. Ask your mom." We both laugh.

"Here's another tip." She points in her book with her pencil. "We're supposed to interview people about their lives. Okay, Mr. Danny Ellis, tell me something about yourself." She holds up her pencil as if it was a microphone.

"Well, let me see . . . I'm very happily married to my best friend . . . with a beautiful family . . . I'm a professional musician . . . a singer-songwriter . . . with a thousand unfinished songs . . . "

"Aha! So you get stuck, too, then, huh?"

"Yeah, totally!"

"Christine, our writing instructor, said that sometimes we get stuck when we've lost touch with our feelings about our subject. Does that happen to you?"

I think about that for a long moment. I say resignedly, "Yes. In every single song I've ever written—except one."

"Play me that one, please." She's excited.

"Oh, it's not something you would enjoy, sweetie. I'll play it for you as soon as I'm finished, I promise."

Irene pouts. I change the subject and soon she goes upstairs to the loft.

Thinking about what just happened, I go outside to my studio.

There's an old oak box beneath my mixing desk where I keep my treasured memorabilia: dozens of notebooks full of lyrics and song ideas. I pick one up and thumb through it. I throw it down in disgust. I pick up another—even worse. The writing seems so distilled as to be almost generic in content. The startling rawness of the new song, "800 Voices"—and the emerging voice of the child within me—make everything I've written till now seem like the worst kind of lie.

Some far-off voice inside whispers urgently, *Throw all your old notebooks away! Do it now!*

That's so scary a line of thought that I jump up quickly and run outside for a jog.

Chapter 6

Yeah, listen! Katie almost jumps out of her skin with the loud knocking.

"Open the door."

We usually never bolt the door except when we know the rent man is coming. Then we have to be quiet till he goes away. This is not him. It's nearly dark, too late for the little fat fellah, the baldy old eejit with the notebook and the bag of money.

"Open up, it's the Garda Síochána." The bloody cops! I'm in trouble now. It's been coming all evening.

Ma left us after supper with her usual *that's my brave big man of the house taking care of things for me.* But the brave big man had disappeared the minute Da came home, and even though Da's gone, he hasn't come back yet.

"Tell us a story Ma, please, before ya go, will ya?"

"Okay, here we go."

"Shush, Katie!" Great anticipation.

"This is a story . . . about Johnny McGory . . ."

Breathless pause.

"Shall I begin it?"

Nods.

"Well, that's all that's in it." Ma laughed.

"Oh, please, Ma, a real story, not a little farty joke of a ting."

"I've told yez all the stories I know, and I'm in a hurry."

"Tell 'em again, Ma, we don't care."

"I'm late, that's what I am. I'll tell yez one tomorrah, I promise."

"That's what ya said last night, Ma. It's not fair, so it's not."

Tears and hugs and more promises. Okay.

After she left, Katie and Patricia played with the Two Twins while I sat on our bed with my box of crayons. Times like this call for the American army: the best fighting men in the whole world.

I don't like Germans, so I'm not drawing any of them. They can all feck off. The lot of them.

Above the battlefield fly the red planes and bombers of the American Air Force. They're dropping bombs and paratroopers at the same time on the American GIs below. No one ever gets kilt, but it all adds to the confusion. Need some more men over there on the right-hand side.

Bombs are easy to draw, like falling fish. There's always a good reason to have more bombs. And there's plenty of room in that sky. The trucks and tanks and planes are harder to draw. I usually save them till I can take my time with the wheels and wings and propellers.

Noise from the living room drew me out of my war decisions: Katie was singing to the Two Twins again. It was a song I liked so I joined her. Patricia had raided Ma's box of stuff under the bed. I looked over her shoulder at Ma's things as I was singing: clothes, old records—His Master's Voice seventy-eights—pawn tickets, letters from America, pictures of Ma and Da, Da in uniform, and me ma with Granny Ellis and Uncle Joe.

"There's no snaps of us in there at all," Patricia moaned. She's a great one for noticing things that are not there. There's no sugar in the tea. There's no butter on that bread. That's not real Christmas wrapping, it's only newspaper. That's not a real battle on the wall, it's only a stupid drawing.

"Not one picture of us anywhere." She was starting to annoy me.

"People don't take pictures of kids," said I impatiently.

"That's not true." There she goes with the *nots* again. "I was in the Carneys's place the other day and there's pictures of Jemser and

Shelagh all over the place." She was angry, as if it was my fault. Such fierce eyes in such a lovely face; that look could stop a train.

I couldn't resist it. "Well, with a face as ugly as yours, it's no wonder. You'd probably break the bloody camera."

"I'm not ugly, Danny Ellis. You're ugly. Ugly as a horrible ol' man with an ugly, horrible face, and everyone hates ya because you're so ugly, ugly, ugly." Okay, that's far too many *uglies* for my liking. She has no sense of proportion. I only used one *ugly*. Outnumbered again. It was time for Steve Canyon to even up the odds a bit.

"All right, that's it! I'm going to blow yez all up. The whole bloody place and everything in it! Where's my hand grenade?" I ran into the scullery and unscrewed the round, black handle off the oven door. On my way back in, I bolted the main door to the landing so there'd be no escape. Patricia was scared now; she doesn't like to be blown up. Katie looked frightened too, but I gave her a little wink that Patricia didn't see. She smiled back. She likes winks. I've tried to teach her, but she can't close one eye at a time. I can, but I have to move me mouth up and me eyebrow down till I look like an eejit.

"This is my grenade that I've been waiting to use on my enemies." I held up the oven door handle. "There's no way out. Yez all have had it. I'm taking no prisoners. Death to all spies and traitors and twins!" I'd have winked at the twins too, but they were asleep.

I opened the window by Ma's bed and put one foot out like I was about to jump. There was someone on the street shouting at me to get back in, but it'd all gone too far to turn back. Once Steve Canyon's blood is up there's no stopping things.

"I'm blowing up this house and all that's in it. Get back cos there's gonna be a mighty blast."

The woman on the street was hysterical. Great! Steve Canyon loves pandemonium. Spread as much panic as possible—it's a hero's best friend. Patricia was wailing and even Katie looked doubtful. I gave her another wink as I threw the grenade into the jungle below, where my enemies had me surrounded. The mighty blast that followed was swallowed up by the sound of Ma's mug shattering on the table where the grenade landed. Feck it! Now I was really in for it.

Patricia was hysterical and I knew I'd gone too far. But she shouldn't have pushed Steve Canyon with all those *uglies*. I climbed back into the room and gathered up the broken mug bits from the jungle floor.

"I'm sorry, I'm sorry. I'm only codding yez. It's just an oven door handle. Look." You'd think she'd be happy it was just a joke, but she wasn't. More screams, and more *uglies*. I know what! I ran into our bedroom and grabbed my yo-yo from my pile of toys in the corner.

"Here ya are. This is yours for keeps, for ever and ever. I'll even show ya how to do it—watch." I did a couple of turns with the yo-yo and Patricia's cries stopped, but she still glared at me.

"Gimme that. I'm still telling Ma when she gets back." She tried to play with the yo-yo, but she couldn't make a proper fist of it. My arm was around her shoulder very sincerely because I didn't want her telling Ma.

"Look. Let's play dress-up. I'll show ya how to do the yo-yo later, I promise." I knew bloody well I wouldn't be able to teach her, even if she'd let me, but my sincerity was growing as I thought of what Ma would do to me. As usual, it was Katie who came to our rescue. She was wearing a funny, feathered hat from the box under Ma's bed. She rolled a bit of newspaper into a pretend cigarette and was puffing on it comically.

"I'm off to the Coombe." Mocking Aunt Deirdre, she moved her wrist backward and forward to her mouth, waving the fag round. We all laughed hysterically at the imitation. Patricia grabbed something from the box and in a few minutes, with Katie leading the way, we're all "off to the Coombe."

But now the Garda Síochána is here. "Open the door at once, like a good man." The policeman shouts again, knocking loudly.

"It's not locked now," says I, struggling with the bolt. Patricia is beside me in Ma's old yellow dress. Katie is hiding back somewhere in the halflight, scared by all the knocking.

The policeman is a big fellah. Taller than Birdie and tougher looking than Jemser's da, he's ready for trouble all right. He says his name is Guard O'Rourke.

"Blowing up the house, are ya? Hanging out the window like a Republican flag? What's wrong with ya, son? Ya could a kilt yerself stone dead. Where's yer mother?"

"She's gone out."

"Jesus Christ!" O'Rourke sounds disgusted. Maybe he was expecting Ma to make a cup of tea for him. "She's not a mother at all."

"She is so. And we're her children, so we are." He's an eejit. How can you have kids without a mother? *Make yer own tea, stupid.*

"Is there no light at all in this house?"

"Ma said we've no shillings for the gas meter. We have candles if you want."

The guard reaches into the pocket of his overcoat and his flash lamp blinds me as he turns it on. He puts it on the mantelpiece, shining up toward the peeling wallpaper and the flaking ceiling. The place looks like a Christmas card with Patricia in the long dress, me in Ma's nightie, and Katie with the feathered hat falling down around her eyes. Guard O'Rourke sits on a chair in the middle of it all and he's not mad any more.

"That baby can sleep through an All-Ireland football final, by the looks of it." He points to the cot.

"It's the Two Twins, Guard," says I, proudly. Mikey and Timmy are sleeping like babies.

The guard sighs wearily. "Five children, at her age. Gawd help her. Gawd help yez all. It's freezing in here. Is there no coal or turf for the fire?"

"Ma doesn't like the fire to be lit when she goes out at night."

"Okay, it's time for bed. I'll be waiting here till yer mother gets home." He takes a little notebook from his pocket and looks at it for a second.

"Danny, you help Patricia and Katie to bed and come back here to me when they're tucked in." Does he have all our names in his book? Still, I'm keen to know why he wants to talk to me. Probably wants to tell me what a big man I am for looking after everyone while Ma is out.

While I'm putting the girls to bed, I turn and call O'Rourke to come and see me American War on the wall. He shines his flashlight from one end of the wall to the other and the battle looks even better than it does during the day.

"The planes are dropping bombs on top of their own paratroopers," says he in dismay.

I'm disgusted at his stupidity. It's my bloody battle and if I want to have bombs and paratroopers falling at the same time, who's to argue?

I tell him so. "Anyway, some of those planes are flying on different days than others."

He raises his eyebrows.

"That one there is flying last week and this one is flying yesterday. They all have different jobs and you can't expect them to just feck off the wall when they've dropped their bombs." Then I add triumphantly, "I haven't learnt how to draw a plane that's not there any more. Besides, the bombs never land on anyone, they're stuck there in the air for ever like fly shite on a window."

He's stunned. That shut him up. He walks out of the bedroom in defeat, leaving us in the dark.

"It's not a real war anyway," says Patricia to O'Rourke's back. He didn't hear her.

"It is too," says Katie.

Once the girls are tucked up in bed I come back to Guard O'Rourke, who's smoking. He's all serious now; maybe he's mad because I outfoxed him with the bombs. Adults always win in the end.

"Now, lad, there's a bone or two I'd like to chew with you. We've been hearing about your gallivanting down at the station and now that I'm here, we might as well deal with it. If I were yerself I'd be very careful with my answers." My tummy's tightening. He looks at his notebook.

"First, there's the bike. Where is it now?"

Ah, the bike. How does he know about that?

"I left it over in Paddywhack Flynn's house on Little Britane Street."

It'd been leaning against a lamppost all day in King Street: a girl's bike; wasn't even locked. It was just begging to be knocked off. I wheeled it from King Street all the way down Halston Street and home to Ma, who nearly had a heart attack.

"Get that bike outa my sight. Ya'll have the Gardai on us, ya will."

You'd think she'd a been grateful.

"Paddywhack said we'd get a pound for it."

"Paddywhack can get a hundred pounds for it, for all I care. Get it off the street before the p'lice come and send ya away to Artane."

Artane! I shuddered. I thought she'd be proud. I wheeled the bike around to Paddywhack's place. "It's all yours, Paddy, good luck to ya," I'd told him.

"Good man, so yer telling me the truth. That's good." The guard is writing in his notebook. "And then there's the matter of Mickey Doyle's prize pigeon, Sparky. Can ya tell me a bit about him?"

Feck it anyway, he knows everything.

"That wasn't my fault, it was young Batty Doyle's idea. He's always bragging that his da's pigeon can find his way home from

China or anywhere on earth. So Batty an' me took Sparky over to the Ha'penny Bridge to see if he could get home from there."

"How did ya carry the bird, son?"

"Under me shirt, Guard," says I.

O'Rourke covers his mouth with his hand. "Did ya let it fly away?"

"Well . . . I kinda did . . ."

"Out with it, lad. What happened?"

"Well, when I took Sparky outa me shirt he was sleeping, so I shook him a bit to wake him up. When he didn't wake up I threw him up in the air, thinking he'd wake up and fly away home."

"And . . . did he?" Guard O'Rourke looks like he's choking on something.

"No, Guard, he didn't. He dropped like a brick into the Liffey. He couldn't fly at all and when he hit that water, he couldn't swim a stroke either." The guard is bent over now, laughing like he's going to burst. I'm enjoying meself now and warming up to the story.

"He floated on his back with his two legs straight up in the air, his arms spread out like a priest and his arse feathers fit to be a Chinaman's fan. Batty and me said a few Hail Marys and Sparky was off down the river head first. He had a good send-off, though, Guard, so he did."

O'Rourke is wiping the tears off his face and doing his best to appear like a stern officer of the peace. He lights another cigarette.

"Okay, that's enough of that for a while." His eyes are kind though as he writes again in his notebook.

"Do ya bet on pigeon racing, Guard?" I'm changing the subject. I don't want him to send me to bed so I'm saying the first thing that comes into my head.

"No, son, I don't gamble. Anyway, I'm saving up to get married."

"What? Ya need money to get married?" First I heard.

"Yeah, ya need a lot of money to get married nowadays . . . and to stay married."

"How much?"

That's quietened him. He scratches his head under his cap and looks very serious for a bit, then grunts, "A hundred pounds. That should get ya started."

Now that quieted me. Maybe that's what went wrong with Ma and Da. They didn't save up properly. I'm wondering how much Guinness costs, but I say, "If I got a hundred pounds from somewhere, would me Da come back?"

The guard sighs wearily and takes his flashlight down from the mantelpiece. He puts his big hand on my head and says quietly, "Money doesn't fix all problems, son. It often starts them, but seldom solves them."

We go quiet. I'm getting sleepy now, and we've run out of things to say. The light from his lamp is on the floor and the room is all shadows and softness and it's nice to have a kind person here with us in the night. I put my head on the sofa and pull Ma's nightie tighter around me.

—ᴡᴡ—

"Jaysus Christ!"

Ma's voice is far away in my dreams. But I'm awake now. She's in the door and there's someone with her. Guard O'Rourke is on his feet and his flashlight is on Ma's face, which looks scary in the hard light. The man behind her in the darkness tries to get back out the door but the guard has him by the collar in a jiffy. *That's right, kick the shite outa the bastard.* O'Rourke pulls the man back in as easily as lifting a coat. He shoves him up against the wall, flashlight on the man's face now. The Two Twins are bawling in the cot.

O'Rourke growls, "Get outa here, ya dirty shitehawk. If I ever see you again, day or night, ya'll be picking yer nose outa the back of yer head." The guard throws him out the door and we can hear him falling down the stairs.

O'Rourke turns to Ma, her hands shaking as she lights a candle. The policeman is breathing heavily from the tussle. "As for you, missus, you should be ashamed of yerself." He's looking at Ma fiercely.

Please don't, Mr. Policeman. Please leave her alone.

"You haven't heard the last of it yet, me girl. The NSPCC will want to be talking with you and you won't like what they have to say. I'll hand in my report to the sergeant in the morning and ya won't like what I have to say either. If you'd a hair of shame on yer head you'd stay at home with yer childer instead of . . . " He looks over at me and hesitates. Then he hisses at Ma, "Instead of betraying the very notion of motherhood itself. I hope for your sake that God is as merciful as they say, woman."

Katie's here now, crying, and Patricia's rubbing her eyes. The Two Twins are getting louder and Ma's crying too. I hate O'Rourke for talking to Ma like that. He's ruining everything. Who does he think he is? But it's my fault he's come here to our flat, and whatever the sergeant and the NSPCC have to do with it, that'll be my fault too.

—m—

Shane is looking a bit tired today as we clop down Parliament Street toward Capel Street Bridge. Larry flicks a spent cigarette past the horse's head and shouts pleasantly, "Git up outa that, for God's sakes, Shane, will ya? D'ya think we have all day? Whaddya say, Dano? Should we kick his arse a bit?" Larry seldom uses his whip. He's just trying to get me to smarten up. Good luck there.

"No! He's all right. Maybe he didn't have a good sleep last night," I say wearily.

Larry laughs kindly. "I think yer talking about yerself there, Dano. Yer eyes are like two cigarette holes in a sheet."

"What's the NSPCC, Larry?" I ask.

Larry hesitates for a full minute before answering in a harder voice. "It's the National Society for Prevention of Cruelty to Children, son." He almost spits the words.

"I think Ma's in trouble with them. They're going to say some bad things to her. Are they nasty people?"

He's taking an awful long time to answer my question, so I'm thinking they must be a really bad bunch. He struggles with his words. "I suppose ya could say they try to prevent nastiness, son, but they cause as much trouble as they fix."

Okay, so they prevent bad stuff but they cause it too. That's just great. Clear as Liffey water.

"What bad stuff do they cause, Larry?"

He's starting to worry me with his pauses. "There are some nosey parkers that think they know what's good for everyone else, son. Sometimes they're right, and sometimes they're wrong."

"What will they do to me ma?"

Another long pause. Shane snorts as a car honks. He lifts his golden tail and lets loose a nice big smelly shite.

"I don't know, son. I don't know. Ya shouldn't be worrying about this stuff, for Chrissakes. Why don't ya lie back and snooze for a bit? With the bloody traffic we won't be in Smithfield till Christmas."

We've come to a stop on the bridge.

"Y'know, Dano, God has a quare way about him. One minute he looks like he's gonna banjax ya, the next he's pulling a lollipop outa his pocket and sticking it in yer gob. It's hard to tell sometimes if he loves ya or hates ya, but in my book tings always turn out for the better. Always. Ya'll see that for yerself as time goes by, son."

What the feck is he on about? He's looking at me in a funny way. He's never an unkind man, but today for some reason he's gentler than usual and it's getting on my nerves. I like people who are gruff to stay gruff. When they start being extra kind it just feels funny. I move back a bit, behind Larry. We start to move ever so slowly across the bridge.

I'm half asleep among the vegetables and fruit boxes, lying on an old sack in the middle of the cart. With my head on an empty egg crate, the Liffey passes sideways to me. It gives me a funny feeling in my stomach, watching the green water, the buildings and the pedestrians all passing by as I'm lying down. It all looks safer from the side, not as dangerous, like it's all just pretend.

I turn my head so everything's completely upside-down now. Sky and city change places. Clouds below and earth above. Chimneys reach down out of the gray sky as if created by their own smoke and spread out along roofs that grow upward into gray buildings and streets. Streets are ceilings where people with magnetized feet walk upside-down and don't fall into the sky. All are hanging down from the ground above. Nothing is real. Nothing matters. Nothing to hang on to. In the gathering darkness, I float off into the soft halftones of the upside-down world, unfettered and free. But scary free: I'm dissolving. It's terrifying. I'm drifting away somewhere, melting into the Dublin evening.

Gerroff! I'm not an evening and I'm not gray and I don't want to melt into Dublin. Shite! It's pulling me away. I can't get back. Lemme go, ya gray bastard. Feck off! I need to get bloody well back. Right now! For Jaysus sake.

I snap out of it—whatever it was—and straighten up so suddenly I cause a crick in my neck. A young lad on a bike is ringing his bell irritatingly as he overtakes us. Pox bottle! He grins mischievously at me as he stretches a hand over the cart in the pretence of stealing an apple from that box there. Overwhelming anguish for ordinary things quickly turns into anger. *Black Daniel, what took ya so long?* That's better.

"Think that's funny, do ya? G'wan, feck away off, ya spotty goose gob," I say under my breath. The cyclist sticks his tongue out at my long, serious face and rides on.

"Did he take something?" Larry is stretching to keep his eye on the cyclist weaving in and out of the Capel Street traffic.

"Yeah, he took an apple from that box there." I'm amazed at the lie, but it's out now and that's that. It feels great. I'm in charge again.

"Bastard! Da dirty thief! He's away up Mary Street; we'll not see him again," says Larry. He stands up, watching the disappearing cyclist, and my hand reaches out to the box and before I know what I'm doing there's an apple in my pocket.

"Do ya know him?" Larry looks around at me.

The lump of the apple in my pocket feels like it's a football.

"No, no. Not at all. Not at all. Never laid eyes on him in me life." I'm shaking and my stomach's in a knot.

"Are ya sure? He was looking at ya very friendly."

Stop looking at me and watch the bloody road, will ya, Larry, for Christ's sakes. "I told ya I never saw him before in my life, didn't I." I'm shouting and nearly in tears.

Not another word from Larry now. He lights a cigarette and gives Shane a gentle little smack on the arse with the whip. It's not Shane's fault; it's all my fault. It's like the whole world and everything in it is tied to my chest with elastic bands that are pulling me all over the place. But when I start lying I'm not being pulled any more. I'm doing the pulling.

The kids on Green Street are playing relieve-ee-aye-o as the cart pulls in on the corner of little Britain Street. "See ya, Larry."

No answer.

He can feck off.

CHAPTER 7

The big man with the briefcase looks like a school teacher with a square coat, square glasses, and a square arse. Ma lets him in and tells us to go and play. I'm about to follow the girls out the door when I notice the initials on his briefcase: NSPCC. It's one of those fellahs who cause trouble by trying to prevent it. Ma looks worried, too, and pushes me out the door and closes it. I run downstairs and make sure the girls are busy playing before I creep back up the stairs and sit on the landing beside the scullery, listening. Ma must be sitting by the window cos I can barely hear her. I look through the keyhole and he's sitting at the table, nearer to me, his briefcase open and papers everywhere.

". . . Many reports, Mrs. Ellis, many of them . . . not just the police, but neighbors too." Pause.

Ma says something I can't hear.

"Maybe not, but I'm afraid it is *our* business, Mrs. Ellis . . . if it wasn't for good people like that there'd be more children suffering in Ireland."

Ma is shouting now and I can hear some of her tearful words:

". . . Bastards . . . why don't they mind their own bloody business. They have no idea what it's like . . . five children and no father. As God is my judge, I love them kids."

Something about the way the NSPCC man says the word "children" sends a shiver down my spine; like it's a crime to be one. It doesn't sound like he's interested in preventing cruelty to children or anyone else.

". . . We have a duty to those children, Mrs. Ellis, a sworn duty. They can't protect themselves, and it's my job to see that they have proper care. You can't deny leaving them alone late at night . . . Your neglect is well documented. Guard O'Rourke . . . neighbors . . . My recommendations to the court . . ." His voice trails off as my heart pounds.

"Oh please, mister, please . . . I do me best . . . it's the loneliness at night."

There's a knot in my stomach that feels like I'm dying. It's not because he's talking nasty to Ma. She's well able for any of that stuff. But this is no fight with a neighbor or relation. In what little I can hear of Ma's voice there's something I've never heard before. She's really scared by this fellah and he's not even shouting. In fact he speaks so soft and slow and singsong that I want to grab him by the scruff of the neck. *Speak proper, ya posh bastard!*

My anger at him turns to fear again quickly cos he's talking about me now. "Daniel . . . completely out of control . . . his irregular school attendance . . . it's no secret that he'll steal anything that's not locked up . . ."

That's right. I bloody well would. Who wouldn't? Just about everyone on Green Street does. Maybe not as well I do it. But it's no good being famous for something that's getting yer ma into trouble. I run down to the street and run and run to stop the bad feeling. Why should Preventing Cruelty care about me and school? Ma has been warning me that something awful will happen if I don't stop mitching from school, but I can't help it. Now Ma's getting blamed.

—✲—

The nuns have just left, thank God. They've been around twice already; nearly as much as the Preventing Cruelty fellah. I wonder what the nuns are preventing. The Brides of Christ, I heard Grandah call them last time. If they're all married to Christ, then someone will have to do some preventing cruelty on Jesus too. I wouldn't want to be married to one of dem even if I did have a hundred pounds. They sit there like they're dying to take a crap but they left their toilet paper at home. And when they talk, their lips don't move. A little hole in the middle of their mouths opens and the words fall out like nanny-goat droppings, small and tight, one by one. I was so mesmerized by their clothes and headdresses I couldn't concentrate on what they were saying. All I heard was, "God's children" and "better off in God's care" and "you'll thank us one day." I'll thank yez to leave us alone. Do us all a favor and go and join yer husband in heaven. I feel sorry for Jesus.

Ma's not as scared of the nuns as she is of Preventing Cruelty. He has something about him, as if he knows what's going to happen because he's the one who's bloody well gonna make it happen. He's always nodding his head, agreeing with himself. Well, with all the agreeing and the preventing cruelty and marrying God you'd think we'd all be happy as Christmas morning.

But the only happiness around here is coming from the Two Twins. Every day they seem more and more joyful. I can even tell them apart now: Mikey is a bit fatter in the face, and Timmy has softer eyes. Mikey farts more too, maybe cos he eats more than Timmy. They're easier to play with, too, cos now they'll laugh at anything. I'll crawl under the cot and come up the far side and they'll be in fits. Then I'll stand on a chair and make faces at them through my legs as I bend upside-down and they'll kill themselves laughing. I'm not famous for my sense of humor but I can make them two laugh all day without even trying. I can't wait to get home and hear their laughter. Today at school I won a little turning plastic windmill thing in a heads-or-tails toss. It spins on a stick in the wind or when you blow it, and the Two Twins are gonna die laughing. Maybe I can teach them to blow it. It's turning in the breeze as I walk up Green Street.

A strange chant comes from an open window above. "Ah, the poor little doggie. The poor little doggie." It's Polly-Polly-Pick-Pick. She's at her window as usual, picking her nose. She's wrapped her torn curtain around her to hide her nakedness.

"Ah, the poor little doggie. The poor little, poor little doggie woggie, doggie woggie, woggie." The sing-song repetition seems to bring some comfort to her mad mind. I feel sorry for her.

But here comes Jemser. I show him my windmill as Polly rattles on with a new chant inspired by Jemser's arrival.

"Ah, the little boys. The dirty little boys. The dirty little, dirty little, dirty little boys."

Jemser wants to try the windmill. Reluctantly, I let him hold it. He runs up and down the street making little engine noises.

"That's mustard, Dano! I've give ya a penny for it."

"No ya won't. Give it back here before ya break it." As if he didn't hear me, he runs down the street with the windmill whirring away to his noises. I join in the fun for a bit till we're out of breath.

"A penny and a gobstopper I've only sucked once," says Jemser, drawing back the windmill from my outstretched hand.

"Gobstopper, gobstopper, poor little gobstopper," says Polly, anxious to join the conversation.

Jemser looks up at her and I snatch the windmill from his hand. "Sorry, pal, it's not mine any more. It belongs to the twins." I head up the street and into number nine.

I run in the door to the living room. The Two Twins are gone. The cot too.

Ma's crying on the bed. She's heaving like she's on her last breath.

"Where's the Two Twins, Ma? Where's Mikey and Timmy?"

No answer. More sobs; cries so full of anguish and despair that I don't know if she'll ever be okay again. Frightened, I decide I'd better leave her alone for a bit. I go outside. I walk across to the park.

Katie and Patricia are playing skipping with Shelagh Carney:

London Bridge is falling down,
Falling down, falling down,

London Bridge is falling down,
My Fair Lady.

"C'mon Danny, jump in." Katie's blue eyes are dancing with delight as she skips over the rope.

"Mammy's crying," I say.

"She's always crying," says Patricia in between singing the nursery rhyme.

"The Two Twins are not there any more."

"I know. I think they're at Granny Ellis's," says Patricia.

I don't know why, but I don't think the Two Twins are at me Granny's.

I walk over to a park bench and sit looking across at the haunted statue of the man with the dog. *Okay, so you two walk around in the night when we're asleep, do ya? We'll see how walkey yez are in a minute.* I pick up a rock and hit the stone man smack on the nose. *Move, ya bastard.* Not an inch. Just a stupid statue with no feelings. I can hear the girls singing away merrily"

Stole my watch and stole my chain,
Stole my chain, stole my chain,
Stole my watch and stole my chain,
My Fair Lady.

I can't stand it any more. I walk back to the street. Something's wrong. Even Polly can feel it; she's stopped chanting and looks down at me sorrowfully. I run upstairs and in the door home.

"Where's the Two Twins, Ma?"

"They were a gift from God himself and he's taken them back and that's all there is to it." Ma's stopped crying but she's mad at me for asking.

"But they're not dead, are they?"

Silence.

"They're gone, son."

"That's not fair. I'll never make anyone laugh like that as long as I live."

But Ma won't say another word.

Patricia is real upset, but Katie is absolutely in bits. I try to get her to play with my windmill but she won't have it. She won't eat her potatoes at dinner either and I can't finish them for her like I usually do. There's a big empty space by the fireplace where the cot used to be.

—⁓—

I'm down by the Liffey again. Yesterday too—and the day before. I leave home and set off running with no idea where I'm going but I nearly always end up here by the river. Here, the world moves like it's supposed to: big and fast and important. Important people with important places to go and important things to do. I'll lose meself in the din: the buses and the horses and carts and bikes and lorries. I'll steal a pint from the milk carts and finagle a cake from the baker's van. I'll spend hours watching the Guinness barges and the little boats wind their way over Dublin's Green Carpet below. I'll shout down at them as they pass:

"Are yez looking for a helper?"

"Give us a lift, will ya?"

"Anyone going to New York?"

They'll shout back every time; no one's ever short of an answer in Dublin:

"Go on back home to yer ma, ya skinny little sparrow fart."

"New York, is it? More like new-monia for you in this weather. Have ya no coat, ya eejit?"

"You should be in school, ya durty mitcher."

That's right. But I'm not. So who's winning here? I'm free as a bird. So yez can all feck off.

—⁓—

The gray stone of the courthouse wall curves around to meet the railings where Jemser's tied up like a captured cavalry scout. But strict orders from Ma: we're not talking to anyone on the street, except Grandah and Mary. The rest of them are all traitors. The words of Preventing Cruelty have put paid to the last of the neighborly friendship. But Jemser's been captured by Indians and that's not something Roy Rogers can ignore on a gray November evening.

"Bloody Apache bastards left me here to die in the desert sun," says Jemser wishfully. The only thing dying in this sun is us dying from the lack of it.

"I'll set ya free if ya don't tell anyone. I'm not supposed to talk to any o' yez. Yer all in our bad books, so yez are. We hate yez all. Have ya any sweets?"

"There's a gobstopper in me left pocket." Before I untie him, I search for it. First things first. There it is—sticky, all kinds of stringy, pockety stuff stuck to it. Still, tastes great.

"Brutal! Thanks, Jemser, I'll get ya down." I untie him. He shakes himself free of the twine.

"Why don't ya come to school any more, Dano? We miss ya."

"What's the use? Roy Rogers never went to school."

"If ya don't learn how to read ya won't get a good job."

Yeah, and if ya don't get a good job ya don't ate and if ya don't ate ya don't shite and if ya don't shite ya'll burst. I've been warned about the dangers of mitching from school by some of the bigger lads on the street. They forgot to mention being sent to Artane for mitching. Ma never forgets that little threat, but lately, even she has given up on that score.

Jemser continues, "Me ma was saying that youse are all poor unfortunates. She says, 'It's not good to talk about dem. They're all just poor unfortunates, that's what they are, poor unfortunates.'"

"I'm not poor." And whatever unfortunate is, I'm not that either.

Here comes Ma, just turning the corner from Little Britain Street. She glares at Jemser, who looks scared and runs off sheepishly.

"See ya, Dano, thanks for rescuing me." He's gone. *So long, Jemser, see* ya.

We go upstairs, and Ma is singing a happy little song. I can't believe my ears. I haven't heard her sing since before the Two Twins were born. She's dancing around the room and hugging me up and down.

'Danny, son, I have some great news—we're going to live in the country. We've been re-housed by the Social Services. Can you believe it? Our very own, brand-new house that's never been lived in by anyone else. A Corporation house."

"I don't want it. I don't care. What's wrong with this house?"

"This isn't a house at all, son. It's a one-bedroom flat and it's not ours, it's rented. You'll love the new house, Danny. There'll be fields and little streams full of pinkeens and fresh air and lots of kids to play with."

"The Liffey is my river, Ma, and I have plenty of kids to play with." *At least I used to before you stopped me.* And what would I bloody well do with fresh air? "Why do we have to leave, Ma, why?"

She smiles in a funny secret way and says, "I nearly forgot to tell ya, son, there's a lovely little girl who'll be living next door to us. Her name is Maggie." Then she starts to sing again; it's the same song she sang earlier: *"I wandered today to the hills, Maggie."*

The girl next door sounds nice, I suppose. Ma's joy, seldom seen, is hard to fight, and soon I'm laughing with her. It's nice to hear her laugh again—and sing. It's a nice song, Maggie.

—⁓—

The damp autumn air wafts upstairs through the hall door, which is held open by a box of clothes. The small moving van is nearly full. Stuff is piled up around the pavement and the two packing men are cursing merrily. Out the window I can see the empty street; all the kids are at school except Katie and Patricia, who are playing skipping round the lamppost. From downstairs I can hear Ma talking to Grandah. Usually I'm very curious around grown-up conversation, but today I don't want to hear them. I stick my fingers in my ears—but too late to stop Grandah's words: "Don't be a stranger now, Frances, ya hear. Rathfarnham isn't the other side of the world y'know."

Rathfarnham—what a horrible name! Sounds like a farm for rats.

I've never said goodbye to anyone except Da and that too many times to take seriously. A strange new feeling is creeping over me. Goodbye is a place: Green Street. The empty flat seems to know how I feel. It looks very queer—bigger. There's nothing left except a few of my toys. I put them in a pillowcase: my comics and my windmill and my box of colored pens. I lie down on my back on the empty living-room floor, looking at the ceiling. I look down at my feet. If I open them wide I can see a new rat hole where Ma's bed used to be.

I lift my right foot and close one eye, aim my foot like a gun, and send a couple of shots through the rat hole. *Take that, ya rats yez.* Raising my foot, I shoot out the gas mantle near the door and then shoot off the door handle. There's a little picture of Jesus over the door to our bedroom that someone forgot to pack. Save yer ammo—he died for our sins and rose from the dead so he's probably bulletproof. I lower my foot and I'm shooting at the American War on our bedroom wall, which I can see through the doorway.

I go into the bedroom. It looks awful funny with everything gone: no bed, no clothes on the floor, no shoes or toys. I sit on the floor looking up at the battle for a long time. All the men are standing or running; there's not a dead soldier in sight. Americans don't get kilt. Da's in America. I grab my box of crayons from the pillowcase and add a few soldiers and a couple of paratroopers. All alive.

I stand back for a minute and look at it all.

Then I draw the tank: the caterpillar tracks and the little wheels inside them, the long gun with the holes at the end, the turret with the man looking up at the paratroopers, and planes above him. I step back again, looking at the best bloody thing I've ever drawn in my whole life.

Then I notice something else: with the bed gone, there's a big space below the battle that looks funny, like it's all up in the air. I take a black pen and move over to the left of the wall where the head of the bed used to be, where Katie used to sleep. Beneath the battlefield I draw a long line from one end of the wall to the other, taking care to have it run under the Perfect Tank I just drew. I step back and look at the long line. That's better. Every good battle needs a ground.

CHAPTER 8

The trouble with buried memories is that they are buried. So you can't really call them memories any more. Maybe memory is a part of our soul: the part we lend to people and places and events. If you bury those memories, maybe you bury a part of your soul too.

Leaving Green Street: what could I do with those feelings? And losing the Two Twins: where would I put that sorrow? In a back pocket or a pillowcase with the other broken toys? It was deeply disturbing to leave the street where I'd been born. In total confusion, I reverted to an earlier introversion that had been somewhat ameliorated by the colorful characters and excitement of Smithfield. No one could remain introverted in Green Street for long; it was far too alive for that nonsense.

My family was re-housed by the Social Services to Rathfarnham, six miles south of the city center. Eighteen Loretto Crescent sat on a bland, brand-new Dublin Corporation estate, surrounded by miles of green fields and bubbling streams. There were half-finished houses everywhere. The mud from the building sites covered the roads and fields. But we had our own tiny house now, although the dust got in our food, our beds, and on what precious little furniture we'd dragged from Green Street. Ma finally had a proper bedroom for the first time since marrying Da. I shared the other bedroom with my sisters.

Loretto Crescent seemed a soulless place to me. There were none of the ancient memories that clung to the Green Street chimneys like fog; none of the mystery of the alleyways and cobbled backstreets. There were a hundred ways to get from any one place to another in Smithfield, where short-cuts and tantalizing diversions were constantly revealing themselves. Loretto was a circle within a square, and once found, the way home was always the same. As were the houses.

The good-natured banter of the ever-vital Green Street was exchanged for the petty discrimination of the self-conscious suburb: thruppence looking down on tuppence, Ballybough frowning on the Coombe. Apart from some genuine kindness from our next-door neighbors, the Tullys—Maggie was beautiful, her dad was a bus conductor who let me ride the buses for free as I pocketed the fare— there was little to remember about anyone. Or at least, little I wanted to remember. The fierce loyalties and edgy competition of the city had been replaced with feigned acceptance and polite platitudes. Where Green Street was tribal and exotic, Loretto was neutral—and neurotic.

The neighbors didn't know the scandalous details of the Ellis family's business—at first. They were friendly enough, but not friends. Ma was excited to get a fresh start and tried hard for a while. But loneliness and strange surroundings soon had her out late with her old friends from town.

Christmas passed in a daze, as did spring and my first Holy Communion. In the summer holidays I was happy enough, running through the fields, robbing the Lamb Brothers' orchards, and catching pinkeens in the streams. Patricia and Katie made many friends, as did I, but there was a foreboding sense of transition; there was no anchoring *thereness* in the Rathfarnham air. Friendships ebbed and flowed with no gravity to hold them. I missed Jemser and John O and the craic. Ma brought us back to Green Street once or twice, but something had changed and old friends seemed distant. The autumn took me back to school in Rathfarnham, which, with earnest entreaties from Ma, I'd suffered at first in the spirit of a new beginning. But I couldn't focus in the drab little schoolroom. Neither the nuns nor their rulers across my knuckles could make me pay attention. I couldn't make friends and didn't care to. I couldn't have known I was simply dead tired from staying up every night waiting for

Ma to come home. I had absolutely no interest or energy for lessons. The window in the school toilets led to the field, which led to the woods and the chestnuts, the streams and freedom.

After a while, I didn't even bother to walk the mile to school. I'd spend the days wandering the fields, playing cards with the men on the building sites, eating my lunch sandwich when I was hungry, and napping in haystacks when I was tired.

Ma's boyfriends had become a part of our nights, and nightmares; their slurred speech and their droopy, drunken eyelids filled the house with dread. Ma's drinking led to such severe food shortages that the girls and I would go from door to door, asking for a slice of bread; *"Mammy sent me over for a bit of bread and butter."*

Unlike Green Street, where it had been offered without the asking, here it was given with a shake of the head and click of the tongue. I buried the humiliation with constant chatter and joking, filling the neighbors' stony silences with absent-minded humming that only worsened the indignity.

Then something happened that changed everything very quickly. That incident still remains blurred in my mind. At the time, I didn't even remotely understand what had transpired. It would be a year before events forced me to face it and decades before I fully grasped it. It compelled the neighbors to report my mother's nocturnal activities and neglect to the authorities. It caused the NSPCC to reopen our case. One day I came home to a silent house.

—⚏—

Yeah, I suppose I should be happy Patricia's not here. She's been acting real strange for ages. She's been avoiding me like I'm the Gas Man. But I'm not happy. I'm really not. She's not here now and neither is Katie. Ma is crying quietly, all alone in the kitchen.

"Where's the girls, Ma?"

No answer.

A cold feeling creeps over me, and I don't know why. I realize I've been fighting the feeling off for days. It was there this morning too. But I shook it off when Ma told me I wouldn't be going to school today.

Ma had left early this morning with her and the girls dressed up like it was Sunday. As soon as we woke she dressed me in my usuals and the girls in their best. She fussed over the girls but in a sad kind of way, like someone fussing over sick puppies. She hardly looked at me at all. But the girls didn't notice; they were glad to be dressing up nicely.

Ma sent me next door, saying, "Mrs. Tully knows yer coming for the day. Be a good boy and don't be touching things and rooting through drawers again. I'm taking the girls for a little trip, and I'll be back early evening."

She hasn't called me *the big man of the house* for ages and I'm sure it's because I've been a bad boy lately. Maybe that's also why she didn't come and get me from the Tullys. Instead, she came on home and cried alone in the kitchen.

She's very upset. She didn't lose the girls somewhere, did she? She's always losing stuff.

"Ma, where's me sisters?" Still no answer. She goes upstairs.

I follow her and she collapses on her bed, moaning softly. I sit on the floor, fingering the tassels hanging from her bedspread. The street lamps come on outside, and she falls asleep. I get the blanket from my bed in the other room, cover her up, and crawl in beside her.

—m—

Ma's very kind this morning. I slept like a kitten curled up around her; so different from the kicking legs and flailing arms of the girls. I've tried to ask about them a couple of times, but Ma just shakes her head.

"I'll tell ya later, son, after breakfast."

And what a breakfast it is: eggs and sausages and rashers and toast and a big mug of tea with three spoons of sugar. All cooked and served with such tenderness that even though I'm not hungry I eat everything up, not wanting to spoil it for her. She won't hold my gaze for more than half a second, but in that half-second is all I've ever wanted to see in her eyes.

Softness. Softer than I've ever seen her, so soft that the silences aren't really bothering me. Not too much.

She gets my nice khaki gabardine coat out—the one we got from the Saint Vincent de Paul—and the nice shirt Aunt Deirdre got me for my birthday. She hardly ever irons anything but she's ironing that shirt, taking the greatest care with it, going over and over the sleeves and collar. There's a button missing and she sews one on, slow and careful. It's a bit of a different color than the rest, but she doesn't notice and I don't tell her. She sews it on so well it'll be there when the rest of the buttons have fallen off from old age.

When she finishes tying my shoe laces, she stands back, smiling. "There's a handsome man. The spitting image of yer da, ya are."

"Where's the girls, Ma? And why am I getting all dressed up? Are we going to visit someone?"

"I'll tell ya everyting later, son." She bends under her bed and drags out the little case where she keeps her make-up stuff. She empties it out on the bedspread: lipstick and powder and puff, lotions and creams, the sweetsmelling bits and pieces of her beauty. I watch them on the bed in a daze; they look so sweet and soft. But there's that queer feeling in my stomach again and this time I can't shake it off. Maybe I ate too much. I'm not used to that much grub.

She fills the case with my socks and underpants, a shirt and a geansaí, a few comics and my old yo-yo that Patricia never wanted to learn. She closes the case.

"I'm going to get ready, son. Go and play in yer room for a bit. I'll be with ya in a jiffy."

—⁂—

Jesus! It's Preventing Cruelty! What's he doing here? I nearly died when I saw him. The courthouse was cold and draughty and I couldn't get a word out of Ma. *What's going on, Ma?*

I knew nothing good would come of anything Preventing Cruelty was involved in. I knew it was a courthouse cos he kept saying *if it pleases the court* to an eejit he called M'Lord. Two men in wigs and two men in black with white collars and all of them standing up and sitting down and *may I please approach the bench* and Ma crying all the time. Finally the M'Lord fellah banged his hammer and everyone looked happy except Ma, who looked so pale I thought she would faint.

Now, after half an hour of listening to the biggest load of codswallop I ever heard, we're all outside the courthouse in the December cold.

It's pretty clear the White Collars are in charge. Ma follows them, holding my hand as they walk over to a big black car. One of them has a limp and gets into the car while the other, a tall skinny fellah with a huge Adam's apple, is talking to Ma. She's crying, and he puts his hand on her shoulder, speaking softly. I feel like I'm going to puke and I'm regretting that big breakfast. Adam's Apple opens the car door and grabs me to put me in the back. In total shock and panic I push his lily-white, hairy hands away.

"Gerroff me, ya bollix. Feck off!"

He couldn't have looked more surprised if I'd kicked him in the balls. He's fuming like he's going to murder me, but he looks at Ma and restrains himself with some difficulty.

There's a young couple walking by on the street. The man shouts, "Leave him alone, will ya? He's only a gossoon, for Jaysus' sake."

Someone else joins in. "Pick on someone yer own size. Trust the Christian Brothers to beat up a child every time."

My heart freezes: *the Christian Brothers.* I'm paralyzed with fear. I start to cry and try to back away, but Adam's Apple has me by the scruff of the neck and pulls me closer.

The people on the street are jeering now and the Christian Brother turns to Ma and says, "Mrs. Ellis, it might be better if you got into the car . . . Please."

Confused and in tears, Ma gets into the car and beckons me to join her. Doubtfully, I climb into the back seat beside her.

"Don't worry, Mrs. Ellis; we'll give you some money for the bus fare home when we get to the school." It's The Limp. He's kinder than Adam's Apple. So I'm going to school, am I? What's wrong with the school in Rathfarnham?

In silence we drive down the village street I've often walked along as I skipped school. My favorite stroke was to look intently down at the pavement with pretend tears in my eyes till someone asked me, "What are ya looking for, son? Did ya drop something?"

"Yeah, me ma sent me out to buy food and I dropped the half-crown and can't find it. We'll have no dinner and she'll kill me, so she will."

"Here ya are, son. It's only a shilling, but sure it'll get yez something to eat." More often than not that's the answer I'd get. There's so many ways to make an honest living here in Rathfarnham. No one would fall for that shite in Green Street.

—w—

I don't know why, but I know I'm in trouble. I know I've done something real bad and it's all catching up with me. As we cross O'Connell Bridge, the car comes to a crawl in the city traffic. Down the Liffey, to my left, I can see Capel Street Bridge, where I stole the apple from Larry O'Toole. That was the start of it, wasn't it? The bike and the pigeon and the vegetables at Smithfield were all fair game, but the apple from Larry was another thing altogether. Something changed forever that day, like a broken egg that can't be mended. From then on it all just went bloody mad. I must be the worst heap of shite who ever shat. My heart must be dirtier than the Liffey.

Don't talk about the Liffey like that. Ah, Sweet Jaysus, just let me go and walk down the quays for a bit. I promise I won't throw stones at the boats, and I won't climb down the ladder and try to catch the swans, and I won't pick up cigarettes from the ground or skip on a bus without paying or steal comics from the shops . . . No, I'll just pop around this wide corridor for a walk and climb these big stairs and—

Ugh! It's the Gas Man. He's standing at the top of the stairs, grinning.

I wake up with a jerk and a punch to his wide ugly mouth, which has turned into the roof of the car and Ma's making a face and telling me *shush.*

She motions with her head toward the Christian Brothers in a warning gesture.

We go quiet again, listening to the sleepy whirr of the engine.

Not a word is spoken as we drive through the city streets. Finally, the car slows down as it passes a long gray wall that seems to go on forever.

"Where are we, Ma?"

"This is the Malahide Road, son. We're nearly there."

Nearly where? We turn left and enter through a huge iron gate. The car stops but the engine's still running. The Limp turns and says to Ma kindly, "It's probably best you get out here, Mrs. Ellis. There's a bus to town every few minutes. Here's two shillings; that should see you home."

Thanks, Mister Limp.

Ma gets out with tears in her eyes but she leans back into the car and says to the others with surprising strength, "I need to speak to my child in private, if it's all the same to you."

The Limp looks at Adam's Apple and nods. Adam's Apple gets out of the car and opens my door.

"Get out, son. Don't take all day." He nods at The Limp, who drives off up the long winding avenue. He nods at Ma and walks off a little way. He's standing and smoking a cigarette as he's looking across the fields of cattle.

Ma's stopped crying and the softness is back in her eyes again. She takes my hand as we walk back outside that big iron gate. With the noise of the Malahide Road traffic behind her, she bends down and whispers in my ear. I can smell her powder as her lips touch my cheek. My nose is in her hair, and I can see the little row of cottages across the street through her auburn strands. "Son, I know yer the best little man in the whole wide world, so I do."

Now I'm really worried. When she starts with that I know something bad is coming.

"Yer mammy's not well at all, at all. I have the TB and have to go into hospital for a while. I have to leave ya here with these people till I'm well enough to come back for ya."

Confusion! Too many things at once! Leave me here? Ma is sick? TB? I'd heard of the TB many times on Green Street. It was always said in a whisper—like now. People die of TB.

"How long will it take to get better, Ma?" I'm crying now. I'm not sure if it's because she's very sick or because she's going to leave me with the Christian Brothers. I try to pull back to see the softness but she holds me close so I can't move.

"It won't be long, son. It won't be long. I'll be back for you at Christmas."

"That's miles away, Ma. Are the girls here too?"

"No, son, they've gone to the nuns." She holds me tighter. "This is Artane. Artane Christian Brothers School for boys."

I can't breathe.

Artane! She's done it, just like she threatened a thousand times. I must have finally driven her to it.

My chest feels like a horse just kicked it in. A cold tightness steals my breath and my mind slips away. From across the street, I can see the black smoke from the chimneys of the cottages rising up lazily into the gray sky. A bus stops nearby and some kids are smiling and waving at me out the window. I wave back feebly. I hear the bell ring and the bus drives off, the black smoke from the exhaust making me choke and cough, which feels better than the . . . than the . . . it just feels better.

I step back to look at Ma but the softness is gone now. She's looking over my shoulder at Adam's Apple, who's finished his cigarette. She lifts her head as if to call him and now he's behind me with his pale, bony fingers on my shoulders. Ma kisses me on the forehead. She walks off. I watch her move down the Malahide Road.

Numb. Cold. Lost.

We're walking. Adam's Apple lights another cigarette as a cow moos to our right. I'm following him up the avenue with Ma's little make-up case in my hand. The huge buildings of Artane are a quarter of a mile away. The brother never says a word or even looks at me. As we draw nearer to the buildings, I hear what I think is the noise of a crowd at a football match. Loudest thing in the world. Uncle Joe took me to Croke Park once and it sounded like this. As we get closer I think, *Jaysus, that's no football match. That's the sound of kids playing, for God's sake.*

We go through another huge gate. We turn around the corner into the playground. My blood freezes in my veins as I get my first look at the kind of kids that could make a noise like that.

CHAPTER 9

The song is finished. I sit Liz down and play it for her. I play it all the way through for the very first time.

> *800 voices echo 'cross the grey playground*
> *Shouts of fights and God knows what*
> *I still can hear that sound.*
> *With their hobnail boots and rough tweed*
> *Angry seas of brown and green*
> *The toughest godforsaken bunch that I had ever seen.*
>
> *I was taken 'cross the schoolyard*
> *In the cold December morn*
> *Through the games of ball and the wrestling kids*
> *All fighting to stay warm,*
> *There I handed in my trousers and my khaki gabardine*
> *Farewell to the last reminders of a home in smithereens.*

Artane Industrial School. At first, it was a mixture of fear and wonder. The paralyzing terror came later. The sight, the noise of eight hundred lads playing, fighting, and screaming was frightening beyond words, and yet, despite this, somehow thrilling. The deafening cacophony echoed between the two huge main buildings. The acre of concrete playground was enclosed by those buildings and the handball alleys to the west, which further amplified the din. A huge outdoor shelter to the north made up the rest of the quadrant.

The roughness of the play, the wild, angry abandon of the kids, is impossible to describe. Everybody was running everywhere: wave after wave of surging incoherence competing for something unattainable. It seemed that the concrete playground itself was an ocean and humanity's lost children were tossed and tumbled in breakers that defied any law of nature. There was nothing of the easygoing pursuit of fun displayed by normal children, whose parents were within earshot; there was a grim desperation in the way these lads went about the business of play—if it could be called play at all. Whatever determined such fierce focus was universal and it imbued the tableau with such purposefulness that I felt weak and faltering.

Within a few moments the initial wonder and awe gave way to utter dread.

Colder than the icy December gloom that hung over the playground and buildings, this dread found its way into every corner of my being. It was impossible to believe that a few short moments ago I was asleep on my mother's shoulder, unsure but safe. Impossible to imagine that a few short miles away, Dublin City throbbed with life and vitality; its shops, traffic, and crowds were now some distant dream. Impossible to comprehend that I'd been left here with no forewarning or explanation. Trembling with cold and fear, all my cocky, Dublin Jackeen swagger, so carefully cultivated and encouraged in Green Street, fell away.

I started to cry.

The Christian Brother who'd just walked me up the avenue told me to get a grip. "Crying won't be tolerated here, boy, the Brothers won't stand for it." And with a malicious grin, "Neither will the lads."

He took me through the screaming kids, across the playground, to another brother—the Slasher, they called him—who stood by a schoolroom with his arms folded, overlooking the outdoor shelter. The Slasher delegated a tall lad about twelve years old to take me to my bed in dormitory number five, and later to the storeroom between the dorms, where a Brother Burke fitted me out with the tweed clothes and hobnail boots. A threadbare shirt, rough woolen geansaí, underpants, and thick socks completed the transformation. Brother Burke said I'd have to get the cobblers to stamp my bed and dormitory numbers on the boots tomorrow. Now dressed like the others, I was brought back to report to the Slasher, who looked me over, pulled my shirt collar over my jacket, and said simply, "Go and play." Turning to the other lad he said, "Keep an eye on him." He didn't.

—⁓—

I wrap the hundreds of kids around me like a cloak and try to move about the playground, but I can hardly walk. These boots, they're miles too big for me and each one's heavier than a sack of spuds. The fuzzy tweed from the trousers is rubbing against the insides of me thighs like sandpaper and if there's any warmth in me body it's keeping itself a secret. In a daze, I walk across the playground to the big silver object in the middle: a lamppost. The only familiar thing in sight, it's drawing me like a magnet. I'm lost in thought when someone pushes me hard from behind.

"Get over that line before Prout sees ya." He's a big lad with long trousers and a hurley stick. He points with the hurley to a faded, painted line that runs down from the lamppost to the huge dormitory buildings and up past me to the outdoor shelter. "This side of that line is for traders—big fellahs. Ye young lads have to stay over there. If Prout or the Slasher catches ya here, they'll tear yer arse off." His accent is strange—none of the easy slurring tones of Green Street or even Rathfarnham, but clipped and sing-song as if he's in a stage play. I have to strain to understand what he's saying. With expert flicks of his wrist, he's bouncing a ball on the hurley. He runs off, still keeping the ball bouncing.

I go back to daydreaming, looking up at the lamppost, thinking of another. A lad about nine or ten runs up to me. He's in short trousers and he's on my side of the line so he mustn't be a trader. He's very nifty on his feet and looks real sure of himself. But he has a good look in his eye and, thanks be to Jaysus, he's grinning. The first grin I've seen since arriving. He gallops around me a few times, looking me up and down and grinning some more. He moves his hands like he's reining in a horse and grins again at me as if to say, *hard to control this bastard.* He stops and sticks his chin in my face and says, "Yer a new lad, aren't ya?"

Nod.

"Yeah, I could tell by the way yer standing there like a frozen duck. Ya better smarten yer hump, or someone's gonna smarten it for ya. It might even be me."

Frightened grimace from me.

"Ah, go on. I'm only codding ya." He winks—a tight, neat wink that fills me with hope. "C'mon, let's go for a run."

Off he goes with me behind. As he runs, the metal heels on his boots are making this great horsey galloping sound: *kiddy-cup, kiddy-cup, kiddy-cup.* His name is Rasher, and I'm holding on to him like a raft in a storm. Down he gallops across the playground to the drinking fountains. Up again by the handball alleys and into the big shelter. We run and we run and we run, till all I can feel is my breath heaving and my heart pounding. But a part of me wants to lie down somewhere and go to sleep.

Tighten up! Don't think. Never mind the tears trying to well up. Put them away. Away behind the sound of the boots on the concrete.

All the time we're ducking and dodging, weaving in and out of the games of ball and chase and wrestling. A ball lands at Rasher's feet and he gives it a good hard kick, sending it flying off in the opposite direction from the lads who own it. They're mad as fire and now two of them are running after him, shouting threats of death and torture. But they're wasting their time; they can't catch him. Still at a gallop, Rasher turns around on his horse and shoots them very deliberately, one by one, with his finger. *Bang! Bang!* He blows the smoke from his gun.

They don't fall down dead cos they're in a different movie than him, but they know they're beat and trail off in frustration. Rasher turns his horse around and chases one, catches up, and whacks him on the head playfully; *take that, ya lug*! The other lad is foaming at the mouth, arms flailing like a mad windmill. He's trying to punch Rasher, who's twisting and turning with such agility that it's impossible even to touch him. Rasher gallops off with a cheeky grin and a whip to the horse's arse. I catch up with him by the churchyard to the north of the playground beside the shelter. I'm panting heavily but he's barely out of breath. He grins merrily. "Ya don't have to be so tough. Ya just have to be fast. The fastest ting since lightning got himself a horse."

I'm amazed. Never in Rathfarnham or even Green Street had I ever witnessed such cocksure tomfoolery. We sit on the smooth, low wall of the shelter and he takes some white stones from his pocket. He calls them jackstones. We play with the stones for a while. A bugle blows, like when the cavalry comes to the rescue.

Ta-ra-ta-ta-ra! Ta-ra-ta-ta-ra!

A lad by the football field has a battered horn to his lips. His cheeks are balloons.

Rasher jumps to his feet. "That's for me, I'm a kitchener, a Moniumer. Monium is the dripping. It gets everywhere: in yer clothes and hair." For the first time I notice the dark, shiny stains of the dripping matted into the legs of his pants. Rasher continues, "That bugle is playing 'The Moniumers Up'—it's the national anthem of the kitchen lads. It blows before every mealtime for the kitcheners to scoot to the refectory to get the grub ready. I'm off to do me duty. See ya later, Dano."

He gallops along by the railing of the football field to the north of the shelter and heads for a long, white, single-storey building beyond. This must be the refectory or whatever he called it. There's a big clock over the entrance—biggest clock I've ever seen.

On my own, I walk around limping. The hard leather of the boots is cutting my ankles to shreds. The waves of kids playing take on recognizable shapes. What at first looked like herds of mad, stampeding cattle, running in all directions at once, I now see as overlapping games of ball and chase, relieve-ee-aye-o and cowboys. I look at it all in a daze.

The shapes run into each other, merging and moving like different colored sand blown by a restless, shifting wind. I walk around in circles, lost. The laughter is too loud and the shouts too harsh and the games are battles. The surrounding buildings frown down with their huge window eyes, unblinking and accusing. The gray clouds above can't belong to the same sky that watches over the River Liffey and Dublin City.

Shite! Something's hit me on the back of the head. It's a ball. I turn to see the two lads whose ball Rasher had kicked—the same ball that just hit me. The two lads are not much bigger than me, but they have a mean look. I'm terrified.

"You're the smart-aleck who pals around with Rasher, aren't ya? Not so smart now, are ya?"

Speechless with fear, I blurt out something even I don't understand. They laugh and one lad grabs me by the coat collar and knees me in the balls. I can't believe the pain and collapse to the ground, crying loudly. They run off, disappearing into the sea of kids. Lying on my side with my face on the concrete, I'm holding my balls. Lads are running around me on all sides, totally indifferent. Through my tears, their black boots are hatchets inches from my head and the sparks flying from the metal studs and heels are daggers.

"What's ailing you, boy?" It's not a brother in black; it's a man in ordinary clothes. He's wearing a tweed cap over his gray hair and, looking up at him from the ground, I can see the gray hairs up his nose. "What happened?"

"Some lads . . . one of them kneed me in the ba—between me legs."

He nods slowly, not missing me correcting myself. "Would you recognize them if you saw them again?"

"I t-t-think so."

"You're a new fellah, aren't you?" His eyes are kind. "What's your name, son?"

"Danny Ellis."

He helps me up.

"Okay, now, Mister Danny Ellis, here's what I want you to do. I'm Mr. Prout, the drillmaster, and I'll be around here most of the time. The next time you see those lads who attacked you, say nothing, but come and see me and point them out quietly. I'll take care of the rest of it. Eh?" He nods slowly.

"Yes," says I.

"Call me 'sir' when you speak to me. The same with the brothers. Say 'sir' every single time, if you want to stay out of trouble. Got that?" His eyes are still kind.

"Yes." He looks sideways at me, warning. "Yes, sir. Yes, sir."

"That's it, son. This is a tough place, but if you learn the rules you'll be okay. Now run along. And remember, next time you see those bowsies, come and tell me."

"Yes, sir."

Before he can walk off, a whistle blows. Whistles are being blown all the time by the brothers: *Stop that! Come here! Stay off the grass!*

"That's the dinner whistle," says Prout.

How the bloody hell can he tell that? All the whistles sound the same to me. The lads all stop playing and fall into straight lines, facing north to the refectory—the ref.

Prout says, "You'll need to line up there at the back, Ellis. The big lads at the front and the little fellahs, that's you, at the back. There's twenty divisions and you'll be in the last one." He starts to shout at the top of his voice. "Okay, now lads, dress to the right. Double quick!" Prout walks up to the front of the what-you-call-them . . . the divisions. The lads are moving back and forth, trying to straighten the lines in front and to the right. I'm at the very back, still almost doubled up with the pain in my balls.

"By the right, quiiiiiick march!" Prout blows his whistle and the lines move forward all in step. Jaysus Christ! The noise of it!

"Left, right, left, right. Swing those arms. Thumbs bent. Left, right, left, right." The sound of the hobnail boots as the lads march in time is so shocking and thrilling that I forget the pain—almost. I can't keep in step, and I limp my way through the refectory entrance under the clock. It's one o'clock.

My division is last into the ref and I follow it as it turns to the right at the middle aisle between the big tables. We march to the back of a huge room, which is surrounded on all sides by large paintings of beautiful Irish scenery, right up to the high ceilings. My division stops at the last table on the left, and we all stand in silence. There's a brother walking up and down the center aisle with his hands behind his back.

Twenty metal plates are spread out on each table. In the middle of each plate is a thin slice of beef and alongside that a sorry looking bit of cabbage. What looks like it's meant to be gravy over the meat is already hardening in the cold. But wait a minute: down the middle of each table are five big plates of steaming hot potatoes bursting out of their skins. I'm looking at those spuds and my mouth is watering like a St. Bernard's.

The brother claps his hands loudly. "In the name . . ." He starts, and the lads join in: "In the name of the father and of the son and of the holy ghost . . ." Grace before meals. I've heard it said before, at school in Green Street and Rathfarnham, but eight hundred lads all at once—this is another kettle of fish altogether. We finish and a whistle blows and we all sit down in silence, hands on our laps. The sound of eight hundred kids being absolutely quiet does a funny thing to the ears—and heart. Another whistle . . . and suddenly those lovely potatoes . . .

those beautiful, steaming, fluffy spuds disappear in a flurry of diving hands and flying potato skins and I'm left looking at a sad, empty plate.

The lad next to me says, "Ya have to be quicker than that if ya want spuds." He takes a bite from a potato. "We're a *diving four.*" He winks slowly as if he was telling me a secret.

"A what?"

"Each table has twenty lads divided up into fours. Each four has different rules and ours is diving. We're a diving four." He's a little fellah, even smaller than me, with sandy hair and a tooth missing in the front. "When that whistle blows just dive in and grab—what's in yer hands is all yours." He grins and I can see my spuds oozing out through the gap in his teeth.

"Another rule we have in this four is *nicking.* If ya look away from the table and someone nicks yer grub before ya see him, that's fair game. If ya want to eat, ya have to keep looking at yer grub all the time. We change the rules sometimes, but right now it's diving and nicking. My name is Tony Gibson. They call me Gibbo. What's yours?"

"Danny Ellis." Then shyly, "You can call me Dano . . . if ya want."

We shake hands and he gives me half of a potato. Thanks. I gobble it up and the slice of meat with it, but I can't stomach the cabbage at all. After one mouthful of that cold, soggy mess I put my fork down in disgust. Gibbo asks me if I'm going to finish the *hash,* as he calls the cabbage. I say no and he reaches over and with a fork and his fingers he shoves the hash into his mouth.

"Ya'll soon learn to eat anything they put in front of ya. Don't worry about that."

We talk for a while and he tells me he's from Ballyfermot, Co. Dublin. "Where are you from?" he asks.

I don't know why, but I hesitate for a minute, confused. Rath . . . Rathfarn . . . The word won't come out of my mouth.

"I'm from Green Street," I say quickly. That's it! From now on, that's the way of it. Feck Rathfarnham—I'm not from that creepy place any more—never was!

"Great! A Dublin Jackeen! There's not many of us here, Dano, lots of country lads. Us Dubs have to stick together." He winks and nudges me with his elbow. "We'll be in the same class; class number one with the Mackerel. He's a bit too fond of the strap, if ya ask me."

"What strap?"

He laughs. "The leather strap! Ya'll find out soon enough. Some brothers have keys sewn into the straps to make 'em heavier."

We grow silent.

The rest of the lads on my table are all about the same age as me. For the first time, I look around the ref at the other tables. Everyone is talking and eating at the same time. The noise of the knives and forks on the metal plates is deafening. Soon a whistle blows. The noise and chatter ends abruptly, as if someone pulled a plug from a loud radio. Another whistle blows, and we all stand. The brother starts us off with the after meal grace.

"Bless us, oh Lord . . ." The eight hundred lads know exactly where they're going with this one. The last line of the prayer gets faster and faster, like someone running downhill, and the final *Amen* is shouted like a battle cry: "Through Christ our Lord, AMEN!" The brother looks pissed and opens his mouth as if to say something, but changes his mind.

We're marched out; I'm reminded of my sore balls. I look at the plates on the forty tables. Every plate as clean as a whistle, not a morsel left anywhere. But under the tables there's enough potato skins to feed all the black babies in Africa. Out we go, and come to a stop in silence one hundred yards from the playground, with the schoolrooms to our right and the football field to our left. A whistle blows and everyone runs for the playground like crazy. Some lads run to be first to the handball alleys, others to the various spots around the playground that seem to be favored as play areas. A number of large motor car tires that are spread around the yard are grabbed quickly, as are some smaller bicycle hoops. Scuffles break out here and there as lads try to pull the hoops and tires from others. *Diving and nicking and grabbing.*

All I can do is watch. I'm feeling a bit funny in the tummy—that bloody cabbage. The one spoonful I swallowed is wriggling around inside me like a worm. And although it's freezing cold, I'm sweating. I'm sitting on the shelter wall when Gibbo trots over.

"Afternoon school will start soon, Dano. I'll show you which classroom you should go to, if you like."

"Thanks." I groan. He wants us to be friends, I suppose. So do I, but I'm feeling so rotten I'm not able to respond with any gusto. I try to give him a grateful wink, like Rasher, but I can't do it properly and he looks at me funny.

"Don't be a die-away-er, Dano, lads will pick on ya."

"A die-away-er?"

"Yeah, it's someone who hangs around the playground in a mood and won't join in games and things. Ya have to keep moving or the brother in charge will have some lads beat ya up. No one likes a die-away-er."

—⟋⟍—

Class one has about thirty lads, all more or less the same age as me; some of them sat at my table in the ref. The Mackerel is a tough man who pretends to smile a lot, especially when he's just finished talking. "First, we'll see who learned what yesterday, won't we?" Fake smile.

He hands out exercise books to everyone except me. When he gets to me he grunts and moves on.

"Okay, open your exercise books. Those of you with more than five sums wrong step out to the line." Another fake smile. Four lads crawl wearily out to the left side of the class like they have lead feet.

The Mackerel spits on his hands and rubs them together quickly. He reaches into his cassock pocket and takes out a black leather strap.

"Hold it out."

The first lad looks younger than me. He holds out his left hand, which is shaking and dropping a little.

"Up higher. Up, I say."

The lad lifts his hand an inch higher. His eyes are scrunched up and his lips are trembling. His hand keeps falling lower and back in fear. The Mackerel brings his leather strap up quickly, hitting the back of the lad's fingers from below. He howls in pain.

"I said, up. Up! If I have to say it again, you'll get double."

The Mackerel lifts his leather strap above his shoulder and it brings it down with all his might. The noise, when the strap hits the lad's hand, rips through the classroom like a gunshot. I'm sick. I felt every bit of that. The lad is crying and blowing on his hand. Huff. Huff. He puts his hand up to the warmth of the back of his neck and lays his head on it, trying to find the life that just left it.

Four more times, on the same hand, the leather rises and falls, one for every wrong sum.

The other three boys get the same treatment. The fear is a frozen lake that will never thaw again.

"Okay, now, step out all ye lads who got four sums wrong."

—ɯ—

Twelve of the lads have been whipped. One of them is Gibbo; two sums wrong; two cracks of the strap. The Mackerel looks pleased with his lesson. He walks up to me and my heart stops.

"We have a new lad with us today. Stand up, man, and tell us your name."

I stand up, red in the face and feeling like I'm going to puke my brains out any minute. I can't stand up straight.

"What's your name, boy? Have you no tongue?" The Mackerel has a high-pitched voice and he puts an a at the end of half his words: *boy-a, tongue-a.*

"Danny Ellis." I can't manage much more than a whisper.

"Okay-a, we have a bit of a shy one here-a, don't we now-a?"

Some lads laugh, some look sorry for me, and others are hoping for some trouble or fun. I'm wishing the desk in front of me would open and swallow me up. I know I'm a sorry sight, if I look anything as bad as I feel. I'm dizzy and the whole classroom is melting, like eggs thrown at a wall. Where am I anyway? How long have I been here? Why do I feel so rotten? Why is everyone looking at me? Did the brother ask me a question?

Oh, shite! Please, not now.

Vomit!

Straight out of me mouth like water from a hose; all over the desk and the lad in front. The Mackerel has me by the back of my jacket, dragging me out of class, half lifting, half pulling. Out to the football field by the ref and I'm hanging over the railings losing my guts on the grass. It's yellow. Out me nose and down me chin in dribbles and snots and . . . Jaysus fucking Christ! Someone is beating me on the arse. The Mackerel is screaming and laying into me with his leather strap. Once. Twice. Three times. Now I remember where I am: *Artane Industrial School.*

The drinking fountains. Turn the tap. Freezing cold water. But it feels good on my face and hair. Beside me is the lad from class, washing my vomit off his head. I can't bring meself to look at him. He doesn't look at me either. Don't ask me how I got here—it's a long walk from class one and I don't remember a thing. You'd think I'd had a huge feast with the amount of puke on me clothes. *Wash it all off, there ya are, use yer sleeve.* My boots, them too, it's everywhere. I'd rather be soaking wet than smelling of vomit. What's that noise?

The lads are out of class and charging for the playground. I'm wet all over now. But there's no more stinky gawk anywhere. That's better, feeling better. Vomiting cured the pain in me balls and the Mackerel's leather strap put paid to me vomiting. Now the water's gotten rid of it all and I'm right as rain. Grand! Where's Rasher?

—⚭—

Supper's over and we're marching down the playground towards the dormitories. I was starving. I ate the whole quarter of the loaf of bread. No diving at supper. Just cut the loaf and spin the knife to see who gets to pick what quarter. Same for the jam: quarter it and spin the knife. Nice big mug of tea too. Not very hot, but better than a kick in the arse. Better than I often got at home. Gibbo says some lads in class thought I was a real eejit and some thought I did good. They liked me.

What was there to like?

Oh. The lad I puked on is a squealer and everyone hates him. Served him right, they said. "Glad to help," says I.

—⚭—

The noise of the boots on the iron stairs leading to the dorms is enough to wake a railway sleeper. There's a brother at the very top in the middle of the stairwell and he's barking something I can't hear. Bigger lads go to the left, to dorms one to four, and my division all turn right into dorm five.

Dorm five is huge. A hundred and fifty metal beds in ten straight lines, all spick and span, not a thread out of place. The brother in charge is called the Whistler by the lads. It's obvious why. In stocking feet, we march along the linoleum of the middle aisle to the boot room at the bottom. We put our boots in numbered wooden cubicles. Mine is number 125, same as me bed.

I find my bed—it was shown to me earlier; in row eight near the statue of the Blessed Virgin. I'm surprised to see my case is still under it. I open the case and nearly fall over.

It's the smell of Ma's make-up.

I fall down on the bed and smother my face in the blanket so no one can hear me. Lads undress around me and get into bed in their nightshirts. They read and talk to each other. I can't bring meself to get up and take off my clothes. My case is on the bed beside me. If I keep my eyes closed, so is Ma.

I slip off to sleep in her smell. But it's not the end of my first day in Artane.

—⁓—

"Hey, Rip Van Winkle, wake up. Wake up. Get your clothes off and get into bed." The Whistler is shaking me roughly. In a country accent he's rattling away as he's pulling my geansaí over my head.

"You're skinnier than a sideways penny." He laughs. So do some lads near by. I'm blushing. He's talking. *What's your name? Say "sir" when you speak to me. That's right, drawers off too. Put your nightshirt on properly. Now, can you get into the bed like a good man? You don't wet the bed, do you? That's good. That's good. You'll be grand after a good night's rest.*

Soon it's lights out. Radio Luxemburg plays for a while. Lovely songs I know; ones Ma used to sing. Suddenly it stops. The single light bulb in the middle of the dorm is the only friend I have in the world. I can't sleep a wink with the snores and the farts, the lads talking in their sleep, and McCarthy, the night-watchman, waking up the lads who wet the bed, marching them out to the toilets in dorm four.

"C'mon. Gerrup outa that, ya sorry lookin' lake of misery, before ya bloody well drown us all."

CHAPTER 10

It must be about six in the morning. I'm finally drifting off in a lovely dream: the little park in Green Street, Patricia and Katie, the kids around the lamppost, we're running and laughing and singing. Someone is clapping very loudly. *Stop it, Katie, I'm trying to sleep.*

But it's the Whistler. He's marching down the middle aisle, clapping his hands loudly and shouting at the top of his voice. Now he's whacking the metal bedposts with his leather strap. Lads are hopping out of bed like their arses are on fire. One boy over in the corner is still asleep and the Whistler shouts to some lads, who upend him on to the floor, mattress and all.

> *Come all ye young lads from Cork and from Dublin*
> *From Wexford and Limerick, from Kerry and Clare*
> *Jump out of them beds all ye lazy good for nothings*
> *Mush into the washroom as quick as you care*
> *Yer mothers and fathers abandoned yer hides*
> *And they left your upbringing to others*
> *They couldn't take care of yer ugly backsides*
> *So you'll do as your told cos your bodies and souls*
> *Now belong to the bold Christian Brothers*

Row by row, after a trip to the washroom, the lads are lined up in front of the Whistler, each one doing a funny little routine: hands outstretched, turning them over, bending heads sideways, left then right, so the Whistler can examine their ears and necks. Okay. Okay.

Crack! The Whistler's hand hits someone's face. "Go back and wash your ears properly, you filthy pig." We're all dressed now and rushing out the dorm door. I find Gibbo and fall in beside him. We march down the iron stairs to the playground and into the outdoor toilets. It's bloody well still dark! Is the whole world gone mad or what? I thought it only got dark at night. My toes are numb inside the boots. We're all lined up under the shelter, waiting to go into chapel.

There's noise from the front: it's Adam's Apple—the Maggot is his proper name. He's shouting, "If any man-jack of ye have even as much as half a teaspoon of water left in your bladders, now is the time to get rid of it. Not during Mass. I don't want to see any blackguard insulting God with a dirty bodily function."

Into the chapel. It's nice and cheerful. Lots of pictures around the walls and the altar looks all shiny. Prayers and answers, kneeling and standing and sitting, and more prayers. I fall asleep on my knees halfway through Mass. Through my sleepiness, my ear suddenly feels like it's being pulled off my head. It's the Maggot. He's crept up behind me. His long skinny arm has reached across three or four lads to remind me of the holiness of the occasion.

"Don't make me come over here again," he screams in a whisper and pulls hard again at my ear.

During a moment of quiet between the answering of prayers, a shaky, husky voice wails out in front, somewhere off to my right: "Oh, Lord, please have mercy on your humble servant . . ." The voice trails off. I'm mesmerized.

"That's Brother Columbus," Gibbo whispers, without moving his head or lips. "He's getting carried away again."

I'm stretching to see Columbus. He's bent and gray and very old. His skin is tight around his face and his thin, feeble hands are trembling. He goes on a bit more. "Almighty father, king of heaven and earth . . ." There's something very sad in his voice. But it makes me feel good.

After Mass, breakfast is the same as supper—except it's margarine instead of jam. I win the spin of the knife. I pick for myself the black, round part of the loaf—the Protestant, my favorite bit of the bread. I'm starving, but I can barely keep me eyes open.

Gibbo takes the time to be sure I know the lads close to us on the table. Ginger Burke, Pat Murphy, Antho Kelly, and . . . I'm too tired to remember everyone's name and nicknames. All of the twenty lads on the table are in dorm five and most are in class one. After the Whistler called me "skinnier than a sideways penny" last night, it seems that my nickname is Skinnier! I'm not pleased, but I'm too tired to object. Maybe I kinda like it. No, feck that.

—⚬—

Rasher's lent me his spinning top. It's made from a pared-down wooden spool from the tailors, with a dowel hammered down the middle hole and a metal stud stuck in the end of it. Colored wavy pen marks on the sides. He said someone from the waxies—the cobblers—made it for him. I have a length of bootlace tied around a stick and I'm whipping it across the playground. I suppose it's fun, sending it flying fifty yards or more, but I'm still not feeling very good. Everything I eat is sticking in me throat for hours. It's hard to give myself to play, but it's freezing cold and I have to keep moving. Lots of lads are playing with spinning tops and we send our little missiles toward each other, back and forth. But ya have to be careful, cos if the other lad is left-handed and he whips your top, it'll throw it out of spin and stop. Lefties have to play with lefties. *Kitoges,* they call 'em.

Pat Murphy is showing me how to spin the top by turning the bootlace clockwise around and around it. With a flick of the wrist, he sends it flying off. Nifty!

I want to be alone, so I coax the top down to the water fountains away from Pat and the other lads. The bootlace is worn at the end, with lots of fine black threads that wrap around the top very nicely. I whip with the threads gently to keep the top spinning almost in the same spot. I get down on my knees to get a lower whip crack and from here the different-colored wavy marks on the top are making a great pattern as they turn. I'm staring.

Whip and stare. The top is alive, making little patterns, circles and figures of eight. Whip and stare. How little effort it takes to keep it spinning! It sends little spurts of dust flying off here and there. *I wandered today to the hills, Maggie.* La la la di da. Whip and stare. La la di da.

Suddenly, the noise of the lads at play stops and the whole playground goes quiet. In surprise, I let the top spin itself out.

Someone smacks me across the head from behind with the palm of a hand. I turn around to see that all the lads are lined up by the shelter and I'm alone at the bottom of the playground. The Monto, the brother who hit me, has his hands on his hips and is saying something I can barely hear because my ears are ringing. ". . . Still playing after the whistle blows. Report to the Slasher at once and tell him I sent you." He used the Slasher's proper name, which I've changed to protect the guilty.

What whistle? And the Slasher, who is he again? I've only managed to catch a few of the brothers' names and I forget them as fast as I hear them. I stagger over to the shelter, where the lads are lining up in divisions ready to march off somewhere—into school, I suppose. Gibbo is in the last line. He looks around at me and says, "What's up, Skinnier?"

"I don't know. That brother over there told me to report to the Slasher. Where can I find him?"

Pat Murphy makes a face and says, "I think he's in the jacks. Watch out for him." He points to the toilets behind the handball alleys. I find the Slasher—okay, now I remember him—he's talking to a lad halfway along the fifty or so urinals. He's laughing and so is the lad, who is about fourteen years of age. The lad walks off and grins at me as he passes. I grin back. Another lad rushes past me to speak to the Slasher before I can get to him.

"I'm sorry, sir, I can't help it," he moans. "I really have to do a job very badly, sir." A "job" is what they make us call a shite. They have no respect for the English language at all. The Slasher nods impatiently and waves him aside. The lad runs into the jacks, loosening his pants as he runs.

The Slasher is very tall and erect, with blond hair under his black hat, and is wearing glasses. His face is red and he has watery blue eyes like a girl. He doesn't look a bad sort, but I can see he doesn't remember me. He gives me a friendly nod. "What can I do for you, young man?"

"The other brother on the playground told me to report to you, sir."

"And why did he do that?" His eyes are suddenly hard as steel.

"I'm n-n-not sure, s-s-sir." My stomach feels queer all of a sudden. "He said something about me still playing after the whistle blew and—"

Crack!

Red lights go on and off in my head.

I'm on the ground, knocked flying by the full force of his open hand across my face. His hand had been in his cassock while we were speaking and I never saw it coming. I hit my head when I fell down and I'm lying in the splashes of piss around the urinals. Dazed and confused, I look up to see his raised hand falling against the gray of the morning sky. A flash of black; it's the leather strap.

When it hits the cold of my thigh my whole leg explodes. I curl into a ball with my arms wrapped around my legs. Again and again the strap comes down on my hands and my legs and back. I can feel him picking his shots deliberately, anywhere he can find bare skin. I plead with him: "Please, sir. I'm sorry, sir. Please."

But he's completely out of control, with bulging eyes, swirling cassock, and flailing arms. He's screaming as he hits me, emphasizing each word with the full force of the leather: "When . . . will . . . you . . .

lads . . . learn . . . that . . . when . . . the . . . whistle . . . blows . . .
you . . . drop . . . everything . . . and run . . . for the . . . lines?"

Sweating and out of breath, he's done.

—⁓—

It was all over in a minute. A minute in which the last shreds of my childhood disappeared forever. As I lay on that cold concrete toilet floor, gasping for a breath that I still search for, a breath that would never again rise freely of its own accord, I knew then the brutality, the vicious, callous cruelty that humanity is capable of.

I can feel them now as if for the first time, as I write these lines: every blow, every single one of them on that cold December morning. How did I ever forget? But I did forget. The incident itself I'd always remembered, talked about—even laughed about. But it had faded into some kind of blasé toleration. How many subsequent beatings did it take before that first one slipped out of the realm of criminal insanity and into the casual acceptance of the Artane norm?

Maybe I never truly knew it until this moment, the damage that mad monk inflicted on me as a child. But the child in me knew it all along; it carried the pain and recognition of that crime—and others that bulldozed me, at eight years of age, into adulthood.

These songs of Artane, they just keep on coming, like migrating birds across a late-autumn sky. But I thought that first song was finished—now I know it's not. I go back to my laptop and open the file "800 Voices—song." I feel the old tightness in my breathing return as I search for the words. Then I write:

> *Marked black by the Christian Brothers*
> *Who stole away my breath*
> *Marked black by their straps of leather*

An inch away from death
Some were only lads themselves
One or two were saints
But too many grim abusers
Had no compassion or restraint.

CHAPTER 11

Yesterday, after Mass, when Rasher asked me for his spinning top back, I suddenly remembered. I apologized for leaving it there on the playground when the Monto clouted me from behind. Rasher shrugged it off. But when I told him about the Monto making me report to the Slasher and the whipping, he threw his hands up in disbelief.

"For fuck's sake, Dano, are ya mad or what? Don't be such a dope. When a brother tells you to report to someone else, don't do it. Nevfucking-ver. They're all too busy to remember who told who to do what. Keep things to yerself, and if you get caught, just say you forgot. It's worth a try, right?"

Maybe. But I got mad at him for calling me a dope. I pushed him and he pushed back. He could've kicked me arse, but he grinned and tapped me on the face so quick I never saw his hand coming.

"Honesty will get ya nowhere in this shithole, Dano." At least he doesn't call me Skinnier, like everyone else.

I didn't sleep again last night, and when I finally did I wet the bed. Thought I'd grown out of that one. I'm in real trouble now. You have to report it to the brother in charge of the dorm when you piss in the bed. This morning, I asked one of the lads close to me, a lad I know wets his bed too. I didn't let on I'd done it meself. I'm getting a name for being a bit of a cry-baby, so I'll have to be careful. He said you get whipped if you piss the bed and the Whistler likes to make a show of you in front of everyone. Also, your name is given to McCarthy, the night-watchman, who wakes you up a couple of times during the night to go. Then after breakfast, you have to get your pissy sheets and walk across the playground with them to the laundry below class number one.

Feck that! Taking Rasher's advice, I'll keep me bed-wetting to myself.

—∞—

A whistle has just blown and all the lads are running to line up by the shelter. I shudder as I run; I won't make that mistake ever again. Whenever I hear a whistle now, I just start running like a lunatic. The first whistle I heard after the Slasher's beating, I was so nervous I jumped up off the ground, where I was playing jackstones with Gibbo and some other lads, and I started running, a hundred miles an hour, in the wrong direction. If it wasn't for Gibbo's long arm almost ripping the coat off me back, I'd probably be in Sligo by now.

"Not that way, Skinnier. Are ya trying to get yerself murdered again, ya amadon?"

Now I always run in the general direction of the shelter, which seems to be where most of the lining up is done. *Line up here, line up there, eyes front, dress to the right.* Prout the driller's hoarse voice is a machine gun. His leather strap across the legs reminds you to straighten the line. Where are we going now? Supper is just over and it's too early for bed—isn't it? Everyone looks real happy for some reason.

"What's going on?" I ask Murphy, who's grinning his head off.

"The theatre, the pictures. We're going to the pictures." He sucks in his breath and grins again.

In our divisions, we march into the theatre, which is directly below dormitory five. The big lads at the back and the younger lads at the front. A dozen brothers are already seated there, most smoking cigarettes. The picture starts to loud cheers and claps and even I'm cheering now cos it's *The Three Stooges*. Then it's Mickey Mouse. In the flickering light, I suddenly notice that some lads are sitting on the floor with their backs to the screen, looking really fed up. I nudge Murphy and point to them. "What are they doing?"

"They're being punished for something." He pushes me away impatiently. "Shush!"

Next it's Gary Cooper and *Distant Drums*. Mustard! Massive! A million years roll back across my mind and I'm back in the Maro in Mary Street with me da and Patricia and Katie. I can smell Da's cigarette and I can hear Katie's sniggers as she and Patricia share sweets. We'll all go back to Green Street in a few minutes and Ma will make us some tea. Ah, Da's gone for a pint and me and the girls walk up the street home. There's that awful smell of gas and Grandah and the men from the pub and Ma getting sick and God bless all here and Pat Murphy elbows me in the side so hard I nearly lose me supper.

"Yer muttering in yer sleep and yer missing the whole thing," he hisses.

"That's all right," says I. "I've seen it all before."

—m—

I didn't wet the bed last night because I woke up dreaming I did. Five times. I've slept so little since I got here that it's hard to tell what's real and what's a dream. I could feel in my sleep that I needed to go. Then I'd dream I was in the jacks and just about to piss.

When McCarthy woke the lads who wet the bed I woke, too, and joined them on the way to the jacks. McCarthy looked at me questioningly. *I'm not one of yer wet boys. This is a temporary ting.* He pushed a lad in front of him who was half asleep.

It's Sunday morning and the lads are more cheerful today, but I'm so miserable I can't look anyone in the eye. I feel like I'm on the verge of crying all the time. But I can't let anyone know that. *Smarten yer hump.* Then when no one's close by I find myself whispering under my breath: "Mammy, Daddy, Mammy, Daddy, Mammy, Daddy," over and over real quick. Into the washroom I go and stick me head and face in the cold water; "Mammy, Daddy, Mammy, Daddy, Mammy, Daddy." What's wrong with me? *Stop it!* I sound like poor Polly-Polly-Pick-Pick, the crazy naked lady on Green Street. Jesus! Wait a minute—did her ma leave her too? A lad next to me in the washroom bumps into me accidentally and I push him away roughly. Gerroff!

Scared stiff of slipping off into that other world in my head—Polly's world—I keep jerking meself out of it, angry at everything. Anger is better than the feeling that I'm disappearing. *Focus on the things ya have to do: tie yer laces, make the bed, lines on the blankets nice and straight, pick up the floss from the floor.* I'm under the bed, reaching for a bit of paper, the sagging bedspring almost touching my little suitcase beneath it. The smell of Ma's make-up from the case sets me off again: "Mammy, Daddy, Mammy, Daddy, Mammy, Daddy."

We all put on our Sunday suits, which are a bit nicer than the others, and down the iron stairs we go and across the playground to the toilets in the cold of the morning darkness.

A warm wind blows out of nowhere, around from behind the dormitory buildings; across the yard it goes and hits us like a shout of good news. Then it's gone. But for the moment it lasted, so warm and surprising was it that a feeling welled up inside me I knew so well: the feeling of Sunday. I know, today *is* Sunday. But it's cold and dark and I've never had a Sunday feeling in the cold and dark before. Sundays are warm and bright and the rest of the day is a promise. I'd felt that warm wind before—many times. Back in Green Street, when I'd ride with Larry O'Toole, it'd come up the Liffey and across Dublin City without warning. Shane's golden tail would twitch and the people walking the streets would brighten up and Larry would take a long, deep drag on his Woodbine and say, "The wind from the Gulf Stream. God bless her warm heart." It cheered me up no end to think she'd blown all the way across Dublin City to find me here on the Artane playground.

—⁓—

Pat Murphy's cap falls from his pocket as he crosses over me in the pew. It lands on my foot and, for maybe five seconds, it's mine. But I like Pat. He's kind and a hair smaller than me. Anyone smaller than me deserves a break. Maybe it'll come back to me. I pick up his cap and hand it to him. He smiles sheepishly and I'm glad I didn't stick it in my pocket.

It's almost impossible to stay awake in Mass. I'm learning to fall asleep on me knees while still able to mouth the prayers. Now that's talent. But remembering the Maggot's threat, I try real hard. I've seen what he can do, but he actually thinks he's fair. "This is going to hurt me more than it hurts you. I'm afraid it is. I'm afraid it is. It's my sad duty to see that the divil doesn't take up residence in your heart, me lad. Hold out your hand now like a good little boy."

The priest turns around and blesses us.

Maybe the Maggot doesn't lay into us as much as the Slasher does, but he takes his duty seriously just the same. If he thinks you're trying to do the right thing, he'll give you the benefit of the doubt. But if he senses any rebellion, even imagines it—watch out.

He's not very fond of our parents. He's always saying, "Your mothers and fathers couldn't take care of ye and they've left your upbringing to the Christian Brothers of Artane." The Christian Brothers, thanks for reminding me. Those bloody words still make me quake. They're almost worse than the real thing. And don't tell me my ma couldn't take care of me. She was sick, that's all. And she takes great care of me.

The priest turns around and blesses us again. We're all very blessed.

Then above and behind me, from the choir balcony, a lone lad starts to sing.

"Kee-ree-ay-ay-ay-ay."

The hair on the back of my neck stands straight up. Jesus Christ! "Who's that?" I whisper fiercely to Murphy.

"Tommy Bonner. It's the Kyrie."

The lad continues singing in a rich, dark voice so sincere and heartfelt that the last shreds of pretend-to-be-brave leave me. I know we're not supposed to look around in church, but I can't stop myself. The Maggot is gesturing angrily at me to face front. I ignore him. I don't care. I have to see the singer.

> *Forbidden to look round us in church, today I have no choice*
> *I have to see what kind of human being stood behind that*
> *angel voice*
> *And in his eyes you saw the place where prayer first began*
> *And you knew that God was listening*
> *When Tommy Bonner sang.*

He's a tall lad with brown hair. His face is sad, but honest and open, and there's not the tiniest trace of the Artane cockiness in his eyes. I'm startled at the naked pain in his voice and face. But he's strong and upright with no hint of self-pity. He sings as if his life depended on it. Everyone's singing now. I don't know the Latin words but I know what they're trying to say. My chest is a sunrise. The purest crystal stream is pouring through my veins and every shred of unfelt sorrow is flushed out into the open by this flood of music. My heart bursts open. Down they come like rain; no sobs—just big, silent tears.

I'm still looking back around at the lad singing, ignoring the stares of the other boys and the brothers behind. The Maggot looks as if he's about to come and let me have it, but an older, gray-haired brother who's next to him whispers in his ear. The Maggot nods slowly and stays put. This older brother has a tough, hard face, but his piercing eyes are full of a steely intelligence that holds me in its gaze. That fierce look rivets me, I can feel it all the way down to my toes. It feels good, scary good; it seems to understand more about me than I'm ready to share. It seems to say, *Yes, this is what music can do. Let it. Now turn around and don't push your luck.*

I turn to the front, electrified by that gaze as the lad's dark, strong voice continues to pierce my heart. I'm more awake than I've ever been in my life.

—⚬—

Before Elvis, before the Beatles, the first voice I ever wanted to imitate was Tommy Bonner's. The raw purity of his singing would frustrate me for years as I tried to emulate it. But, of course, raw purity can't be emulated; it springs from a well—a well I'd been forced to cover over. In Green Street and Artane, feelings were something to hide, to bury beneath a joke or collapse into in despair. But here, singing in this lad, was a glorious sorrow. A strong thing you could almost feel good about displaying; no shame, no pretended nonchalance. This was a sturdy lad caught up inside a pain he didn't deserve and wasn't afraid to show. When he sang you could feel the lads let go of something; Tommy's voice gave us all permission to feel what we were so afraid to feel. He knew what to do with his pain, and his music was holding him as he allowed it; a candle holding the flame, the light drawing fuel from the hurt below. I'd seen Ma do something similar when she sang. But this was different; Ma would cave in with her own emotional gravity. Tommy was upheld by his.

—⚬—

Mass is over. We're all lining up in the shelter to march to the ref for breakfast. But here comes the Maggot. Jesus. I'm in for it.

"What's your name again, lad?"

I tell him. He's not too mad. Thanks be ta God.

He grabs my cold ear, twisting it almost off my head. "Okay, now I know Tommy Bonner's Kyrie can break a heart in two, but that doesn't mean you can break the rules, ya hear? If I see you turn round again in church, you won't be able to sit down for a week. Get it?"

"Yes, sir."

The Maggot blows his whistle and we march off to breakfast.

—⚹—

"Mustard, there's gonna be a parade." Rasher nudges me roughly. We're all lined up outside the ref just after breakfast, between the classrooms and the football field. He's pointing as a commotion starts up at the front of the ranks.

"What's that?" says I.

"It's the band—the Artane Boys Band. They'll march us round the grounds. Smashing!" He rubs his hands together.

On tippy-toes, I'm reaching up to see past the hundreds of lads in the divisions. Up front there's the noise of band instruments warming up. Little farty squeaks and deep blares and rat-tat-tats of drums. It goes on for a few minutes. A whistle blows.

Silence.

It's cold. I put my hands in my pockets. A lone crow caws its way across the gray sky and lands in the football field. No one is breathing. Another whistle blows.

A drum roll: *Trrrrrrrr . . . rrrrrrrr . . . rat! Trrrrrrrr . . . rrrrrrrr . . . rat!*

Holy Mother of the Baby Jesus in the cold crib with no pajamas! The loudest bloody thing I've ever heard in my life. Trombones and trumpets and tubas, saxophones and clarinets and drums. And more drums. Bigbelly bass drums loud as cannon guns. Fifty mad lunatics, each one trying to play louder than the other—and succeeding.

The noise tears across the playground, bounces off the dormitory buildings, slams into the handball alley walls, and around again it goes, echoing in the most glorious blast of rebel cacophony lost ears could ever hope to hear. It's an old IRA song we used to sing back in the Halston Street classrooms: "Twenty Men from Dublin Town."

The shivers running up and down my spine send waves of goose bumps up my back and across my arms and down my legs into my freezing toes. We're all marching with great gusto, swinging our arms high and banging our boot studs and metal heels into the concrete as if we could break Artane into smithereens. The music is screaming through me like scalding tea. I feel like I'm ready to take on the divil himself. Black Daniel of the Liffey is back.

Out the gate we go. Left past the brothers' quarters and the chapel and down toward the farms and infirmary. Back again and up by the refectory. Everything in the world has disappeared and there's nothing left but this blasting music, this beautiful, angry marching.

> *Discarded by my family I was giving up the fight*
> *But music made me hers that day, adopted me for life*
> *On the Sunday-morning concrete*
> *My life in strangers' hands*
> *My soul was captured by the Artane Boys Band.*

The December wind rips through the ranks like a razor, but we don't feel it. It can fuck off. Our mothers and fathers have left us here, but we couldn't give a shite. They can fuck off. We're bossed around by a bunch of lunatics who'd kick us stupid without a second thought. They can fuck off too.

Fuck yez all! The music is a sword and I'm a Roman Centurion—no, I'm Robin Hood—no, I'm Genghis Khan. Anyone except Skinnier Ellis with a snotty nose and a pocketful of *I want my mammy*.

Down we go by the classrooms again. Then as we turn left by the shelter and down toward the playground I see him. It's the gray-haired brother who whispered to the Maggot in church: Piercing Eyes.

He's up front with the band and he's calling out orders to them. He gestures angrily to a band lad who smartens himself up quickly. Piercing Eyes has a fierce air about him of a fellah who means business.

"Who's that?" I ask Rasher, shouting.

"That's Brother Joseph O'Connor. Joe Boy, we call him. He's in charge of the band. Hard as nails." He makes a face. "You should try out for the band, Dano."

"Why aren't you in it?" I shout. We're screaming above the blast from the band.

"I was—for ten minutes. Got thrown out for popping someone. Joe Boy tore me arse up." He grins. "Ya don't get a second chance. Everyone wants to be in the band. You should try to get in, Dano, it's an easy life."

I fall silent for a few minutes. The band's stopped playing. Then I say, "It's hardly worth me while. Me ma is coming to take me home at Christmas."

—⁊⁊—

Row after row of excited lads are walking down the long avenue toward the Malahide Road for the Sunday walk. The cows stop grazing to see the sight. In the fields to our left they've all gathered near the fence. In front of us, that big iron gate of Artane is wide open and we go through it gingerly, holding our breath as if it might bite. Jaysus, we're actually outside—Donnycarney.

After all I've been through in the last few days, I'm amazed the world still goes on as usual. The buses are still running. Mothers are still walking their babies in prams and fathers are still slipping off to the pub. Little girls are still playing skipping and little boys are still disrupting them. Shops are still selling comics and sweets and street kids are still robbing them blind. I drink it all in like lemonade.

"Don't let go of your partner's hand." The Monto reminds us that we're not free. "If he runs away off somewhere, you bloody well better report it to me or you'll get it—hot and heavy."

I'm holding Pat Murphy's hand and he's agreed to let me walk on the outside near the street, where I can smell the petrol from the cars. To me it's like perfume.

Down we go into the belly of Donnycarney village with its hundreds of terraced houses. We can smell the Sunday dinners through the doors and windows. Even though the Monto's stern gaze watches over us like a hawk, the wall-to-wall Artane dread can't follow us here. The air is too sweet and the noise of the kids playing is too happy.

Like drunken sailors on leave, we stagger through the housing estate, laughing and saying silly things we'd never dream of uttering on the playground. Donnycarney—your arms hold me like earth holds new grass. The ordinary beauty of humanity turns your narrow streets to spacious avenues and your tiny front yards to gracious gardens.

But smell that lovely roast. I'd give anything for a bit o' that.

"Catch!" Murphy throws a piece of chewing gum in the air between us. For a second, we're not holding hands as I reach to grab it. Shite! Can't do that! Shudder! For a minute, the Artane feeling creeps back in as I imagine the Monto's leather strap across me arse. I grab Pat's hand quickly and he laughs. "It's not that bad, Skinnier. Relax, for fuck's sake."

A lad in front of us, Willie O'Reilly, delirious with high spirits, is joking with a girl swinging on her front gate. "Hey, young one! What are ya doin' tonight? Are ya up for a bit of *divarsion*?"

"Gerrup the yard, ya ugly lump of mutton." She laughs. "Ya must be joking with a face like that."

We're all laughing but the Monto has crept up behind and heard it all.

"Okayeeeeeeeee, Mr. O'Reilly, you know what's coming to you now, don't you now? Think you're Tyrone Power, eh? Well, report to me in the boot-room tonight after lights out. We'll see how chirpy you are when I'm done with you." Who the fuck is Tyrone Power?

O'Reilly looks like someone hit him with a sledgehammer. Sick with shame and red in the face, he goes very quiet. We all do. The long hand of Artane has reached across into the Donnycarney Sunday.

Murphy and me play a word-guessing game, but it's a long walk back for Willie O'Reilly.

—⁂—

Back on the playground, some lads I don't know rope me in for a game of cowboys.

"OK, you . . . skinny fellah . . . what's yer name?" says a fat lad with a moustache.

Wait now, it's not a moustache, it's a snotty nose.

"Danny Ellis," says I.

"These lads are rustlers. Right, lads?" He points at the others. He's obviously the leader.

"Right ya are, Fatser," says one of the rustlers, a little fellah with glasses.

Fatser grabs the lad by the lapels. "Don't call me Fatser or I'll banjax ya." He pushes the lad away roughly.

Fatser turns to me and says, "You stand over there and when I come into the bar, you say, 'Howdy Roy, just in time to arrest these dirty varmints.' I'm Roy Rogers, ya see, and you're Gabby Hayes."

Something's wrong here. I'm Roy Rogers and always have been. I hate Gabby Hayes. Anyway, Roy Rogers doesn't have a snotty nose. And he's not fat either.

"I'm only going to play if I'm Roy Rogers; I can do him real well. Listen. 'Reach for the sky and pronto,'" I say in my best cowboy drawl.

Everyone laughs. Fatser points at my boots. I look down like an eejit and his fist hits me in the Sunday dinner, which wasn't nice going in and isn't nice coming out. Jaysus! I'm becoming the world's champion vomitor.

Fatser jumps back to avoid my puking peas and gravy. Everyone is laughing harder now. I stand there wiping my mouth, fighting the tears. Roy Rogers doesn't cry.

"Do you want to play this game or not?" says Fatser as they all move away from my puke.

I want to run away and cry somewhere. *You'll have to join in the games sooner or later or you'll freeze to death.*

"Y-yes, I do," I croak.

"Okay," says Fatser. "Here I come, riding in on me horse . . . and I walk into the pub . . . I mean bar." He gets off his horse and says to me, "Howdy, Gabby."

Everyone looks at me. My tongue's a plank. My heart is beating real fast.

"I said, 'Howdy Gabby.'" Fatser's snotty nose is so close to me it's the only thing in the world.

My voice is a shaky whisper. "H-howdy Roy, you're j-just in time to arrest these dirty varmints."

"You lads—I mean varmints—are all under arrest," says Fatser, pointing his gun at them. He turns to me, his moustache shining as the sun sets below the Rocky Mountains. "Tie 'em up, Gabby."

"Sure thing, Roy."

CHAPTER 12

If Monday happened on any other day of the week, it'd be great. Or if we could all agree to come to school on Wednesday and skip the other two days that'd be great too. Then we'd all hate Wednesday. But still not as much as we hate Monday. My first Monday in Artane is the longest day of my life so far and it's not even ten o'clock yet. The classroom is the Mackerel's little kingdom, but his rule stretches well beyond it. He keeps us all in constant fear by punishing us for things that happened outside it, things we couldn't know were being watched.

First thing this morning it was "Ellis, stand up like a good man. I couldn't help but notice how fond you are of talking at Mass. Go to the back and face the wall. I'll deal with you in a minute." Oh, Sweet Jesus.

"Ginger Burke, as you well know, the only thing you're allowed to eat in chapel is Holy Communion. Face the wall." Burke stands beside me, his red, freckled face as long as mine.

Just the thought of that strap—in this cold it doesn't take much of a bang to make your hand feel like it's falling off. We've been standing here facing the wall for half an hour; each minute's a week long. The Mackerel is talking and writing on the blackboard. It's about the Pope and infallibility, whatever that is. It's probably something I should be learning, something he'll beat me for not knowing later. It's enough to make me wish I was one of the Photo People who can't feel anything. I'm starting to shake and in my head I'm doing my *Mammy, Daddy, Mammy, Daddy* thing again.

Some lads are asking the Mackerel questions about the Pope and a long explanation comes out of him. He's probably flattered that anyone gives a fiddler's fart. The lads pick up on this and pretend to be very interested.

It's Antho Kelly, the class comedian. "Sir, if the Pope can't be wrong, then all he has to do is say, 'Drinking Guinness is a holy thing and good for your soul,' and Bob's yer uncle, everyone in Ireland is a saint." The class howls.

You can hear in the Mackerel's voice that he's not sure if Kelly is taking the piss. But still flattered by the interest, he gives him the benefit of the doubt. "The Pope's infallibility is only true in matters of faith and morals. In other words, when he speaks on matters of right and wrong then he can't be wrong." The Mackerel pauses triumphantly. Even though I'm facing the back wall, I can feel Kelly's mind working this one over.

"So, if the Pope says it's wrong to go to sleep, then we'd all go to hell if we did?"

The Mackerel's voice is getting a little shrill, but he's trying to keep cool cos he doesn't want to give the Pope a bad name. He's caught between wanting to skin Kelly alive and kissing the Pope's arse. But that's where Antho wants him. Ginger winks at me. This could go on all night.

"The Pope is not going to rule on how we sleep. He only rules on matters of great importance." I glance around real quick. The Mackerel's fake smile is uglier than ever as he tries to keep his bad temper out of the Pope's business. But Kelly has the whip hand and he's not giving it up without a fight.

"But isn't sleeping a matter of great importance, sir?" Kelly's voice is a fountain of innocence. I have a feeling I'm learning something very important here.

"Sleep and food and drink and work are all matters of great importance, but they're not matters of faith and morals and so the Pope won't rule on them," the Mackerel hisses. He's imploding like a fart that's not allowed out.

Someone else takes up the battle, but they don't have Kelly's wit and I lose interest. But I'm happy enough, I suppose, as long as they can keep the Mackerel talking and the leather strap stays in his pocket. On he goes and on he goes, and suddenly the clock above me strikes ten. I nearly shite in my pants with the noise of the gong.

The door opens and in walks a brother with wavy hair and glasses. He has a little hump on his back and his cassock is all wrinkly and full of chalk marks. The Mackerel's cassock is always spotless, like dirt is afraid of him. Humpy says something to the Mackerel in Gaelic and they talk back and forth for a few minutes in their secret language, which they force on us till we hate it.

The Mackerel walks out and Humpy says, "Sit down, you two at the back. I don't know what ye did, but the brother seems to have forgotten ye, so you're off the hook." He grins good-naturedly. "I'm sure your chests are very grateful," says he.

"What, sir?" says I in surprise.

"Oh, you're a new fellah, aren't ya? Your chests. Gibson, show him where your chest is," he says.

Gibbo stands up, sticks his arse out comically, and points to it, grinning.

"Looks like you were going to get your backsides whipped for your sins. We call that part of the body *the chest*. We don't use dirty words here, lad, or talk about dirty parts of the body. Understand?"

I nod, still puzzled. But I can't believe it. I'm in tears with relief. Ginger rubs his hands and makes a sucking noise through his lips. Everyone in Artane makes that noise when something good happens.

Humpy is cheerful, but he's as fussy as an old woman. That's fine with me.

"It's time for the *Do-Re-Mi*, lads," says he.

The what? says I to myself.

He clears the blackboard and starts to write some letters on it. D-R-M-F-S-L-T-D. When he's finished, he takes a tuning fork from his cassock pocket and bangs it on the desk in front of him. He holds the fork to the desk and a musical tone rings through the wood. His eyes are shining. "That's your *Do*, lads. Let me hear ye sing."

The whole class goes, "Do."

It's beautiful. That roomful of blackguards and chancers and bowsies and bullies turns into a choir of angels. The note echoes round the room and I'm singing now too.

"Again lads." Humpy is waving his hands.

"DOOOOE."

The sound of my voice mingled with thirty other lads' voices is beyond anything I've ever heard or felt. It's as if all our bodies melt into this one long note that rises above the class like a golden cloud. The tears of relief I was holding back are now doing their very best to come down my cheeks. *No need. Put the tears into the music. Hold strong, like Tommy Bonner.* The fear of waiting for nearly an hour to be whipped rushes from my belly and chest up into my head and out of my mouth in a stream of melting, musical chocolate.

The brother points to the symbols on the blackboard: D-R-M-F-S-L-T-D.

"This is the musical scale, lads. Remember, we went over it last week. For the sake of the new lad, let's try it again . . . What's your name?"

"Ellis, sir." I'm red as Geronimo, but the other lads are looking at me kindly now. What's happened to everyone all of a sudden?

"I'm Brother Fallon," says he with a slow wink. "I'll be teaching ye singing." Fallon. That's better. I won't call him Humpy any more.

We sing. *D-R-M-F-S-L-T-D*. Again. *D-R-M-F-S-L-T-D*.

Fallon is writing again. "Let's try it backward now, lads."

With some difficulty we do. *D-T-L-S-F-M-R-D*. Again. *D-T-L-S-F-M-R-D*. Then we do it forward and backward, up and down. After about five minutes we're all red in the face and as I look round the class everyone's eyes are glazed over, deep inside some inner world, soft and safe. No leather straps in this world of music.

Fallon is writing again. "Okay, now we're going to go through some variations of the scale—'modes,' we call them." He sings with us and we try to follow the "variations," with surprising success. *M-F-S-L-T-L-S-F-M.* And so on, through the scales we go. The success is making me dizzy. Holy Mother of God, this is great!

After a while he says, "So lads, if you like we can do this singing once a week or twice a week. It's up to ye all to choose. What's it to be, once or twice?"

To a man the whole class shouts, "Twice, sir!"

He grins. Class is over.

—᧞—

Out on the playground I'm playing cards with Rasher—gin rummy. Cards are the one thing that I'm almost better at than Rasher—almost. I keep breaking into the D-R-M-F-S softly under my breath. My head's still reeling from Fallon's lesson.

Rasher's impatient. "What in the name of Jaysus is up with ya? Ya sound like a broken record. Shut the fuck up before I *canonize* ya!" He has a funny way of adding a new word he's just heard into sentences. Lots of lads do it, throwing odd words in all over the place; leave me alone or I'll *vaporize* ya!

But I can't stop singing. In between looking at me cards and humming, I say, "It's Brother Fallon. He's teaching us the *Do-Re-Mi* thing. It's mustard! He's showing us how to find the notes in the air. It's like . . . I know where to find me boots in the boot-room, even though there's millions of other boots there, because I know the number of my boot box. The notes are the same. The music, the notes have names and addresses, just hanging there. When you know where they live, you can go back to them any time you bloody well want. Listen. D-R-M-F-S. And backwards: S-F-M-R-D. Ya can play with them just like cards. Ace of diamonds?"

He shakes his head. He's looking at me like I've gone crazy. But he has a funny look in his eye and says, "Maybe you should just join the band, Dano. King of spades?"

Yeah, music is grabbing at me from all sides; first it was Tommy Bonner and the band on Sunday morning. And now Fallon's *Do-Re-Mi* is filling my head with dancing notes that I can shape and play with like magic putty. I think about it for a moment as I look at my cards. No! I shake my head hard.

"I told ya before, me ma is coming to get me at Christmas. I'll be home fishing in the Dodder long before I'll learn to play anything. Ace of clubs?"

Rasher has gone quiet, like he does when I speak of Ma. He's looking at his cards for far too long. He snaps, "No. Now do ya have the fucking five of spades or not? Okay. Hand it fucking over before I *latitude* ya!"

—m—

Rasher is the best at swearing I ever heard. Even better than me—and Ma. Ma could curse pretty good when she had a mind to. I remember one evening in Green Street, just before the Two Twins were born. Ma was really fed up. Me and the girls were trying to play, but it's not easy when the air is a heavy coat of thick, sad stuff. We were used to shaking off that coat and cheering her up, but that night it was too much.

After a few bottles of Guinness, Ma started to let it all out. One of the neighbors had said something that she didn't like.

"That fucking woman is the stupidest fucking bitch I ever fucking laid eyes on in me whole fucking life. She fucking well is and that's a fucking fact."

The thick, sad coat fell off my shoulders in a second. The relief was a sunburst.

Patricia and I started laughing helplessly, Katie joined in without knowing why, and soon Ma was laughing with us.

Ma threw herself into it. "I never said a fucking truer word. That's the fucking truest fucking thing I ever fucking said in me fucking life," she laughed.

"Yeah, Ma, and she's fucking ugly too. She's so fucking ugly, her fucking nose is bent back around to her ugly fucking arse," said I loudly. Everyone went real quiet suddenly. *Jaysus! I've gone too far,* I thought.

Ma went very serious. "If you're going to say *fuck,* then fucking well say it properly." She got louder as she went on. "You have to blast whatever you're cursing to smithereens. It's 'ffffuck,'" said she, shouting and laughing hysterically. "Go on, man, say it. Say it properly."

On fire with her excitement, I took a huge breath. "Ffffuck!" said I fiercely and correctly, forcing my bottom lip against my top teeth as I blew air into the *uck* in an explosion. Ah, that's it. It's the long *f.*

Massive!

"Ffffuck! Ffffuck! Ffffuck!" said Katie, jumping up and down.

"And ffffuck the begrudgers, the fucking lot of them," said Ma, jumping up and down with her.

"Ffffuck them all," said Patricia. "Ffffuck them all."

How we laughed and laughed. United by a forbidden word that had become our secret weapon against the night, we spat it out, over and over again, till we couldn't breathe with the laughter. Red in the face and hot in the chest, we danced and cursed as if we hadn't a care in the world. In that cold, dark flat, surrounded by shadows real and imagined, the very air itself seemed to burst into light, ignited by the flames of our blazing new freedom.

I learnt a great lesson from Ma that evening. The right words, said properly, in the right place, make all the difference.

But Rasher has us all beat there. He can curse for five minutes without repeating himself once. He knows more curse words than everyone else in the world put together. And when he says "fuck that," that, whatever it is, is truly fucked. He's a great man. My hero. He must've had a great Ma too.

—⁊⁊—

Classroom eleven is a general common room and is never used for school any more. It's Sunday evening, and for the last hour lads have been drifting back from spending the day with their parents or fosters. As Rasher and me are seated at the front, at one of the double desks playing cards, I watch the returning lads with confused feelings. I envy the happy looks on their faces, their eyes lightened by a day at home. But I can also feel the despair they have to bury as they're forced to return to a place they hate.

The Maggot is standing at his tall desk, writing in the Book. That's where he keeps track of everyone's money, debit or credit. He's the Artane banker. Lads just back from home are lined up in front of him and he checks their names as they approach him.

"Duggan. One shilling, please." Duggan hands over a shilling to the Maggot, who writes in the Book and Duggan moves on. "Next," says the Maggot. "McGuiness. One and sixpence."

"Lads borrow money for the bus fare," says Rasher. "They have to get it from their parents and pay it back to the Maggot when they get back."

A lad in line winks over at Rasher. It's Willie O'Reilly. He works beside Rasher in the kitchen and plays with us sometimes. He's got his hair all greased back, different than it was before he went home to visit his parents earlier. O'Reilly's a wee bit daft, but he looks very pleased with himself.

"O'Reilly. One and thruppence," the Maggot barks without looking up from the Book.

O'Reilly winks over at us again and says confidently, "Sorry, sir, I haven't a penny to me name, sir."

"What?" The Maggot can't believe his ears.

"No, sir, not a single penny. I'm lucky to be alive at all," says O'Reilly cheerfully.

"What are ya talking about? Do you have the money or not?" the Maggot says impatiently.

"Not a penny, sir. They cleaned us out, they did. Top and bottom decks on the bus. We were lucky to get away with our scalps, sir. But they were happy enough with the money and they galloped off and left us in peace."

"Who the hell are *they*?" shouts the Maggot. He's reached into his cassock and pulled out his leather strap.

"Indians!" says O'Reilly triumphantly. "Indians attacked the bus!"

Despite the awful stupidity of O'Reilly's story and the trouble he's in, Rasher and I are laughing hysterically. The Maggot's ugly look stops us dead.

"You think that's funny, do yez?" he shouts at us, then turns back to O'Reilly. "Do you think I was born with the stable-door open? What kind of an eejit do you take me for?" He moves around from his desk to lash out wildly at O'Reilly with his leather strap—legs and thighs, anywhere, everywhere, he doesn't care. For good measure he moves quickly over to us and whips our legs beneath the desk.

"The three of ye can sit with your backs to the screen on Saturday at the theatre. And O'Reilly, write and tell your parents they owe me one and thruppence, or you won't be visiting them again in a hurry."

The three of us go outside to the playground. It's freezing!

"Stupid bastard!" says O'Reilly. "Some people know nothing about history."

"History?" says Rasher, puzzled.

"Yeah, everybody knows that Indians are always attacking stagecoaches and robbing banks and stuff like that." O'Reilly is disgusted at the Maggot's stupidity.

Rasher shakes his head in disbelief. "Couldn't your parents afford to give you the bus fare?"

"Of course they could. Me da is rich. He has a great job in Cleary's in O'Connell Street. He gave me the money all right, but I'm not giving it to the Maggot. He can fuck off." He shows us the shilling and thruppence. He runs his other hand through his oily hair and continues slyly, "*Teds* borrow money, but they never pay it back." Now I get why O'Reilly's hair is greased back: he's talking about Teddy Boys—fellahs who grease their hair and wear funny clothes.

"So you're a Teddy Boy now, are ya?" says Rasher, winking at me.

"That's right. And Teds never pay back debts, they don't do homework and they never wear drawers either."

"Why don't Teds wear drawers?" I ask. It seems like Teds don't have any brains either.

O'Reilly blushes and looks like he's said too much. I've heard about some lads not wearing drawers, afraid of soiling them accidentally and getting whipped by the brother in charge of the dorm, who examines them every week. O'Reilly must have learned that lesson the hard way.

Rasher nudges me and says to O'Reilly, "Do Teds play cards?"

—·—

Jimmy Cranny, the lad I vomited over on my first day in class, is in for it again. He's always getting beaten by the Mackerel. He's the world's worst at arithmetic. If the leather helped with learning, he'd be a genius. It's night class and we're correcting each other's work. The Mackerel has written the answers on the blackboard, saying with an evil grin, "Hand your exercise book back to the lad behind and we'll see what's what, won't we?" He enjoys teaching us very much. But looking at Cranny's work, it's obvious he's not learning. Remembering my vomiting and feeling sorry for him,

I erase some, not all, of his wrong answers, and write in the correct ones, checking with the Mackerel's answers on the blackboard. *This will make up for me puking on his empty brain,* I'm thinking, feeling pretty proud of meself.

We hand the exercise books back to their owners and the Mackerel starts off on his usual rant about who got what wrong and step out to the side if you got more than five wrong, blah, blah, blah. The leather is doing its work and lads are getting slapped and are crying. I put my hands over my ears to block out the madness. I move my hands in and out, blocking and allowing the sound in a *wah-wah-wah* manner. It's like turning a radio volume dial up and down real fast. It would be fun at any other time. Cranny looks around at me and stands up, saying something to the Mackerel. I can't make out what he says with my hands over my ears, but the next thing I know, the Mackerel lets fly with the leather and it hits me in the side of the head under my eye.

"Fuck," I shout before I can stop myself. The Mackerel's on top of me now and the leather is landing on every part of me like bombs. "What did I do?" I scream though the tears.

The Mackerel stops and walks back to the blackboard. Pointing at Cranny, he says, "Tell him what he did."

Cranny stands up again and says, "He changed my answers, sir. He cheated. I had some wrong sums and he made them right."

The bastard! He turned me in! I tried to save his hide from the leather and he turned me in. What's wrong with me? Gibbo warned me he was a squealer. I put my hand up to my face. I have a huge bump, big as a turnip, where the leather hit me when the Mackerel threw it. The lads are looking daggers at Cranny, but he ignores them, grinning, happy to be in the Mackerel's good books. *That'll be a short grin,* I think to myself. Artane, I'm quickly learning, is not a place to make hard enemies: for every twenty or so lads, there's a monitor, a boy in charge who can turn you in: make you report to a brother who will beat you on his word. They feel pretty protected from the rest of us, but there's no such thing here. A punch on the nose in the middle of a crowd of lads, and no one any the wiser as to who threw it. A stone in the back of the head as you walk out of the jacks, impossible to trace. Or a pint of water in your bed when you crawl into it in the cold, who can you blame? Oh yeah, I know I don't have to worry. The lads will sort out Cranny soon enough. I almost feel sorry for him.

My thoughts are interrupted by the door opening, and a big lad comes in, panting. "Sir, Danny Ellis's mother is here to see him . . . in the main office."

What? Me ma! What's she doing here? Christmas is over a week away. Am I going home tonight? The Mackerel looks like someone kicked him in the balls. The usual sing-song menace has left his voice as he says quietly, "Ellis, come here, let me look at your face." He takes my head in his hands in what he imagines to be a gentle touch, examining me like a doctor. He runs his hands over my bump, and I yelp in pain. His face is red as a beetroot and he looks genuinely worried.

"Why don't you go down to the drinking fountains before you meet with your mother, son. Give your face a good dash of cold water. You'll feel better," he says almost kindly. It's taken me a while to catch on as to why there's this sudden change in him, but I'm too excited about seeing Ma to take advantage of it.

The Mackerel turns to the big lad who brought the good news, "Take him to the fountains and then to the main office. Make sure he puts plenty of cold water on that lump."

The big lad and I gallop down toward the fountains in the dark. "Do you mind if we don't go to the fountains?" I plead. "It's freezing."

"I couldn't give a shite," says he. We're at the concrete steps to the office door in a few minutes and I run up as the lad runs off. I burst through the door excitedly, but Ma is sitting on a chair looking very sad. A very old, gray-haired brother—oh, it's Brother Columbus—has his hand on her shoulder and is speaking to her very quietly. He nods his head soothingly and says, "Of course,

I understand, Mrs. Ellis, I understand." He turns and leaves. Ma turns to see my face and she stands up with her hands to her mouth in horror.

"Jesus Christ, what's happened to your face, son?"

"A brother hit me with a leather strap. Don't worry, Ma, it's okay now."

"That's right, that's right. Always my big man of the house." She slurs the words and hugs me.

Oh, sweet Jesus! She's drunk. My knees go weak as she holds me too tightly, but I stiffen up immediately as the Guinness breath banishes my joy. I'm torn apart; I want to hold her forever and kiss her and tell her I love her, but I'm pushing her away in confusion. She's hurt by this. Ashamed of my rejection, I reach to hold her again awkwardly, but I've ruined it and the moment has gone. I'm always messing things up. I'm the worst person who ever lived. She shrugs off the hurt and tries to smile as she puts both hands on my shoulders. What's that shitty smell creeping up between us, behind the Guinness? I look down at her shoes. They're covered in cow shite. A noise behind the office door jerks my head around. It's a man. I didn't see him when I entered; he was behind the open door. He's unshaven and his shoes are full of cow dung too.

"We came too late for visiting hours and they wouldn't let us in the main gate. So we climbed the wall and walked through the fields." She giggles like a little girl. "They can't stop me from seeing my big brave man. I had to see ya once more before I—" she stops herself suddenly, putting her hand up to her mouth. "I had to see you once more before I go into hospital." There's little black marks at the edges of her mouth, like the ones I used to see on the mouths of everyone in the pub in Green Street.

"I thought you went to hospital straight away, Ma." I'm crying and I don't know why.

"They . . . they didn't have a bed for me, son. I'm going in tomorrow morning after breakfast."

Breakfast! The word fills me with memories that turn me to jelly and here come more sobs and more tears.

"Don't cry, son. Your mammy is here. Look what I got for you." She takes a comic out of her overcoat pocket. It's all wrinkled and dog-eared. It's *Steve Canyon*. I take it from her hand, turning the pages absentmindedly, my mind running back to another *Steve Canyon* comic, floating in the River Liffey, so long ago. Behind me, the man coughs and I turn to glare at him. The picture I've just seen in the comic—Steve Canyon punching someone's face with his huge fist—explodes in my mind and I have to control myself. But he smiles crookedly and his eyes are soft. Guinness soft. He slips what looks like a two-shilling piece into my pocket and I don't have the heart to tell him to fuck off.

"What about the girls, Ma? How are they keeping?"

"They're all grand, son, grand. But can ya read a bit of the comic for me?" she says quickly, changing the subject. My stomach turns. I can read a little bit, if the writing is big, but I'm very slow and I don't want to let her down. She opens the comic randomly. "Go on, son. Read that page for yer mammy. Go on."

I start to read the words Steve Canyon is saying, but the writing looks really small all of a sudden. The tears in my eyes are blurring the whole page. Before I can stop it, I'm crying and crying and crying.

"That's all right, son. That's all right."

"No, it's not!" I cry. "Let me try again . . ." I'm squinting through the tears, trying to read. "If . . . I . . . ever . . . see . . . you . . . again . . ." I stop, exhausted from the effort, but Ma is over the moon.

"Massive, son, that's smashing! That's my big man. They must have great teachers here, so they must."

The other door opens, the one that leads to . . . I don't know where it leads. But Brother Columbus comes in and says, "It's time to go, Mrs. Ellis."

Ma stands up too quickly and nearly falls over. My heart drops to my stomach in shame as the old brother tries to hide his disgust.

"I'll have Mr. O'Brien open the gate for you," Columbus says.

"Thank you, Brother, thank you very much." Ma bends down to look into my eyes for a long time. She turns me around so that I'm standing between her and Columbus. "There's not a braver man in the whole world. You know how proud your mammy is of you, don't ya?" I nod. She gives me a big sloppy Guinness kiss on the mouth. The man stands up behind her. He's actually smaller than Ma, and he's twiddling his cap like an eejit.

Ma whispers in my ear so neither Columbus nor the man can hear: "No matter what anyone tells ya, son, just remember: I'll be back to take you home—real soon." There's a fierce light in her eyes and she's not slurring her words all of a sudden. "Just remember that. I'll be back soon." She's crying now. She says goodbye.

"I'll see ya on Christmas day, Ma, right? Right?"

She kisses me again on the head and, without another word, she and the man stumble out the door and down the stairs into the December night.

—m—

"How did you do that?" Irene shouts incredulously.

"Magic!" I laugh, shuffling the cards.

"No, it's not. There's no such thing as magic. It's a trick, isn't it?"

"No. It's magic, pure and simple." I pull the cards back from her as she tries to snatch them from my hands.

"Then do it again. I want to see you do it again." She's screaming at me, laughing, but her eyes are wide and unsure.

Liz is smiling in the background as she chops up some vegetables. She's seen me do this card trick before. After a surreptitious glance at the bottom card—the five of clubs—I lick my fingers. I shuffle again, moving only the cards from the middle of the deck while the bottom card stays put, held there by the wet fingers of my left hand. There's a hundred variations to this little trick that simply requires you to know the bottom card and keep it there while you shuffle. "Okay, tell me when to stop," I say, as I turn cards over on the table one by one, face up, from the top of the deck.

After I've turned maybe twenty cards or so she screams, "Stop! Stop right there."

"Okay, the next card I'm going to turn over is the five of clubs," I tell her, grinning. I put my thumb on the top card as if to turn it over, but instead I quickly pull out the bottom card with my index and ring fingers, turning it over triumphantly. She didn't catch the switcheroo.

"No way!" Irene is beside herself with disbelief. "No, no way." She looks over at Liz, who is bent double, laughing. "Okay, smart ass, what's the next card?" Irene is standing now with her hands on her hips, just like her mother does when she's mad.

"Ah, that's not the way magic works," I say, standing up. "Twice is enough for magic. Any more than that and the magic works against you."

"How–did–you–do–it?" she says deliberately, looking at me intensely.

"Okay, okay. Sit back down and I'll tell you how to do it." I shuffle the deck again. "And while I'm at it, I'll tell you who taught it to me."

CHAPTER 13

Andy "Fatser" McBride is only ten years old, but he looks much older, with his big belly and wide shoulders. No moustache this time though. We're playing poker—me, Rasher, Fatser, O'Reilly, and another lad whose name I haven't bothered to learn yet. You can't know everyone. Fatser had sat his big arse down smack in the middle of a hand. "Deal me in," he said menacingly.

While he turned aside to secretly count his pocket money, I whispered to Rasher, "That's the bollox who punched me in the gut the other day—Roy Rogers."

Rasher gave a long slow wink.

We're a few hands into the game now and Fatser is ahead. We're sitting in the shelter with lads running around us playing ball and chase. Everyone plays cards here; the brothers encourage it, thinking we're learning math. But math will have little to do with this particular game. Rasher's dealing now, and just like we practiced, he's shuffling the deck in such a way as to let me see what card ends up on the bottom. No one notices. I scratch my nose repeatedly until a jack of hearts shows up on the bottom of the deck. Then I clear my throat loudly. Rasher stops for a second, licks the fingers of his left hand, and continues shuffling, but now only from the middle of the deck, keeping the jack on the bottom with the wet fingers. "How many cards, McBride?" says Rasher.

"Two," says Fatser, sucking the air through his lips in a dead give-away. He's got something good. Rasher deals him two cards and asks the same of the other lads and deals their cards also.

"What about you, Dano?"

I pretend to hesitate, remembering the tricks the men in the park in Green Street taught me. "Give me two . . . nah, fuck it, give me three," says I, throwing three useless cards into the middle. Rasher, talking all the while, quickly deals me three cards; one is the jack from the bottom of the deck, too fast for the eye to catch.

Fatser is far too impatient as he throws thruppence into the pot.

"I'll see ya," says I, doing the same. The other two lads fold.

"I raise ya thruppence," says Rasher, throwing in a sixpence.

Fatser looks hard at his cards. "How many did you buy again, Rasher?" That's allowed.

"One."

"Okay, I'll see your thruppence and raise you six." He grins, thinking Rasher has two pairs at the most. He's completely forgotten about me. I shift my weight off me arse on the cold concrete.

"I'll see ya, and I raise yez six," says I, my heart thumping. Fatser looks like he's going to choke.

"I'll see all that there and raise you six, Dano," Rasher says, throwing out a shilling and a sixpence.

By now, Fatser's face is gray as the playground and he's stopped breathing, looking at his cards like they were death threats. After a long silence he says, "I'll see yez," throwing down a shilling.

"Me too," says I, throwing sixpence.

Enough is enough. Rasher turns up his cards: a pair of sixes and a bunch of nothing else.

Fatser laughs, showing three tens, reaching for the pot.

"Hold your horses, Fats—I mean McBride," says I, throwing down my three jacks.

Fatser jumps up like a scalded cat, shouting and screaming bloody murder. I know most curse words, but I'm learning some new ones here. Rasher pulls out some gum and sticks it in Fatser's hand. "Come on, McBride, it'll be your turn next time. You'll see." Fatser sticks the gum in his mouth and walks off in a daze.

Rasher winks at me and the game breaks up. I can't believe it. It worked! Three days of hard practice and we turned it into a small fortune—the first time too. It all started over the weekend.

Rasher had been walking along by the lamppost in the middle of the playground. He had something tucked in his trousers, a comic or something papery. He saw me and called me over. "Dano, c'mere." He hesitated, looking around as if he didn't want anyone to hear him. "Have ya any money?"

"Yeah," said I carefully. I still had the two-shilling piece in my pocket from Ma's . . . I don't know what to call him . . . Ma's . . . Okay, the shite-hawk who was with Ma when she came to visit. But I should be careful with Rasher. He's a genius at relieving you of stuff you don't want any relief from at all. Instead of being careful, I said eagerly, "Yeah, I have two bob. Why?"

He dipped his hand into his trousers, pulled out a book, and held it up to me. I strained to read it. "Easy . . . Card . . . Tricks. Where the fuck did you get that?" I laughed.

"I stole it from a Donnycarney shop on our Sunday walk. When we get through reading this bugger, it'll make us rich."

"Yeah? How?"

He took out a deck of cards from his pocket. "Just wait till you see this." He licked his fingers and started shuffling. "Keep yer eye on that bottom card."

—w—

I'm tired. I'm always bloody tired. Every time I slip off to sleep, the Gas Man is there to greet me, grinning at the top of his big staircase. Once he's arrived, I know it's useless trying to get back to sleep. I lie there, holding my breath to prolong my life. I heard someone say the other day, *don't waste yer breath!* What? You mean to tell me breath can be wasted? Like food or money? You only get a certain number of breaths and after that you're dead? So I don't waste my breaths. Not me—I hold them and save my life. I'll live to be a hundred. But I'll be a tired old man if the Gas Man has anything to do with it.

But the cold and the snow this morning snap me out of my tiredness. I've never seen anything like it. It started last night in little flurries, like the ash that would fall over Green Street when folks too poor to buy coal or turf would burn newspaper. As we were marching to the dormitory stairs after supper in the dark, a tiny snowflake landed on my nose. I looked up to see a million white specks sailing around the playground lamplight. Before we got to the dorm stairs, the ground was covered with them as the noise from the hobnail boots got quieter and quieter. Until we got to the stairs, that is.

"Shake that snow off your boots, lads. Don't traipse it into the dorms or you'll be in big trouble with the brother in charge. Shake it all off," the Maggot shouted. Big mistake. Well, the noise of it: lads gleefully banging their boots against the iron stairs as we march up. Any excuse for a bit of blackguarding. The Maggot was mad as fire, but couldn't do much. The lads, realizing this, made the most of it, creating a din that'd cure the deaf.

It must've snowed all night, and by the time we reached the chapel for Mass next morning, we were all two inches taller. Kneeling down in the wet pews, we cursed the melting of it as we shivered through the Mass.

And there it is again, still falling after breakfast. We're all lined up in our divisions outside the ref, waiting for the Maggot's whistle to send us galloping to the playground. But he's keeping us waiting longer than usual this morning. Something's up. Maybe he's taking pity on us with the cold and snow and he's going to say something like, *Okay, now lads, it's a bloody terrible day, so why don't you all go up to the dorms and crawl into bed for the rest of the day and enjoy yourselves.* Instead he says, "Okay, now lads, march into the football field and line up behind the goal posts, half of you at each end." The Maggot is joined by half a dozen other brothers in hats and scarves and long coats and gloves. They usher us into the field, dividing the lines in two and directing us to stand at opposite ends of the pitch. Puzzled, I'm standing with four hundred lads, looking across the acre of snow at the other four hundred opposite. A strange thrill runs through me as I watch the sight of it. I say to Gibbo, under my breath, "Like cowboys and Indians, lined up on the prairie, ready to go to war."

The Maggot, as if he heard me, shouts, "Okay, now lads, we're going to have a battle. And I mean a real battle. Not some little fiddly excuse for a battle. Ye lads on the left are the Germans and ye on the right are the British. So when I blow the whistle I want to see a snow fight to end all snow fights. So make your snowballs now, lads." I was trembling before, but now I'm actually shaking like a dog just out of the water. I'm so scared I can't even breathe. I search out Rasher, who's down to my left a bit. I move over to him and he winks at me. "Stay close to me, Dano." Too scared to answer, I nod my head wildly to disguise my shaking. He winks again and the whistle blows.

A roar goes up across the field and we charge each other, waving our snowballs in the air. When I say we I might be stretching the truth a wee bit. The only thing I'm waving is my head, in helpless shakes, and the only charge I'm interested in is charging the Maggot with criminal lunacy.

A snowball, hard as stone, hits me smack in the gob and my head stops shaking. I don't see who threw it, but I blindly let rip with mine, hitting someone—anyone—in the back of the head.

"That's one of ours, Dano, for Christ's sake," shouts Rasher, pushing off the poor lad, who's hell bent on revenge and trying to murder me. Rasher pelts him in the face with his snowball and within a minute there's no telling who's on whose side and the whole place has gone mad.

The Maggot and the other brothers are screaming at us, "Go on, give it to him! Take no prisoners!"

Someone stuffs a cold handful down the front of my shirt and whacks it, breaking it up. As the snow slithers down my back, I see Jimmy Cranny, the squealer from class, about twenty feet away.

I bend down to gather a snowball, but before I can stand up, Gibbo and Antho Kelly and two other lads from my class pelt him around the ears and I swear I saw a fist in there with the flying snow. Kelly winks at me as they run off. Cranny's on the ground, crying, too pathetic to waste my ammo on.

Some lads have rolled up snowballs till they're as big as me and they're making a wall across the middle of the field. They're up on top of the wall now, letting rip at everyone below. A gang has gathered around the snow wall and it's like the fall of the Alamo, with lads climbing on the wall and throwing others off until everyone is fighting everyone else and all loyalty and friendship has gone to the wind in this mad tide of snow and snot.

There's a white halo over the football field, the gray sky releasing more and more of its confetti, the flying snowballs colliding in mid air with their free-falling younger brothers, gathering them up in flight. The noise of the shouting is muffled as the sky itself sinks lower and lower and the air becomes thicker and colder. No snowflake is the same, they tell me. The millions and trillions have only one thing in common.

That's right! They're all fucking well freezing cold. I'm snapped out of it by a white blur that explodes in my eyes. This is all bollox. I'm so scared I could shit meself and I'm not sure I haven't, but I'm too cold to check. There's snow in my ears, up my nose, down my pants, around my balls, and up my arse. I'm a snowman.

Everyone is getting slaughtered by everyone else. One lad is singled out for a really bad bashing. His name is Fran Dunne—at mealtimes he sits on a table near mine in the ref. For some reason, four or five evil-looking bowsies have pinned him to the ground, pummeling him with snow and fists. He somehow beats his way out of the middle of the madness and manages to climb up on top of the crumbling wall of snow. His nose is bleeding as he shouts through his tears, "Any one of you . . . I'll fight any single one of you bastards." The fighting suddenly stops around him. Everyone is surprised by his outburst. The bigger battle continues all around, but this little group has suddenly become very still. We all stare up at him but Fran has no takers for his brave challenge. I'm not sure if they've all suddenly become cowards or have come to their senses. My own fear has disappeared for a minute as I, too, am mesmerized by the sight of Fran, bravely standing alone on the wall, covered in blood. Fragile but defiant, his little figure is silhouetted against the morning sky. I don't know why, but something is stirring up my insides till I'm ready to burst. Before I know what I'm doing, I'm on the wall beside Fran and suddenly so is Rasher. Rasher lets fire at someone below and I do the same. Fran kicks out at the wall, sending showers of snow on the lads beneath, and I do the same. Rasher is yelling and so am I. I'm laughing and screaming and kicking, and when the Maggot's whistle blows to finish the battle, I'm surprised to realize that I'm sorry to hear it.

I look around me at the battlefield. Some lads are out cold on the ground. Others are crying, many are bleeding, while some are walking around aimlessly in a daze. Another whistle blows and the Maggot shouts, "OK, now lads, it's time for class. A grand battle it was! I want every man to forgive and forget what happened out here this morning. Don't go around bearing grudges. It's over now, so forget it. A little bit of good, clean fun never did anyone any harm."

"Tell that to these lads here," says I, under my breath. A dozen or so badly injured boys are being helped toward the back road to the infirmary.

"A grand battle indeed," the Maggot repeats, slapping his knee.

—ᴡ—

"What do you want for Christmas?" Rasher nearly knocks me over with a mighty slap on the back. I'm walking along by the churchyard with my hands deep in my pockets from the cold.

"I want to go home to my ma," I say, pushing him back as hard as I can.

"Okay. Come on then," says he, putting his shoulder to mine. He starts to lean into me with all his weight and we both crouch low in the Artane wrestle stance. We all do this to keep warm, hardly moving as we push against each other. In a matter of minutes we're both red-hot as we lean into each other's shoulders, the tension keeping us from falling. It's massive! A great way to stay warm and toughen up without getting your arse kicked. There's no win or lose in this game. You don't want to knock each other down or anything silly like that. No, this is a dignified meeting of friends at play. Suddenly, Rasher moves his weight back and I fall flat on the ground. "That's not fair!" I shout, glaring up at him.

"That's allowed, I forgot to tell you." He grins. "You can't push someone to the ground, but you can move out of the way and let them fall. Anyway, you get my goat up every time you talk about going home to your ma. You need to forget about that shite and join the band."

I climb to my feet and try to push him, but he moves out of the way and I fall down again. Almost in tears, I'm ashamed to hear myself say, "My mammy told me . . ."

Before I can finish, Rasher lifts me up by my coat collar and shakes me hard. "My mammy told me, my mammy told me," he mimics cruelly. I'm crying now. Rasher is shouting, "Do you want to hear what *my* mammy told *me*? Do ya? Do ya want to hear what *my* mammy told *me*?"

I stop crying in surprise. I've never seen him like this. Now *he's* almost in tears. "Go on, tell me. What did she tell ya?'" Suddenly I feel like I'm the big fellah.

"She . . . she told me . . ." he stammers, with tears in his eyes. "She told me that when my da gets home from England . . . . Oh, it's all me arse, I don't give a shite any more." He's shouting as he lashes out with his fist in the air. Then in a second he's himself again; his eyes narrow and he grins crookedly. "I really don't give a shite any more. If you've any sense you'll do the same."

He pushes me hard and we're wrestling again.

CHAPTER 14

It's Christmas Eve. We're all lined up in the long hall that runs along the back of the classrooms. Big, fat Brother O'Driscoll, who's in charge of the kitchen, is dressed up as Santy Claus and everyone's pretending not to recognize him. I noticed earlier, as we sang Christmas hymns in chapel, that he looked very pleased with himself. When he's not in chapel, he always wears a bashed-up little hat on the top of his head like a farmer. He's a mean old fart, with a big strawberry whiskey nose and a neck like a tractor tire. Speaking of tires, instead of a leather strap, his weapon of choice is a tire from a pram's wheel. That's right. A pramwheel tire! Rasher works under him in the kitchen and tells me there's strands of steel wire running through it, and when it hits yer hand on a cold morning you'd think it'd been chopped off. But O'Driscoll doesn't scare me, for some reason. He reminds me of someone . . . . When he prays in church, he looks very sad, and I think he's just acting mean to hide some old sorrow. Maybe he used to piss his bed too, when he was a lad.

Earlier, in the chapel, one of the hymns was called "Gloria in Excellus" or something foreign like that:

> *Come to Bethlehem and see*
> *Judas hanging on a goose gob tree*
> *Mary and Joseph having their tea*
> *Any leftovers give it to me.*

When we got to the chorus, as if they'd planned it, the lads all barked out like staccato gunshots:

Glow-Oh-Oh-Oh-Oh-Oh.
Oh-Oh-Oh-Oh-Oh.
Oh-Oh-Oh-Oh-Oh-Ria.

The brothers were running up and down the center aisle, glaring at the lads and telling them to sing proper and have some respect. But O'Driscoll was unusually good humored, saying, "Ah, come on now, lads, don't be like that."

Now, as I watch him in his Santy suit, I know why he was being so nice. He was practicing being Santy. He's dipping into a big sack and handing out Christmas boxes and shouting, "Ho, ho, ho." Eagerly, the lads grab their presents and rip them open. Up in front, I see Rasher get his package and run off into the crowd of lads. There's Willie O'Reilly now, shoving someone in front of him. Everyone is pushing forward impatiently.

The line slowly moves forward. I'm the very last, probably because I'm the youngest lad in Artane. In front of me is a fellow from the same class as me, Peter McGowan, a little taller and nearly as skinny as me. We get our presents and sit down on one of the wooden benches that line the walls of the hall. He opens his package and holds up a pair of wire spectacles with no lens, a golf ball, a cap gun, and what looks like two legs from a hen and a bunch of little egg-shaped white balls. I can't help laughing and he glares at me, watching as I open mine. I pull out a wornout old table-tennis bat, a doll's head, a dirty comb with hardly any teeth left, a handkerchief, and a tin hen with no legs.

Now it's his turn to laugh, but not for long. He stops suddenly and says, "That's the rest of my hen to go with my eggs and legs. They must have shoveled them into separate packages at the Saint Vincent de Paul's. Gimme that hen, it's mine." He reaches over, trying to pull the hen out of my hand. I push him off. He jumps on me and we fall to the ground. Next minute we're both being lifted up by the scruff of the neck by O'Driscoll, who's huffing and puffing, spilling out of his Santy suit like putty.

"Stop that, lads, for God's sake! It's Christmas, the season of peas and goodwill." First I heard. "Whatever is ailing ya both, sort it out quickly and shake hands." He's looking at us pointedly, waiting for us to *sort it out*.

"I'll tell you what," I say to McGowan. "If there's caps in that gun, I'll swap you my hen for it."

McGowan fires off three shots from the gun into my chest— not my arse, mind, my real chest, the one beneath my chin. "That's enough," says I. "Don't waste all the ammo." He hands over the gun and I give him the hen. To tell the truth, I don't care much what presents I have or don't have. Ma is coming tomorrow, I'm going home, and we'll all have a proper Christmas.

—᎕—

Dorm five feels very strange. I'm not really supposed to be here, but I need to pack my case. All the beds are made perfectly and the colored lines of the blankets are all straight and even, as usual. For the first time, I'm here alone, and I take a long look around at the huge room. Every one of the 150 beds has a little clutter of toys beneath. The treasures of the sons.

Now if only I wasn't going home today, I might have a root about and see if anything would be better off in my pocket. But stuck here in this hellhole, the lads will need their toys more than me. I'm a bit droopy though; I never slept a wink last night with the excitement of going home. Tossing and turning, I kept staring at the Christmas tree in the middle of row ten. The colored lights and the silver angel on top of the tree made the feeling of going home as real as the cap gun I held in my hand all night. I took the few remaining caps out of the gun in case it went off in the middle of the night. McCarthy, the cranky old night watchman, wouldn't understand. I had to fight to stay awake at Mass and couldn't eat a thing at breakfast. The lads at the table were excited too, not just because I gave them my bread, but because the whole of Artane School has been invited downtown by the Lord Mayor of Dublin to see a Christmas pantomime at the Gaiety Theatre. The lads were so worked up about it, I almost wished I could go with them.

"It'll be massive, Skinnier," said Ginger Burke. "We might even get presents from the Mayor." Everyone sucked in air loudly through pursed lips, rubbing their hands.

"Well, I hope yez all do. But I won't be there with yez, so I won't," I said, grinning.

"And where will you be?" Gibbo asked, his mouth so full of my bread he could barely talk.

"I'll be on the bus back home with me ma."

Gibbo gave up trying to chew and stared at me with his mouth open. "Yer going home?" Everyone else stopped chewing too. Maybe they were all too excited about the pantomime to eat.

I spent the next ten minutes explaining things to everyone. Some said they'll be sorry to see me go and some, with a queer look in their eye, said I'll be sorry I missed the pantomime. I brushed the funny feeling off and we all shook hands, saying goodbye. At least *I* said goodbye; some lads just shook their heads and never said a word. Jealousy is a terrible thing. We all marched out of the ref into the Christmas cold.

I searched out Rasher on the playground. I really didn't want to explain everything to him again, but I couldn't leave without saying goodbye to my best pal. He was in a great mood. This bothered me as I wanted him to be sad I was leaving. I tried to shake hands, but he pushed my hand away.

"Don't be fucking stupid, Dano. C'mon downtown with us. It'll be mustard! Don't hang around here like a fucking eejit." He started to push me with his shoulder like he always does, but I shifted my weight and he fell on the ground, laughing.

"Look at ya." He grinned, picking himself up. "Yer just starting to learn the ropes. Another week and you'll be as good as the best of them."

"Another week and I'll be picking pockets in Rathfarn—" I could barely bring myself to say that word but I forced it out. "In Rathfarnham village."

I didn't want to drag this out. It's bad enough knowing I'll never see him again, without us arguing.

"Goodbye, Rasher."

My best pal in the whole world turned and walked off without a word. I ran up the iron stairs to dorm five, confused.

—⁂—

Now in the dorm, I'm wondering if Ma will bring me back to Artane from time to time, to visit my friends. I get my case out from under the bed. I can still smell Ma's perfume if I stick my head in it. I reach down under the bed covers to get my *Steve Canyon* comic. I pack the case with all the funny presents I got last night. I head toward the dorm door. On the way through I pass Fatser McBride, who bumps into me on purpose.

"Watch where yer going, Skinnier!" He growls.

"I *was* watching," says I. Then, like a little girl, I blurt it out before I can stop myself: "My ma is coming and I'm going home today. So I'll never see your ugly face again, thank Jaysus." Why did I tell him about Ma?

He sneers. "Yeah? I'll believe that when I see it." He pushes me and runs off down the iron stairs.

The Whistler comes out of his tiny room at the back of the dorm and sees me. "And where do you think you're going with that case, young man?" He walks over to me real fast, with a look as if he's caught me stealing something.

"I'm going home, sir."

"Is—that—a—fact," says he very slowly. "And who told you that?"

"Me ma, sir. She gets out of hospital today and she's coming to take me home."

The Whistler's face completely changes. "For the love of God . . ." He goes to say something else, changes his mind, and looks at me all worried. "Why don't you just come along with the rest of us to the pantomime, son? There'll be cake and lemonade and lollipops and it'll be great craic. You can't go hanging around here on your own in the cold."

"Sir, when me ma gets here, I can't be away off at a panto downtown somewhere. She'll banjax me if I'm not here when she comes, sir. Please, let me stay, sir. Please."

The Whistler sighs deeply, looking at the Christmas tree for a long while. "In the name of God, son, if that's what you want to do, then I'm not going to be the one to stop you." He squints his eyes and lowers his voice like he's letting me in on a secret. "Why don't you hide here in the dorm till the lads have all gone to town on the buses? Then off you go and wait at the gate for your mother. Don't go knocking off stuff from any of the other lads' beds, ya hear?" He winks and walks off.

"No, sir. Thanks, sir." For some strange reason, the whole thing with the Whistler has made me feel all warm and safe. I lie down on the bed and in minutes I'm fast asleep.

The twelve o'clock bell snaps me up and awake like a jack-in-the-box. Jesus, I've slept for nearly an hour. I run downstairs with my case. My boots make an almighty clatter, echoing between the buildings and the empty playground. I let out a loud shout just to hear it echo off the handball alley and back to me again.

How weird the place looks and feels without the hundreds of lads running around, screaming and fighting.

Goodbye, gray playground, I won't miss ya a bit. You're too big and too hard and the hundred years of play that echoed around you haven't softened you a bit. No, you turn play itself to war and games to revenge and lads to bullies who've forgotten that they are still children. You feast on the sound of a thousand leather straps falling on cold hands and legs, and the million tears you've greedily sucked up haven't quenched your thirst.

I can almost feel the ground opening its mouth to swallow me up as I run across it. I shake it all off in a shudder and quicken my pace.

Fuck away off playground, ya gray old bastard, may lightning strike and crack ya in a million pieces.

I bolt across the dividing line between the playground and the churchyard and come to a sudden stop at the gate. I feel real silly to have run so hard and stopped so suddenly. But no one's around to see me looking stupid. The churchyard is really part of the playground, but it's normally out of bounds unless you're going to the chapel. The outdoor shelter marks the churchyard boundary on one side and the dormitory buildings on the other. A high railing on each side of the gates stretches from the dorms to the chapel. There's three main gates here in Artane. This one, where I stand, is a secondary gate that looks down the long avenue to the Malahide Road, where the main gate and Lodge House are. That's the gate Ma tried to enter when she came that night. It's locked every evening at eight by Mr. O'Brien, who lives in the lodge and who also teaches carpentry in the trade shops. There's another gate, close to the infirmary, leading to Kilmore Road—the north gate. So I'll be waiting here till Ma comes. That way I can keep an eye on all directions, just in case she comes in the north gate. You never know with Ma; she can be contrary when she wants. I lay my case on the ground and start to walk back and forth to keep warm, practicing the *Do-Re-Mi* scales.

I can't wait to sing 'em for Ma, and she's gonna die laughing at these crazy toys I got last night.

> *Oh, I just can't wait to show you*
> *What Santa brought last night*
> *Well he must've been half drunk*
> *Or his glasses weren't on right*
> *I got half an old tin hen*
> *And a rather toothless comb*
> *But you' ll see them all yourself*
> *On the Bus Back Home.*

CHAPTER 15

I wish I'd remembered to ask Rasher for his deck of cards. I could be practicing the tricks now, instead of worrying about Ma. But it's cold enough to freeze the balls off a Kerry mountain goat, so maybe card tricks aren't a good idea. You need nimble fingers for them shenanigans, not these red lumps of solid ice. Each finger feels like one of my feet, and stop, for Christ's sakes, don't talk about your feet, they feel like they've merged with the concrete churchyard. So, with feet for fingers and churchyards for feet I'm in a bit of a state here. It's after three o'clock and there's still no sign of Ma.

Then I spy a lone figure down the quarter-mile-long avenue, coming through the main gate. It walks very slowly toward me. *Too slow for Ma,* I think in disappointment. Then I remember. She just got out of the hospital. She's in pain. I run toward her, but stop suddenly after a few hundred yards. It's only a very old brother I've never seen before. He nods and goes into the office in front of the gate.

Cold is something I know very well, but there's usually a good reason to ignore it: wrestling, a football match, a game of cards, or a comic you've only read three or four times. Wait! That's a good idea! I open the case and take out the *Steve Canyon* comic. I sit down on top of the case, flattening it. Ma won't mind. *Where are ya, Ma?*

I'm a slow reader, but I'm about halfway through the comic for the third time when the chapel door opens behind me. It's old Brother Columbus, the one who spoke so quietly to Ma when she came that night. He's always trembling, and he's always praying. There, he's at it again.

"He's a hundred and fifty years old," Rasher told me one day when Columbus was praying out loud as he shuffled through the churchyard. "He's on his last legs and wants to get his money's worth before he kicks the bucket."

Columbus sees me and says kindly, "What in the name of God are you doing, son, sitting there in the cold? Why didn't you go downtown with the rest of the lads for the Christmas pantomime?" He walks up real close to me, trembling with each step.

For the tenth time in a week I explain that my ma is coming to bring me home. He listens very carefully, and for once, his hands have stopped trembling. His eyes are kind and very soft and set deep in his head. I'm often a bit scared of really old men, there's something skeletony about them, but Columbus has a light around him that shines through his eyes and skin. As I'm telling him about my ma, his face gets sadder and sadder as he nods his head. "Are you hungry, son?" His gray eyebrows rise up real high, willing me to say yes.

"I'm starving, sir."

He puts his hand into his cassock and takes out a brown paper bag. It's full of boiled potatoes. I've heard about this habit of his from other lads. "I like to share my lunch with those who need it more than I. Put these inside you, lad, you'll feel the better for it."

I gobble them up and he's right, the spuds are a door to a whole new world.

"Leave your case there by the gate, son, and come along with me." He puts his hand on my shoulder and gently ushers me alongside him.

"But I'll miss me ma when she comes, sir. Please let me stay till she comes."

In a chatty voice, as if he was still talking about potatoes, he says, "Your mother is not coming, son. You're not going home. She's left you here and she's not coming back." His tone is so ordinary, so matter of fact, that the meaning of the words doesn't reach me. In a kind of spell, I fall into step beside him as we walk along the narrow path between the football field and the chapel, toward the refectory.

"She simply can't afford to keep you, son. You're in God's hands now. He singles out some of his children for special attention and you're one of those." He speaks those last words like they're so full of good news that I'm still not quite sure what I'm hearing. "The sooner you put your trust in God, the better off you'll be. He's your true father, you know; your heavenly father . . . and He wants you all for Himself. He's been with you since before you were born, and He'll never let you down, no matter what. No, don't think of home. Heaven is your only home, lad."

I look up at him. His sad, sunken eyes are glowing and it finally dawns on me what he's saying. All hope drains from my heart.

Stop.

Stop walking.

Stop thinking.

Stop breathing.

Stop world. Stop, while I feel this. I've been trying not to feel it for weeks. Ah, there it is, cold and sharp like the frosted grass in the football field in front of us. The truth. It sinks down inside me till I can feel it in my belly and my toes.

I'm all alone in the world. A world that's not my home.

No ma. No da. No sisters or twins. No Larry O'Toole or friends on Green Street. It's just me. Only me. It almost feels better than the belief that Ma is coming. More solid than the helpless hope I've been clinging to, night and day, since she left me here. My gaze wanders past Columbus in a daze, across the ghostly haze descending on the football field. It comes to rest on the big refectory clock. I'm being held by a clock. It seems to radiate beams of light from its center. The light holds me till there's nothing in the universe except me, that clock, and this cold certainty.

For a long, silent moment I allow my soul to embrace this huge emptiness.

And for a long, silent moment I'm completely free.

Oh, there's Roman numerals on the refectory clock. I suppose time is time, whatever kind of numbers you use to tell it. It's a beautiful clock, though. *Hello world*, it says. *Here's some time.*

Time: the little black dots for the minutes, the bigger dots for the hours, the big hand a spear, and the little hand a dagger that guards the passing. Time is a warrior king on the most perfect clock I've ever seen.

Suddenly the big hand moves. The warrior king speaks the truth: TOCK. It's four o'clock.

—⁕—

In one sacred moment that I would spend most of my early life fighting against, that saintly man carried me across the divide between my infinite soul and my tiny, tortured identity. Annihilation. Nothing was ever more real—or certain. But as hopes for my mother shattered like thin ice, the void they opened was filled immediately with this new nothingness of Columbus's God. As I grew older, every beautiful melody I ever heard would hold the sacred architecture of that emptiness within it. In time, and out of it, I would learn to treasure that solitude, seek it out like an old friend. But it was all too much for my eight-year-old heart and mind to embrace for more than a few seconds. I came screaming back to my old broken self; bound and lost though it was, it was better than that terrible freedom— that endless horizon—my soul was offering. Some part of me knew I didn't belong in that detached state. Columbus must have known it too. A million miles away, I heard his voice reaching to find me.

"Listen, son, listen. Why don't you go and join the school band? Go and see Brother O'Connor and ask him to give you a try out. You'll be very happy there."

—⁕—

No, I won't. I won't be happy anywhere. Jesus Christ! Everyone wants me to join the fucking, stupid, shitty band. It's like, "You're stuck here forever, so you might as well join the band." Well, you can all fuck off. You and that stupid, fucking clock. I'm not here forever. I'm going home with me ma. She told me so, didn't she? She must still be sick, but when she's better, she'll be over here on the first bus and I'm going home. I'm not alone. I have a mother, a ma, a mammy who's not well. So what do you know about it anyway, ya shaky old bastard?

I glare at Columbus, but he smiles warmly.

"Tell Brother O'Connor that Brother Columbus sent you. Go and see him in the band room, first thing Monday morning, and tell him I sent you."

I'll tell nobody nothing. Not Brother O'Connor nor you, ya gray-faced old gimp. I have nothing to say to nobody. I turn and run back to the gate, where I left my case on the ground. I look down the avenue. *She could come any minute. Don't give up. Ever.*

Columbus has disappeared into the brothers' quarters. It's freezing. I blow into my hands. It's getting dark and the cold, damp air is seeping through my clothes. After about ten minutes, my teeth start chattering. *Stop teeth. Stop that.* I clench them, but my eyes start watering. My nose is running too. It's the cold. It's the cold.

Here comes Columbus. He can fuck off.

"Would you like a cup of tea, son? It'll warm you up."

"Yes, sir, I'd love one." The words are out of my mouth before I can stop them. Someone else took over my tongue, someone who's suddenly more hungry than angry, more cold than lonely. Columbus takes me through the gate and up the stairs to the office where Ma came that night. We cross the tiled floor of the office and go through a door. Ah, so it leads into the brothers' quarters. Everything is wood. Shining, dark-brown wood from floor to ceiling, with statues and busts everywhere. The smell of incense is strong till we go through another door into the kitchen. Now the smell of food is enough to make a statue's mouth water. Brother O'Driscoll is passing through the kitchen and looks at me, scowling as if to say, *What are you doing here?* Columbus whispers in his ear and O'Driscoll grunts, turns to a stout lad in an apron who's hovering nearby, and says, "Michael, make this lad . . . what's your name, child? Ah, Danny. Michael, make Danny a nice cup of tea with plenty of sugar."

The lad looks like he just stepped on a turd.

"And a nice big slice of bread and jam too," Columbus adds, as he pats the lad's head.

Soon I'm in the brothers' dining room, stuffing my face like it's . . . Oh, I nearly forgot—it *is* Christmas.

—⚍—

Full of hot tea and bread and jam, I walk toward the gate where I left Ma's case on the ground. The grub has buried the thought of how much I was looking forward to showing her these crazy Christmas presents. It's buried the words Columbus poured over my waiting for her. It's buried my dreams of going home again anytime soon. But nothing will ever bury the memory of her softness or her last words to me in the office: *No matter what anyone tells ya, son, just remember, I'll be back to take you home—real soon. She's coming . . . . Just as soon as she gets better. But how sick are ya, Ma? How long will it take ya to get better?*

A dull hum, a distant noise from down the avenue, creeps up toward me from the main gate. It's the lads, back from the pantomime. The buses have dropped them outside the main gate on the Malahide Road and they're walking quickly up the avenue, laughing and shouting. I watch the nameless hundreds hustle past in a blur till I see Rasher.

"Howaya, Dano. Great panto! Except for Tommy Dando and his stupid 'Keep Your Sunny Side Up, Up.'" He sings the song and skips along merrily, ignoring my long face. *Go on, Rasher—tell me you told me so.* He doesn't.

"C'mon, let's see if we can find some eejits to play cards with," he says. I fall in beside him as he walks briskly across to the shelter.

"Slow down, will ya?" I complain. "I'm going to do it . . . I'm joining the band. I might as well . . . at least till me ma gets out of hospital."

He ignores me, saying, "Y'know, Willie O'Reilly got a five-bob postal order for Christmas. Now, where is he?"

"I thought you'd be glad. Aren't you the one who keeps telling me to join the band?"

He stops dead. "Join the bloody band, for Jaysus' sakes, Dano, but stop talking about yer ma, cos she's not taking you home."

I ignore *him* now, looking intently at the refectory clock across the football field. I feel the emptiness creeping back. *Tighten up, will ya!* Christ! That's the ugliest clock I ever saw in my life. Rasher looks at me, waiting for an answer.

"Gimme them stupid cards. I just had another idea for a great cheat trick. We mark every single high card—ten and over—in the deck, and those eejits will never cop on, cos we'll use Roman numerals."

CHAPTER 16

Monday morning. Saint Stephen's Day. The band room. To get here, I had to go through the wooden gate by the theatre that leads down to the trade workshops. My God! It's hard to tell what the room looks like with fifty or sixty lads packed in here like sardines. But the walls are made of shiny brown wood. So is the floor. The ceiling, like all ceilings in Artane, is high enough to give you a crick in the neck. There's raised platforms for the brass sections and drummers while the woodwind all sit below them. Everyone's seated except the drummers. The crammed bodies of the lads look like a single living thing; a giant crashing wave about to fold over itself. I feel like a tiny boat about to be capsized. *Tighten up.*

In the distance, from the playground, I've heard the band practicing here almost since the minute I arrived. I've heard them blast the bejaysus off the handball alley walls as they marched us around the grounds. I've even spied on them from a dormitory window as they practiced their figure-marching in the field outside the secondary gate. It's a grand and mighty noise. Just what I need. Enough to smarten yer hump and straighten yer spine. But to be in the same room with them is like sticking your head in an airplane engine. *Don't even think of talking. Don't think about Ma or feeling bad. Don't think at all. You're wasting your time. Your thoughts are all mixed up with the millions of notes hammering at your skull. Five trombones, four tubas, six trumpets, seven . . . no, eight saxophones, and don't even talk to me about the clarinets or the halfdozen snare drums. Funny, twisted, backward-facing horns, and . . . a baby tuba?* Each lad is practicing a different piece of music and trying to play louder than the next fellah. If the war on my bedroom wall in Green Street could talk, it'd be proud to make a noise like this. A tall lad jumps down from the raised platform where the trombones are seated, and when he sees me staring, he points his trombone at me like a bazooka and lets out a blast that sends shivers up and down my spine. I'm riveted to the spot. He rubs my head cheerfully and walks off, grinning.

Brother Joseph O'Connor—Joe Boy, they call him, but not to his face—is talking to someone behind the drum stand and he spots me hovering shyly. He says something to the lad, who nods. They must be lip readers. Here he is now, walking toward me.

"I bod bungling ben jude gum hear," he shouts.

"I beg your pardon, sir, I can't hear a word you're saying." I'm screaming; it's almost fun.

He pushes me by the shoulder to a small room behind the drum stand and closes the door.

"I said, I was wondering when you'd come here. I saw the way you looked at Tommy Bonner in church a few weeks back. Music is in your soul, lad, isn't it?"

A nod from me.

"So, what can I do for you?" he says. He knows why I'm here, he just wants to hear me say it.

"I want to play in the band, sir. At least till my ma comes and takes me home when she gets out of hospital."

He's looking at me with his hard, steely eyes for a long time as if he's making up his mind.

"Brother Columbus told me to ask you if I can join the band, sir," I blurt.

No answer. Just eyes. Thinking he's hesitating because of my bad manners, I add in a tiny voice, "Please, sir." Christ, why am I begging him like this? I must want this more than I know.

He shakes his head impatiently and his eyes fill with that scary intelligence I saw on that first Sunday at Mass. "I don't care about the 'please' or 'thank-you' nonsense. I just don't want to waste my time on someone who doesn't really want to be a band lad."

"Oh, I do, sir. I really do." There I go again. What do I care about his silly band? "I want to be a band lad, sir."

"I don't think so, boy. I think you'd rather be on the playground, wasting your time like the rest of those blackguards."

I want to tell him to go and shite, but I hear myself say, "Oh, no, sir. Honest to God, I really, really want to play in the band, sir. I love the music and the marching and the . . . the sound of the lads blasting away and all that there, sir." Either my mouth has lost all connection to my brain or it knows something my brain doesn't.

"Let me see your teeth. What's your name, anyway? Where are you from?"

"Danny Ellis, sir. From Green Street, Dublin," I say through my teeth as he takes my chin in his hand. I can smell the carbolic soap on his pale fingers. His nails are spotless.

"Good strong teeth. Maybe a brass instrument. A trumpet? Or a tuba or euphonium?" He's looking at me carefully as he lists the brass instruments. "How about a trombone? . . . There! That's it! Wait here, lad." He leaves and returns in seconds with a battered old trombone that must have been played at Brian Boru's funeral. "Fire away on this, lad. Blow like you got a hair on your tongue."

I let out a farty little squawk that I'm sure has ended my musical career on the spot.

"Don't be afraid, lad. You won't do it any harm. Whatever's going on in that fighting Dublin heart of yours, put it down that trombone."

For some reason, those words get to me. He sees it, his keen eyes boring into my soul. Nearly in tears, I let rip down that old horn as if the hounds of hell were charging out of my lungs. The sound sears through my body and echoes around the room like a thunderclap. I'm suddenly ten feet tall, and before O'Connor can recover from his surprise, I let loose another blast, louder than the first.

O'Connor tightens his thin lips and nods his head. "Well done, boy. Welcome to the Artane Boys Band."

—◊—

Rasher nearly faints when he sees the cut of me. Brother O'Connor had taken me to the washroom beside the band room and made me scrub my face, hands, and legs, wet and comb my hair, and rub it down with soap to hold it flat. Then he had me polish and shine my boots and button the top button on my shirt. I'm clean as Sunday morning.

"Janie Mack, Dano. Where the hell is Black Daniel of the Liffey? Now it's more like White Daniel of the Band, eh?" He laughs.

"I know, it's worse than Holy Communion day," says I, sheepishly. "But wait till you hear me play the trombone. I can turn your ears crossways on your head. It's massive!"

—◊—

Being in the band is the best feeling since . . . since I don't know when. For three days, Joe Boy had me study music notes with a band lad at a blackboard—*a minim is a white note with a stem count two. A crotchet is a black note with a stem count one.* Then O'Connor gave me the bashed-up trombone and had me sit at the end of the trombone section—who ignored me to a man—and told me to practice away, saying, "Don't worry about reading music yet. Just blow away to your heart's content and get your lip strong." This I did for a week. In a room with sixty others, all individually practicing different pieces of music. I didn't need any encouragement. I made sure the trombone lads didn't ignore me for very long. The wild honks and sliding blares from meself soon had them stretching in their chairs to catch a glimpse of the lunatic at the end of that old horn. I'm not sure whether their looks were of respect or disgust, but I felt so good I didn't care. I'd think to meself, *This is me, me lads. I have this trombone and, by Jaysus, everyone will know I'm here.* But my lips soon swelled up so much they could hardly fit in the mouthpiece and my warrior blasts withered to a few pathetic, floppy farts.

One day the lad to my left, a handsome, stocky fellah, leaned over and shouted, "You're gonna blow your lip out, man. Take a rest, for God's sake." At first, I thought he was being spiteful, but his eyes were kind and he winked. I stopped blowing and looked around the room. Everybody looked cleaner and neater than the playground lads and the way they sat, all straight-backed and dignified-like, made them look like soldiers instead of a bunch of lawless blackguards. I like lawless blackguards, but soldiers are good too. The other thing was, they were all mixed up, age wise. On the playground, older lads were separated from younger ones, but here, nine year olds were seated next to fifteen year olds, and I don't know why but that felt good. There was something else that I was slowly noticing: Everyone's eyes looked a wee bit softer than the playground lads'. More dreamy. It was the same thing I'd been noticing in Brother Fallon's singing class twice a week for the last month. Music makes everything softer. Even loud music. *Especially* loud music. Now why is that?

"How the fuck would I know, Dano," says Rasher impatiently. He's always asking me about the band and then he gets angry when I tell him. "Soft eyes, me arse. *You're* not turning soft on me now, are ya? Now that we have the card tricks down, I'm not gonna have to train some other eejit, am I?" He's more than half serious.

"Ah, stop it, will ya? I can't play the trombone every minute of the day." I shove him hard and soon we're shoulder to shoulder, pushing against each other and the cold of the evening.

—⁊⁊—

"So yer ma is coming to take you home, eh? She probably couldn't stand to be in the same house as ya." It's Fatser—Andy McBride. I can't believe it. He's in the band—a trumpeter. It'll be hard to steer clear of that shitehawk now. I wink at him like he's my best pal and make my way to the trombone lockers.

There's three different bands: Band One, the main band that plays outside at events and marches around the playground; Band Two, made up of lads who are not quite ready to play in the main band yet; and Band Three, which is not really a band at all, it's the lads just joined and starting to learn an instrument. I'm in Band Two and so is Fatser. We all meet in the afternoon, under the direction of Mr. George Crean. He's a lovely, kind old man, and the lads in the trombone section are nice too: Smasher Magee and Itchy Reynolds. But in the morning, us really new lads are allowed to sit with our sections in Band One and learn how to read music from the older boys.

"My name is Ernie Fanning," says the lad sitting next to me, offering me his hand. Fanning is the lad who told me to ease up on my blasting the other day. His older brother, Tommy, also plays trombone beside him to his left.

"I'm Danny Ellis—you can call me Dano." I winked. Rasher's been teaching me to wink properly and I can do it as slyly as anyone. Ernie's much older than me. O'Connor has told him to help me to read music. He's kind and patient, but he laughs a lot at my loud playing. He warms his trombone up, blowing hot air through his mouthpiece. He points to a note in the music book on the stand in front, which looks like gibberish to me.

"This is B flat and it sounds like this." He plays a sweet tone without moving the slide. "Go on, give it a try yerself."

I blast out a note that is louder and higher in pitch than his.

"No. That's a D, Dano. Loosen your lips a bit." He plays his B what-you-may-call-it again. Copying him, this time I get it right. He points to a bunch of notes in the book, all going up and down like stairs, and says, "This is the B-flat scale and it sounds like this." He plays the scale and I'm so excited I let out a yelp.

"Wait, now! That's the *Do-Re-Mi* thingy that Brother Fallon teaches us in singing class."

Fanning looks at me like I'm crazy. "It's the B-flat scale. Simple as that. It starts on B flat, and don't call it anything else. Listen, if you want to read music, learn the notes of the scale first. This scale is B flat, and the notes are B flat, C, D, E flat, F, G, A, and B flat again."

Now I'm really confused. I decide there and then to completely ignore the note names and just nod my head, pretending to try to read. I'm only interested in learning the note sounds and their positions on the trombone. After a while he loses interest, and turns away to practice on his own music. I'm happy to be blasting away on my own. But I'm really excited cos I'm starting to realize that, although I've no interest in reading music, if I learn the trombone positions of Fallon's *Do-Re-Mi* scale then I'll be able to play some of the songs he teaches us in class. I know four or five of his marches in my head already, and I know deep down in my guts I'll be able to play them on the trombone real soon. So the B-flat scale can feck off. It'll always be *Do-Re-Mi* to me. Down the scale I go. This is magic!

—⟋⟍—

Tonic Sol-fa, or Solfège, as the *Do-Re-Mi* notation method is technically called, had a profound effect on how I approach music— even today. Thanks to Brother Fallon, I was extraordinarily well versed in it, even before I got my hands on an instrument. So I was immediately able to translate musical sounds to Tonic Sol-fa. As soon as I learnt the positions on the trombone, I could play a song— whose notes I knew in Tonic Sol-fa—within a few moments. This caused some raised eyebrows in Artane, especially as I wasn't able to explain what I was doing to anyone. But my adherence to it made it difficult for me to read music.

It was astounding to see how differently everyone approached music—and everything else, including loneliness and abandonment. Some boys—like Rasher—seemed to take everything in their stride, while others—like me—carried pain around like a badge.

One of the ironic blessings that still linger from living in an institution with hundreds of others is an acute understanding of different natures. Exposed to that wide, mottled swatch of humanity over a period of years, recognizing the templates of the male psyche became second nature to me. In Artane, every kind of personality, even the most guarded, revealed its secrets over time. Today, four decades later, I'll come across someone I'm struggling to understand and suddenly I'll remember: *Oh! Don't trust him. He's just like Jimmy Cranny.* Or: *Yeah! He's cool. That's Jack McDonald.* Or: *No. Don't play cards with him, that's how Rasher scratched his nose.* It's uncanny how accurate the comparisons have proved to be over the years.

But this kind of intuition doesn't work with the fair sex. I never realized I was using the wrong yardstick till I met Liz.

Now, as I watch her listening to the rough demos of some of the songs from my *800 Voices project*—new songs keep springing up from the same well—I can see that something is bothering her.

Liz takes the headphones off and turns around from the mixing desk. She has that look on her face and I know she's going to say something I don't want to hear. To be fair, her instincts are usually spot on, but I'm never ready for them. I keep adding more and more material to my original songs. Some are a tad long. But I've got a lot to say.

"Everything is beautiful, sweetie. But I can't shake the feeling that there's something wrong with the new last verse you've added to '800 Voices.'"

I pick up the lyric sheet, squinting without my glasses:

> *Then there was Brother Joe O'Connor*
> *Gave me music, strength and pride*
> *He was almost like a father but he was quick to tan your hide.*

"What's wrong with that?" I say slowly.

"*Almost like a father?*" she says. "It's a mite strong, isn't it? Is that really what you want to say here?"

I sigh wearily. She has very strong feelings about the Irish Christian Brothers. So do I, but hers have a fire that makes mine seem pallid.

To be honest, I could never quite figure out Brother Joseph O'Connor. Although hard as nails, with a fiery temper and as quick with the leather strap as any of the brothers, he had a code of honor that was easy to understand. I'm not saying he never lost his temper or lashed out viciously for little reason, but for the most part, he seemed to act with restraint. This was in stark contrast to the senseless brutality of many of the other brothers. His arrival in my life changed everything; I started to feel like I wanted to please him, which was a big surprise to me—and to Rasher.

— ∙ —

Band practice again. The band is taking over. We practice three times a day, after every meal. I just gobble up my food and hare it down to the band room to practice while the other lads are playing on the playground. Brother Fallon never comes to the band room, but to me, he's every bit as present as the seventy or so lads who attack their instruments with as much gusto as they attack the grub in the ref. The *Do-Re-Mi* rebel songs he taught me are sounding better and better on my trombone, especially my favorite, "Twenty Men From Dublin Town."

I just can't seem to learn how to read music properly though, and I'm starting to worry. Nobody bothers me about it except Fatser McBride, who sneers at my efforts every time. It's hard to focus when he's in my face.

But I'll have to learn to read music sooner or later. George Crean hasn't really got the time to give me any help in Band Two and Ernie Fanning has more or less given up trying to teach me. The main band travels outside the school to play at other Christian Brother schools, football matches, and concerts. I really want to be good enough to go with them one day. Although . . . I'll probably be home with Ma before that, right? But there's no harm in trying to get better, is there? With the rest of the band blaring away at the new songs they have to learn, I'll just keep on doing the *Do-Re-Mi* rebel songs on my own. Nobody pays me any attention in the deafening din. Day after day, I whack away at that rusty old trombone.

—⁓—

"Now boys, every of you knows what the word 'conscience' means don't you?" Joe Boy is talking to the band from the conductor's stand. He does it every day at some point, and usually I wish he'd bloody well shut up. I came here to play. Whenever he speaks, his eyes gleam like traffic lights and his words rip through us like alarm clocks through sleep.

"Every one of you has a conscience put inside you by Almighty God. He knew we couldn't be trusted to do what's right, so He planted an awareness of his Law within our souls, and that's your conscience, and when we follow it we are in line with God's will and our lives become full of grace and happiness and we know we're on the right track because it feels good, and when you're feeling good God is happy, because God is good and wants you to be happy too. See?" He likes long sentences.

He's been going on like this for ten minutes, but today, for some reason, what he's saying feels good to me. He's always talking about "the ring of truth." When something is true, you can feel it. It rings true, he says. This talk of feeling good rings true to me, makes sense. If feeling good is what God wants from me, then He'll get it. I'm game for a bit of that.

A Jesuit priest came to speak to my class before Christmas and he certainly didn't talk of God wanting us to feel good. According to that screaming eejit, God was more interested in finding any excuse to send us all to hell for the rest of eternity. His eyes rolled around in his head as he shouted about the horrors of hell fire and the "sins of the flesh." When he was through with us, I was afraid to scratch my balls for fear of God writing it down in his Book. "The Judgment Book," the Jesuit called it. Our only hope was to "deny the flesh." Even taking a piss was dangerous: "any more than three shakes is a mortal sin on your soul."

But Joe Boy's talk of feeling good feels good. I'm putting my money on that one. The only things that make me feel good are cheating at cards and playing music. So they're both fair game. When I blast my life's breath down my trombone, I feel like I've just been made king of the world. Same thing when I deal Rasher a king of spades from the bottom of the deck and Willie O'Reilly a two of hearts. Feeling good is great. And it makes God happy too.

But wait now, don't forget about Ma. You don't want to get too happy without her. Ah, now. A little tear. No one's looking.

Okay, that feels good too. Feeling bad about Ma feels good. She goes down the trombone too, and the bad feeling feels good. Her notes are long and slow and I slide them down till my arm nearly stretches off my shoulder. I wish she could hear me. *Where are ya, Ma? What are ya doing? Are ya still sick?*

O'Connor is shaking me. "Wake up, lad, this isn't the dormitory." He's finished talking. The lads start up with their practicing. I must've dropped off. *Please don't throw me out of the band, sir, I won't do it again, I promise.* But he's grinning and so are the lads in the trombone section. He opens the book of scales on the music stand that Ernie has been trying to teach me and says, "Let's see how you're getting on. Play this." He points to some notes on the top of the page. They still look like gibberish to me. Jesus, I'm in trouble. I still can barely read a note. Wait, that's B flat . . . which is Brother Fallon's *Do.* Okay. I play it. It sounds nice. The next note . . . what the hell is it again? I look around the room. All the lads are blasting away individually. Joe Boy's eyes hold mine fiercely. "Go on boy, play your trombone."

Fuck it anyway. To hell with trying to read the music. I can play this trombone without a stupid piece of paper that sits looking at me as if it wants to eat me. Something explodes in my head and I throw away my fear and blast one of Fallon's rebel songs in *Do-Re-Mi* notes. It's "Twenty Men From Dublin Town":

S—LS–D–M–RD—D—TT—LL–S–M
S—LS–D–M—RD—D—R—MFRTSD—

Brother Joe Boy O'Connor looks like someone hit him with a turnip. He starts to laugh. "What the . . . ? Where the bloody hell did you learn to play that? That's not on the page here."

"I can't . . . I can't explain it, sir. Brother Fallon taught me the *Do-Re-Mi* notes for the song and I've crossed them over on to the trombone, sir. It's all in me head." I feel silly.

O'Connor puts his hand on his hip. He looks around the room at the other band lads, who are all blaring away like mad bulls. He turns to Ernie, seated on my left. "Fanning, I want you to teach Ellis to read music till he can read a fly's droppings."

"Yes, sir," says Ernie. "I'll teach him everything real quick."

"And Mr. Ellis, it's all well and good doing your *Do-Re-Mi* thing, but I want to hear what's on the paper coming out the end of that trombone. If you don't learn to read music, and fast, you'll be back on the playground with the other bowsies before you know what hit ya, understand?"

CHAPTER 17

O'Connor smokes cigarettes, as do most of the brothers. Today, he's run out of matches and he sends me to go and ask the Slasher on the playground for some. Off I go merrily. Just before I get to the wooden gate that leads to the playground, I spy the two lads who beat me up on my very first day in Artane: Hennessy and Murphy. They've been doing something behind a large wood pile when they spot me. Every time I see them, I'm certain I can still feel the pain in my balls. These two bowsies have made a point of pushing me around every chance they get—when Rasher's not around. Many times, I've been tempted to point them out to Mr. Prout, the drill master, like he told me to, but no one abides a squealer. Instead, Rasher and I and Willie O'Reilly just square up to them belligerently on the playground from time to time, amid the games of ball and chase. But I'm alone now and here they come.

For some odd reason, today I'm not afraid. Maybe it's because I've just been blasting the trombone for the last hour and all my blood is in my head. Maybe that's what they mean by *headstrong*. Hennessy, the bigger lad, steps forward as Murphy bends and picks up a thick stick. But I'm still feeling pretty good. Hennessy stops advancing as he sees my strange confidence and turns to Murphy as if to say, *Come on, will ya?* Murphy is looking at Hennessy as if to say, *Go on, will ya?* Holy shite! They're hesitating! As Hennessy is looking at Murphy, my fist lands so sweetly on his jaw that I almost cry with joy. Before Murphy knows what hit him, I hit him. I turn to Hennessy, who's picking himself off the ground, and I hit him again.

Murphy swings wildly but his stick misses me and hits Hennessy on the arm. They're both falling over one another in the madness and I pop them, one at a time, till they run off like the rats in Green Street. Jesus wept! I can't stop laughing. That might just be the very first fight I ever won in my whole life. Either Hennessy or Murphy could have kicked the bejaysus out of me, but each one was waiting for the other and each one was in the other's way. Too many cooks spoil the broth. Chew on that broth for a while, ya gob shites.

I run up to the playground looking for the Slasher. It'll be the first time I'm speaking to him since that . . . that hiding he gave me. But fuck it, Black Daniel is in fine form, I've just won a grand fight so I'm ready for him. Suddenly I see him, through the running lads and the flying balls. His black shape stands out against the gray of the handball alley wall, and his long arm is rising and falling. Yeah, he's whacking some lad with his leather. The lad is withering with the blows to his hand. I'm brought to a sudden stop, just yards away, by the all-too-familiar sight. The fire in my belly from winning my fight disappears through my feet into the cold playground, and I'm shaking. The Slasher turns to me.

"What are you staring at? Are you looking for some of the same medicine?" he says coldly, pocketing his strap. I can barely hear him with the roar of the lads playing around us.

"No, sir. Brother O'Connor sent me to ask you for some matches."

"Oh, you're a band lad, are you?" he says, suddenly all friendly, his whole manner changed. I hear he favors the band lads. But who the hell wants to be liked by that crazy bastard? He doesn't even remember me.

"Okay, now where are they?" He rummages through his pockets and takes out a bunch of keys, a rosary, and his leather strap. Oh, please God.

"Hail Mary, full of grace, the Lord is with thee," I hear myself say insanely. *Eejit!*

"What did you say?" he asks absentmindedly as he searches for the matches. I have to pull meself together here or I could be in trouble.

"Oh, I'm just saying a little prayer for the black babies, sir. Whenever I see rosary beads I'm reminded of the poor starving children in Africa who don't know Jesus and walk around in the nude with no clothes on and have no manners or toilet paper to wipe their chests and can't play cards or talk English or go to Mass on Sundays—"

"Ah, here they are. There's only a few matches left, but there's enough for a few smokes, eh?" He's actually beaming at me as if I'm his best friend. "Please remind Brother O'Connor that I'd like to come and hear the lads play 'Boolavogue' again soon. I'm from Wexford, you know." He winks and starts singing, "At Boolavogue, as the sun was setting, o'er the bright May meadows, la, la, la, la." He walks off into the waves of screaming lads, singing to himself, as if he was going for a Sunday stroll by a river.

—⁓—

"He's just another crazy bastard like the rest of them, Dano, don't trust him," Rasher said angrily. What's ailing him? I'd been telling him about O'Connor when he exploded suddenly. I'm almost sorry I shared O'Connor's liquorice sweets with him.

O'Connor seems to like me, for some reason, and trust me too. When I brought him the matches from the Slasher the other day, he took me into his office behind the drum stand and lit up a cigarette. He sat down on a thick-legged wooden chair, crossed his legs, and fixed me with one of his piercing stares through his cigarette smoke. I sat bolt upright, electrified by this fierce attention.

"I think if you practice hard, you could be in Band One in no time. Don't you think?"

"Y-yes, sir." I stuttered. Five different things were pulling me in different directions at once. It felt real good knowing he thought I'll be good enough to play in the band, but I'm going home soon and probably won't have time for all that. But I want to play in the band, for God's sakes! I love it! The sound of them all blasting away is the best thing in the world. Even better than grub or playing cards. Even better than the pictures they show us on Saturdays in the theatre.

"We'll have a brand-new trombone arriving soon." O'Connor interrupted my meanderings. "It'll be handed out to the lad on first chair and his old instrument will be passed down the line to the other trombonists and so on, all the way over to Band Two. So, if you play your cards right, you'll have a real trombone soon enough. It'll be Itchy Reynolds'."

That very first glimpse of a trombone up close, on my first day in the band room a month back, jumped clearly to my mind. The big, smooth, golden bell and that great blast as that tall lad—Dessie Tate, his name is—poured his heart down it. Jesus, one of those could be mine, instead of that farty old stovepipe. O'Connor just said it: if I play my cards right, I'll be playing Itchy's trombone.

"What do I have to do, sir?" I heard myself say, like a gob shite. *Get a grip, ya lump.*

He looked at me sternly, as if I'd said something wrong. "You have to practice like yer life depends on it. Learn to read music as easy as reading a comic, and above all, keep yer nose out of trouble. I don't care what kind of gallivanting you get up to on the playground, but round here, you're my responsibility and I won't take any nonsense." Seeing my scared look, he softened, "Ah, sure you'll be grand, son. God will guide you if you can ask Him for help now and then." He half closed one eye and made a little face, which made me think he knew what he was talking about. "Everything we want is in God's hands, son, and if we don't grab at

it, He'll let us have it. And what you want is to play in the Artane
Boys Band."

It wasn't a question, so I didn't answer.

Then something happened that sent my mind reeling.

O'Connor shot me a look I didn't understand as he reached out
and opened the left-hand drawer in his desk. He pulled the drawer
out completely and put it on his desk, on top of some papers. He
reached into the very back of the empty space left by the drawer
and pulled out a small metal box. He opened the box. It was full of
pound notes and coins. *Jesus, he's rich. I wonder if he has a hundred
pounds and can afford to get married.* He took out a half-crown and
handed it to me. "I want you to go out the north gate and turn right up
Kilmore Road. You'll come to a shop on the left called Maher's. Tell
Mr. Maher Brother Joseph O'Connor sent you for ten Sweet Afton
and a box of matches. Get yourself a pen'orth of sweets while yer
at it." He put the metal box back into the drawer space and returned
the drawer itself. "I'm taking a big chance with you, Ellis. Don't
make me regret it. Off you go. Don't take all day."

Stunned, I walk out the band room and down by the brothers'
quarters, past the farm and infirmary, and run out the north gate on
to Kilmore Road. My brain is going crazy as I pass Brother Morgan
coming in the gate. He's in charge of the farm. He nods at me, barely
taking any notice. Oh, that's odd, he doesn't question my running out
the gate. I must look like I'm on an errand. Maybe the permission
that O'Connor gave me drapes around me like a cloak that adults can
see. Must remember that.

But I'm free, my mind on fire with the possibilities.

Is O'Connor stupid or what? *Keep yer stupid pen'orth of sweets.*
His half-crown will get me a bag of chips and a lemonade and a
Crunchie bar. Maybe even a bag of Tayto Crisps. *But don't forget to
keep enough for the bus fare, stupid.* Stuffing my face, I'll get the bus
home. Ma won't be out of hospital yet, but I know how to open the
windows and break into the house. I've done it tons of times when

Before the storms. Ma and Da in shock. Me in blessed oblivion.

Ma with Cousin Simon
on O'Connell Bridge,
circa 1953.

Da in US Army uniform.

1954: Black Daniel of
the Liffey is ready for
trouble—not!

With my sisters, Patricia (L) and Katie (R) in Rathfarnham, just before the orphanages, 1955.

Artist's sketch of Artane.

Artane Industrial School, my "home" for eight long years. From the air, the place looks almost benign.

Assembly in front of the main buildings.

The public attends Corpus Christi celebrations in front of the main building.

The chapel where I first heard Tommy Bonner sing.

In our Sunday tweed, confirmation day, circa 1960. I'm in the back row on the far left.

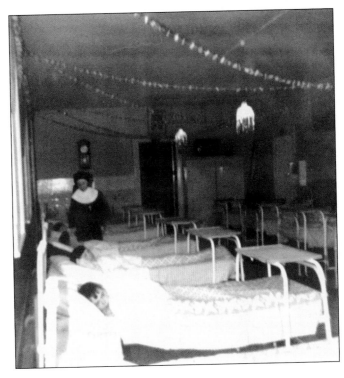

The infirmary, a place to pretend and get some rest.

With twenty hungry lads at each table, the refectory was the most popular place in Artane.

Cold and sterile, the dorms had at least 150 beds each.

The iron staircase led to the dorms. The noise of the hobnail boots could wake the dead!

The imposing "Long Hall" beneath the dorms.

One of the school rooms off the Long Hall.

Lads on the football field in front of the refectory, winter 1962.

Artane concert hall and band #2 rehearsal room.

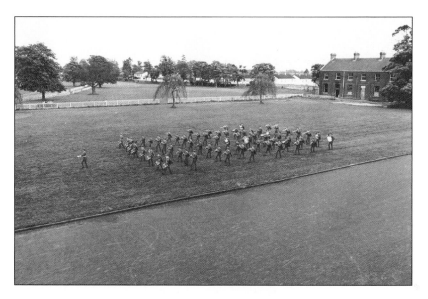

The band marching in front of the main buildings.

The band director, Brother "Joe Boy" O'Connor—scary and inspiring in equal measure.

My first trombone, circa 1959.

The band at the Irish Hospital Sweepstakes, Ballsbridge, Dublin.

The band, circa 1961. I'm in the back row on the far right.

Band lads, circa 1962. I am in the front, third from the right.

Artane Boys Band board a plane for the United States, May 1962.

New York, 1962. Me and Da listening to my first tape recorder, a treasured gift from him.

1963: sixteen years old and practicing my mean and moody look.

1963: just out of Artane and trying to look like I'm
not scared to death.

A new start with the Jim Farley Showband.

Rehearsing for my *800 Voices* concert at the National Concert Hall in Dublin, 2010.

At home with Liz and Irene in Asheville, North Carolina.

Ma forgot her key. *That's my big man of the house.* Thanks, Ma. I'll
live on apples I'll knock off from the Lamb Brothers' orchards till Ma
gets out of hospital. Boy, she'll be surprised to see me. I can't wait to
show her how I can play the trombone.

But wait now, I don't have a trombone at home. Oh, Sweet Jesus,
I'll never play the trombone again, will I? Itchy's golden horn jumps
across my mind with no manners at all. I stop running like I ran into
a stone wall.

I'm halfway up Kilmore Road when the tears start. They roll
down my face as I walk along past the tiny terraced houses, dragging
my feet, the kids playing on the street pretending not to stare at me.
I'm stuck. And I'm fucked. Fucked if I stay and fucked if I leave.
It's not fair. Nothing works out, no matter how hard I try. I walk to
Maher's and stand outside the shop for a few minutes, looking in the
window. I go inside. The smell of sweets, after nearly two months
in Artane, nearly knocks me over. If I wasn't so bloody fed up, my
mouth would be watering.

"What'll it be, son?" Maher asks kindly. "We got some nice new
liquorice sweets that'll melt in yer mouth."

"No thanks," say I wearily. I'm real tired all of a sudden. "Just
give me . . . give me ten Sweet Afton and a box of matches."

Maher raises his eyebrows.

"They're for Joe Boy . . . I mean Brother Joseph O'Connor."

"Ah, yer a band lad, are ya?" His grin gets bigger. "Say hello
to Joe Boy from me, will ya?" He winks. Why does everyone
change when they find out you're a band lad? "Here, try one of the
liquorice sweets for free." He's right. It melts in my mouth. I want
more, but I'm skint. Oh, wait now, I nearly forgot: O'Connor's
penny reward.

"Give me a pen'orth of those, please." The bag of sweets Maher
gives me looks much more than a penny's worth.

I ran back through the north gate. As I enter the Artane grounds,
my body gives a little shudder. I can't believe this—I'm actually

coming back to this shithole willingly. The tears come down again as I pass the infirmary and I feel a real eejit, running and crying and eating liquorice all at the same time. *Tighten up, man.*

It's unusually quiet when I enter the band room. O'Connor is talking to the band again. He finishes up and walks straight over to me. He stops and looks at me strangely for a few minutes, ignoring the cigarettes and matches in my outstretched hand.

"Good man, Ellis. What's that black stuff round your mouth?"

"I suppose it's liquorice, sir," say I, wiping my mouth with my sleeve quickly. He grins and takes the fags and matches from my hand. He puts them in his pocket and sticks his hand out again with a raised eyebrow.

"Oh, yes, sir, the change. I nearly forgot. I wasn't trying to keep it, sir, honest to God." Why does my stupid mouth keep saying stupid stuff on its own when I'm talking to a brother?

"I know you weren't, Ellis. I know a man I can trust when I see him." He gives me that hard look with those piercing eyes again.

Back in Band Two, Itchy lets me try out his trombone—with my mouthpiece. The slide moves like a dream and it sounds gorgeous. Itchy and me have become friends. He's a little older than me and surer of himself. But then, who isn't?

—⁓—

"He's okay, I tell ya," I'm saying to Rasher again, handing him another liquorice sweet. "O'Connor talks about different things than the other brothers and he makes me feel like I can do hard things easily. What's wrong with that?" I'm surprised at how loud I'm talking. Maybe it's the noise of the lads watching the football match in the field in front of the ref.

"Don't be stupid. I've seen him in action, pal, he'll tear your arse up quick as blinking."

"Yeah, but that's the thing. With him, you can get things right and he won't beat you up for nothing. If you do what he says, you'll be all right."

"If you do what he says, if you do what he says," Rasher mimics me hurtfully. He's gone a bit mad here, wagging his finger in my face and sticking his blackened-by-liquorice tongue out. Next thing I know we're wrestling and it's not the friendly kind. He's much stronger than me and soon he has me in a headlock, pulling me around till I'm dizzy. He lets me go suddenly and I stagger and fall.

"What's bloody well wrong with you?" I'm ashamed and I'm crying. Why is everything so mixed up all the time? Between Ma and the trombone and Rasher and O'Connor, I don't know my arse from my elbow any more. "All I said was Joe Boy wasn't a bad fellah and—"

"Where was Joe Boy O'Connor when you were dying away in the corner of the playground, crying for yer ma? Where was he when you were afraid to stand up straight or even walk across the yard on yer own? Who taught ya how to wrestle and curse properly and make the giddy-up noise with yer boots and cheat at cards and make an honest living? Ya can't let him turn you into a smooth-nice-lad shitehawk like the rest of the band eejits."

Now I get it—he's jealous. I want to cry again with relief. "Yeah, but weren't you the one who couldn't stop telling me to join the band, join the band, join the fecking band."

"That's because you wouldn't pull yerself together, ya *amadon*! You were muttering away to yerself day and night about yer mammy and daddy who don't give a fuck about ya and ya needed something to hold on to. Now yer in the stupid band and yer kissing Joe Boy's arse like he was a saint. He's not a saint; he's a bad-tempered old bastard who'd murder ya as soon as look at ya."

"You forgot something, Rasher." I laugh. He's puzzled. "He's as ugly as a mongrel run over by a lorry and his breath smells like shite, and his nose hairs are down to his ankles." Now we're both laughing. Before I know what I'm saying, in the giddy joy of seeing my best pal's jealousy, I blurt, "And I know something you don't know . . . . He's rich and I know where he keeps all his money." Jesus, what am I doing? I feel real sick all of a sudden.

Rasher's stopped laughing. He winks real slow and says, "Where?"

CHAPTER 18

The Mackerel has just left class. Fallon is here. Thank God for his music. I wish I could read my English lesson books as well as I could read the *Do-Re-Mi* notes Fallon writes on the blackboard. My hands are still sore from the Mackerel's leather strap. He didn't take kindly to my spelling skills earlier. It's every day. Either you get caught talking or laughing when you shouldn't, or you get a few sums wrong, or you wrinkle your nose and some eejit brother thinks you're being rude. Or, you might have skid-marks on your underpants as you turn them in—once a week—for a clean pair; as the line of lads moves forward and the brother in charge examines each and every pair of drawers, you drag your feet in shame and fear, knowing you're going to get it for not wiping your arse properly. Some lads, like Willie O'Reilly, don't wear drawers at all, fearing an accident and a beating. But the leather strap is everywhere: on the playground, in the refectory, even in the band room. I dream about it at night, and when I wake up, the dread of knowing that I'll probably get it again today makes me sick to my stomach. Then I try to think of singing or the trombone and I don't feel so bad for a while. But that won't last for long. Some lad will do something wrong—oftentimes he won't even know what—and the leather strap will rise and fall and you'll feel like it's *you* getting beaten.

But the boot room is the worst. Sometimes a lad will step out of line, and instead of whipping him there on the spot, a brother will tell him to "report to me after lights out in the boot room tonight." It'd be in whatever dorm the brother was doing duty in that night. You'd lie in bed, with Radio Luxemburg playing away cheerfully, and hear the terrible screams from the boot room. *Please, sir, I'm sorry, sir . . . Not as sorry as you're going to be, me bucko . . . I won't do it again, sir, I promise . . . I know bloody well you won't do it again.*

Last night, it was Batty McGeehan's turn—with a new brother who everyone hates. Because every second phrase out of his mouth is "I'll flatten ya!" he's been nicknamed the Flattener. Poor little Batty was being beaten real hard and he seemed to lose his marbles, screaming and screaming. The Flattener went berserk, shouting, "Stop screaming, ya stupid bastard. Stop screaming, do you hear." You could hear him beating Batty with every word he shouted. "Stop screaming. Stop it! Stop it! Stop it!"

The beating went on and on and the screams and shouts were enough to set your blood boiling. The tension ripped up and down the bed rows till one brave lad could stand it no more. He shouted from the back of the dorm, "Leave him alone, ya fucking bastard!" Some other lads took up the cause and soon we were all screaming our heads off. "Shitehawk! Fucker! Murderer! Poxbottle!" The noise was glorious. It felt like our heads were exploding and our voices were daggers, flying down the dorm and ripping the Flattener to shreds. The screaming and shouting from the boot room stopped dead.

Silence.

The Flattener came out the big doors of the boot room, dragging Batty by the hair. Batty's night shirt was torn and covered in blood. He shook himself free and ran off to his bed and crawled in. Speechless at our rebellion, the Flattener stood glaring down the dorm, visibly bracing himself against our waves of silent disgust. Even good old Radio Luxemburg had drifted off station in protest and was hissing static at the Flattener.

"You haven't heard the last of this, me buckos. I'll deal with you all later. Every single one of you."

I won't need the Gas Man to keep me awake tonight, I thought.

—⁂—

Fallon bangs his tuning fork hard on his desk, snapping me out of my dreaming. "Ellis, pay attention like a good man, please. I won't warn you again."

Soon the beautiful streams of music are flowing around the room as we bathe in the safety of a force that won't hurt us. Now he's trying to teach us to recognize the rhythm of the notes he writes. Oh, yeah, they're the same as the quavers and semi-quavers that Fanning teaches me in the band. My mind wanders back to the times when I used to play with the Photo People at home in Green Street. Music is kind of the same as the Photo People. It lives in a perfect world all of its own. The notes are always the same, right there for you whenever you play or sing them, and no matter what happens in the real world, music takes it all and covers it with a soft coat of sweetness like snow covers the hard gray playground.

"Ellis, stand up and hold out your hand. I'm tired of you drifting off in class."

I can't believe it—Fallon is actually slapping me with his leather strap. They're not hard, angry slaps like the Mackerel's or the Monto's or the Flattener's. Like a girl throwing a stone at you, Fallon's slaps are weak and half-hearted. They still bloody well hurt. But that's not why I'm crying.

That same big lad who before Christmas announced in the Mackerel's class that Ma had come to see me has just come in the door, interrupting our singing.

"What is it, man?" Fallon is in a bad mood today. He should sing more.

"Sir, the mass X-ray unit is ready for class number one now." I'd heard about it from the lads at breakfast a week back, when I asked what that big, long van thing was doing parked on the road down by the poultry farm.

"They're going to take our X-rays." Pat Murphy had said, as if they were going to take our tonsils.

"What's that?" says I.

"They have a big machine that can take snaps of yer insides. They can see if ya have diseases like new-monia or leprosy or stuff," says Willie O'Reilly with his usual expertise.

They'd started with the older lads a few days ago. You could hear them laughing as they made their way down past the ref to the X-ray unit—anything is better than class. Now it's our turn. The brothers say it doesn't hurt, but I don't believe them. Everything hurts in this place. Even sleep. Fallon marches us down to the unit, where we stand outside in the cold, and one by one we go inside to have our skeletons photographed. *Smile, ribs.*

—ᴍᴍ—

It's been nearly a week since the X-ray unit left the grounds and I've been called from morning band practice to go to the infirmary to see the nurse. I've never been here before. It's a huge two-story building beside the farm. Inside, the dim, dreary rooms are enough to make a sunny day feel sick. Behind the disinfectant, the musty smell of old bed linen and mattresses creeps up on you like a fart in a flower shop. The infirmary is not as big as the dorms, but between the couple of wards I've wandered into, looking for the nurse, there must be sixty or seventy beds. Most are empty, but there's about fifteen lads in various wards with various illnesses. I reckon half of them are faking it, by the glint in their eyes. I find the nurse in an upstairs ward, beside a lad in bed with a lollipop stuck in his mouth. She makes some fussy noises when she hears who I am. Something's going on here.

"Let me tend to my patients for a minute and I'll take you down to the doctor," the nurse says as she takes the lollipop out of the lad's mouth. Ah, it's not a lollipop. It's glass and has numbers and lines on it. She looks at the thing that's not a lollipop and writes something down on the back of her hand. She takes me to an office beside one of the downstairs wards. There, she sits me down with the fat doctor who's called in occasionally when things get too much for the nurse to handle. He and she look like that time has come.

"Do you know if you have any family members who have had TB?" My heart sinks. The doctor seems worried as he looks over his glasses at my X-ray.

"Yes, sir. My mother is in hospital with TB."

"What hospital is that?"

"I don't know, sir."

"What's her address?"

I force myself to say it: "Eighteen Loretto Crescent, Rathfarnham, sir."

The doctor turns to the nurse. "I'll alert his mother. Send someone to his dorm to get his things and put him to bed immediately. He's not to get out of bed till I come back tomorrow. I've got to speak to someone about this."

No. No. No. Ya can't do that to me.

"But sir, the new trombone is coming tomorrow and I'm going to get Itchy Reynolds' old one." I'm almost shouting.

"Itchy's old what?" says the doctor as he's writing.

"Trombone, sir, trombone. Tommy Fanning will get the new one and he'll pass his old one along to Dessie Tate and Ernie Fanning will get Dessie's and I'll be at the end of the line getting Itchy's old one, which is a million times nicer than my old one." I'm out of breath.

"What are ya blathering about?" He looks at the nurse, shaking his head above his fat chins. "You have Job's patience. They're all mad." The doctor groans.

Fuck Job and his patients, wherever the nurse keeps them. Job's patients may be mad, but I'm not. I've never felt saner in my life. I want Itchy's trombone and I'm not staying here in this smelly place while someone else gets it.

But no one wants to hear what I have to say. After a word from the nurse to a big tall fellah with a bandage around his head, I'm taken upstairs. We pass a ward. All the lads there are laughing and going crazy. *They must be Job's patients,* I think to meself. *Don't put me in there with those mad men.* He doesn't. He takes me down the corridor to another ward with only one person in it—a big tough-looking fellah. He's about thirteen, with a broken nose and red hair. He nods at me sourly. He looks as fed up as I do. But the bed is nice and clean and at least I'll be away from the Flattener for a bit. He's been picking on us all in the dorm for any little excuse: dirty ears, beds made badly, or any small thing at all. He's been getting back at us one by one for taunting him over the boot-room beating last week.

It feels good to get into bed at eleven o'clock in the morning. In minutes I'm asleep and dreaming of Itchy's trombone.

—⁓—

I watch my trombone student climb into his dad's car and they drive away. "See you next week, Billy." He's fallen in love with my trombone: a King 3B Silver Sonic. It's a beautiful instrument. He's trying to talk his parents into buying him one. I've had mine nearly forty years and I can't imagine what it would cost nowadays.

I put my horn away and open my laptop to read my emails. As I've gotten up the courage to play some of my orphanage songs for my friends over the last weeks, I've been getting more and more emails from those who love to Google every new thing they hear about. I'm one of those myself, so I shouldn't complain. But this is getting silly.

It seems that there's been a huge fervor in the Irish press over the last five years regarding abuse in the Irish orphanage system—in particular, the industrial schools, and even more particularly, Artane Christian Brothers School for Senior Boys. I've never, up till this point, Googled "Artane School" for any other reason except to look for old friends, like Rasher or Tommy Bonner. But some of the stuff my friends' emails have directed me to has turned my stomach—and Liz's.

"You need to read this post I've just found."
No I don't! I was there, for God's sakes!

—⚹—

O'Connor's going to flip! They rushed me off to the hospital so fast I never got a chance to tell him.

And that's only the half of it!

We're driving through Dublin in the school car, the same one that brought me here with Ma from the courthouse. They call it the Black Maria. The Limp—the same brother—is driving. As we cross the Liffey going south, I swear I see Larry O'Toole's horse and cart crossing Capel Street Bridge in the distance. I squint to see if it's Shane in front, but we're in Westmoreland Street in a second and he's gone.

The last two days are a blur. I didn't stay long in the infirmary and I've waved goodbye to Itchy's trombone and I'm not sure I'll ever play in the band again. I didn't even get a chance to say goodbye to Rasher. It started when I woke up from my eleven o'clock nap the other day in the infirmary ward.

The lad wheeling the metal cart with the food on it had bumped my metal bed pretty hard. Almost before I was awake I sat bolt upright to find my Sunday clothes on my bed and Ma's suitcase beside them. It was dinner time and I was starving. The evil grin on the face of the bowsie responsible for my rude awakening didn't change that. I'm getting used to that carryon. The slice of meat, the cabbage, and spuds were even colder than they usually are in the ref, but I wolfed the grub down hungrily. The big lad with red hair in the bed beside me—his name is Jimmy "Redser" Redmond—wasn't very hungry so I ate most of his dinner too. I made a friend for life there. "If ya ever get in trouble on the playground," he said, "come and find Redser Redmond and I'll sort things out for ya."

It was all because of the radiator. There was a funny feeling in the ward, from the minute I came in, that I couldn't figure out. Halfway through Jimmy's spuds, I got it. It's warm in here, for God's sake! The rest of the school is bloody freezing all the time. There's radiators in the dorms, classrooms, and ref, but they couldn't warm an ant's arse if he sat on them for a week. I reached my hands down behind the bed and Jaysus, the radiator was actually warmer than my hand.

Redser was a talker. He was much bigger than me so it made me feel good to have him trust me with his story. Seems he'd been beaten pretty badly by the Monto yesterday, but that wasn't why he was in the infirmary. He whispered that he was faking illness to get away from class and the leather strap for a while. *I'm with ya there, Redser, lad.* But he was worried that he was about to be thrown out of the infirmary because his temperature wasn't high enough.

"Your *what* isn't high enough?" I asked, through his cabbage.

"Temperature! It's how hot your body is. The hotter your temperature is the sicker you are. They stick a thermometer in yer mouth and it can tell how hot you are." *Oh,* I thought, *that must be the thing that wasn't a lollipop I saw in a lad's mouth earlier.*

"Yeah," said Redser. "The nurse said if my temperature wasn't higher the next time she took it, I'm outta here on me arse."

"Does she stand around watching you as she takes your temp . . . as she finds out how hot you are?"

"No, she usually leaves the thermometer in yer mouth for ten minutes while she arses about doing chores."

"Then we'll make that thermometer hot enough to keep you here till Easter," said I with a wink.

"What do ya mean?"

"Here," I said, "stick your hand down behind your bed."

He reached down behind the bed and searched about for a second till his hand touched the hot radiator.

"Jesus Christ, Dano, I never thought of that."

A friend for life! But I won't be able to use that help where I'm going. The next day the doctor told me I'm going to the hospital for a long time.

"You've got TB, me lad. It's very serious. You could die."

That did it! Stopped me from thinking about Itchy's trombone. Ya have to be alive to play that. Stopped me from worrying about the leather strap. Ya have to be alive to be beaten up. Stopped me from singing *Do-Re-Mi* in my mind all day long. Stopped me from thinking about everything except Ma and going to the hospital.

"We're almost there," the Limp says. He's the Brother Superior, the big boss of all the other brothers, but still, he's not a bad bastard. He gave me a sweet earlier. In the back of the car, I touch the seat where Ma sat, so long ago. Christ, it's only been a couple of months. *Where are ya now, Ma? You're not going to die from TB, are ya?*

We're here. Nurses and wards and beds all go by in a blur. There's a nice smell of medicine in the air and it all feels very safe. "Here's your bed, Danny." I put on my new pajamas the Limp gave me and crawl in for the best rest I ever had. The rest of my life.

—⁕—

His name is Cormac O'Riordan and he's a sissy. For nearly six months he's shared this tiny two-bed ward with me and it's more than a man can bear. Some people die of TB, the doctor said. *Stop it! That's a mortal sin on your soul.* Sorry, God, but I can't stand Cormac. He wouldn't last a second on the playground with his mop of long, blond, curly hair and his big, wide eyes and long eyelashes. On visiting days, his ma comes and showers him with enough sweets and fruit to last the lads in dormitory number five a week. He sits up in bed giggling while she dotes on him, running her hands through his hair. And who, in dirty Dublin City, calls their son Cormac? And who in the whole of Ireland calls his ma Mother?

"Mother, that's not the comic I asked you to bring. Can't you get anything right?"

"Mother, how many times do I have to tell you that I hate apples?"

Don't speak to your ma like that, ya spoiled little fart. And the way she looks at him and speaks to him: "I'm so sorry, sweetness."

Sweetness? If Ma ever called me that I'd roll up and die on the spot. They look into each other's eyes sometimes and say dreamy, going-nowhere, sing-song stuff I don't understand. The whole thing makes me want to puke. It's not natural. She brought him some jam the other day and some Marietta biscuits. When she put the jam on a biscuit she acted like it was the most important job in the world, spreading the jam right over to the very edge, all slow and careful. "Here we are, sweetness." Not a word of thanks from him as he stuffed his face.

Wait, here's his ma now. What's she doing here? It's not visiting day. Jaysus, she's carrying a cake with candles in it and the nurses are behind her, singing a song I should know. Okay. It's "Happy Birthday." Cormac is pretending to look surprised. I'm not. I'm surprised, all right—surprised to remember that I forgot my birthday—and so did everyone else. Nothing new there. Ma would forget our birthdays all the time, only to be reminded days later by a card from an aunt or uncle. Birthdays are for sissies anyway. Who cares about that shite?

"Would you like a piece of cake, dear?" Cormac's ma offers me a slice on a paper napkin.

Stick it up yer arse. I'm trying real hard to say it but my lips have other ideas. "Yes please, Mrs. O'Riordan. Thank you very much." *Have ya no shame, Ellis?*

She's gone now and so is the cake. I've kinda wanted to say "happy birthday" for a while but my lips just won't let me. Who gave lips a mind of their own?

"Would you like a biscuit, Ellis?" says Cormac with a twisted grin.

"Yes, please," say my lips before I can stop them.

"That's too bad, isn't it? Cos there's only one left and it's all mine." He stuffs it in his big mouth and laughs that horrible high-pitched laugh that always makes me look around the room for the nanny goat.

I want to wring his fat neck till the biscuit comes out his ears. I hate him more than I've ever hated anyone in my life. If he had the brains to see the daggers I throw at him with every glance he'd be dead as a dartboard. If hate had teeth he'd be biscuit crumbs. One of these days I'll—

The nurse enters and interrupts my plans of murder by dropping my Artane clothes on my bed. "Get dressed quickly, Danny. The Brother Superior is on his way. You're going home in an hour. We need your bed immediately." She smiles at me as if it was good news. I look at the clothes as if she's dropped a dead rat on me.

But wait. Did she say home? "Home? You mean home to me ma?"

"No. Home to Artane."

Jesus! "Am I better?" I ask. I'm feeling terrible.

"No, Danny. You were never ill."

I never felt worse.

"What about all the X-rays that said I had TB?" There'd been dozens over the months.

"Your last X-ray is showing the same dark spot that it showed in the beginning. It's not TB at all. It's just a cloud thing on your lung. The doctors have suspected it for weeks but wanted to be sure. Now they are. You're perfectly healthy."

"No I'm not. I don't feel well at all," I snap, almost in tears. I look over at Cormac, who's so busy eating something he never heard a word. Suddenly he looks completely different. He did give me some chewing gum once. He even used to lend me his comics sometimes—after he'd read them fifty times. And when I sang a song for the nurses he joined in the chorus. And remember the time he lent me his deck of cards to do the tricks and he let me keep them when I showed him how to deal from the bottom of the pack? With his nice, shiny, brand-new deck, I practiced that bloody trick till I could do it in the dark with one hand tied behind me back. All thanks to him. I'm going to miss my friend.

"Happy birthday, Cormac."

CHAPTER 19

I can't believe it. Six months of swallowing the worst-tasting medicine in the world; six months of so many injections up my arse it started to feel like a pin cushion; six months of choking throat swabs that made me puke every time; six months of lying on my back looking out of the window at the same crows in the same trees in the same distance; four of those months spent pissing and crapping in a bed-pan without standing or walking; and now I'm getting fully dressed for the first time.

In all that time, not a word from Ma. The nurse said the doctor's letter to alert her about my TB was sent back marked NO LONGER AT THIS ADDRESS. That shook me up for a whole week, till I realized she probably hated Rathfarnham as much as I did. Besides, *she* really has TB and she's probably in bed somewhere like me. I asked the nurse to check if Ma was in the same hospital as me. She did and she wasn't. The nurse said she could have gone to the Cappagh, another hospital where they treat TB. Or, maybe she was sent to a hospital way out in the country somewhere. The fresh air is better for some people, she said. I tie my bootlaces. I'm dizzy when I stand up. I look through the big window that divides my ward from the next. Through it, I can see to all the other wards, right down to the end of the wing. I'd felt good in the hospital. I'd sung for the nurses and taught them the *Do-Re-Mi* and nobody beat me or shouted at me. It was nice.

I'd had some visitors. Da's sister, Aunt Molly, came to see me with some toys Da sent me from America. She'd stood outside the ward, looking in, and I turned around in bed to be lit from the inside out by her sweet gaze. Lovely, dancing blue eyes and blonde hair, just like Da. I don't remember seeing her before, but as she stood there, looking at me through the ward window, her look felt like sunshine in the middle of the night. Then she left.

My Uncle Matty, Ma's brother, came to visit too, bringing me a golden rosary. He said he'd write to the school and get permission for me to visit him and his wife, Aunt Margaret, when I got better. But he didn't know where Ma was or how she was doing. Aunt Molly neither. I don't know why, but Molly obviously didn't like Ma.

"Your mother had a lot of secrets, Danny." Her lovely face went hard when I asked her about Ma.

Yeah, Ma liked secrets. *A secret is like money,* she used to say with a wink. *Never tell anyone you have it.* Maybe there's secrets that nobody knows. The nurse told me that the doctors looked through a microscope at the saliva they made me spit in a metal cup every day. There must be millions of secrets that can't be seen without a microscope. Even with one. Maybe everything's a secret. Maybe I'm one too. *Shush, now! Don't tell anyone.*

—※—

The ground has no manners. It won't stand still. Ah, it's not the ground at all, it's your legs. Your legs forget how to do their job when you've been in bed for six months, not walking at all for most of the time. Watch those concrete steps! The only walking I did in the last weeks was to go to the toilet and take a shower. A hot shower! Not like the freezing-cold ones at the back of the schoolrooms that the drill master Prout marched us into every Saturday morning. Ugh! The schoolrooms! My tummy turns. I stop trying to walk.

"Keep going," the Limp says. He has his own problems walking so he doesn't offer to help. I feel like dithery old Brother Columbus walking across the parking lot to the car.

We're driving now. The city looks sad. The people on their bikes, the people walking the street, the people on the buses looking out the window—blank faces, going nowhere and knowing they've nothing to do when they get there. Is that someone from Green Street on a bike? Can't tell, they're gone too fast. *Take your time, car. Slow down.* Everything is too fast. The hospital was lovely and slow and kind. "Oh, you're almost asleep, Danny. Okay. I'll come back in a few minutes and we'll change the bed." The nurses taught me to read properly. I can read the writing on the buses now. GUINNESS IS GOOD FOR YOU. Not for me, it wasn't.

We're on the Malahide Road. There's that long, gray wall. It blurs past as I turn my head all the way to the left to look straight at it. We're very near now. I'm sick. It must be from looking at the wall pass by so quick. Blurry, blurrier, slow, slower, nearly stopped now . . . . The gates of Artane. They swallow the car greedily and I'm back in the belly of hell. The gray giants of the dormitory buildings bend beneath the gray weight of the morning sky. The car stops outside the office, in front of the secondary gate. The playground is a sea of tweed, the screaming hundreds a frightening welcome. The Angeles bell strikes twelve. The refectory clock is two minutes fast. Everything is too fast. The Limp talks to a lad sweeping the steps by the office door. He runs and gets the Whistler from the brothers' quarters. He comes down the steps, wiping his mouth. He nods at me and takes me past the fighting and the shouting and the galloping giddyupping and up the iron stairs to the dorms. *Wait, now . . . what's this?* Instead of turning right into dorm five, where I used to sleep, he's turned left, past the balcony overlooking the Long Hall, to dorm four. I'm too sick to ask why. He takes me to a bed near the end of the dorm. I crawl in and go to sleep.

—✵—

"Would ya look at the cut of it! Back from the jaws of death." Inches from mine, a face grins at me as I wake. It's Rasher—he looks bigger

and his cheeks are fatter. "I heard you were back and I snuck up to
see ya. How's she cutting?"

"Ah, sure she's cutting rightly," I lie.

"Well, ya look fucking *evaporated.*" He's learnt a new word. He's
bursting with life and I feel ashamed of the dead feeling in my mind
and body. I agree with him, I'm fucking evaporated.

"You're still sick then? I thought you were cured from the TB."

"I never had fucking TB. It was a fucking stupid, pox-bottle
mistake." I'm feeling better by the second. It's been months since
I cursed out loud. Fuck the hospital and fuck TB. Oops, sorry Ma.

"Never mind all that shite, yer grand now." He grins. "Here,
Dano, wait till ya see this new trick." He takes out a deck of cards
from his pocket and starts shuffling. "Think of a card—any fucking
card in the whole fucking deck."

—⁂—

Oh, yeah! It's the lovely noise of sixty lads blaring away on their
horns. Take that! And that! That'll sort ya! I'd forgotten what happens
in my chest when I hear it. My stupid, constant aching for the hospital
bed slips away for a minute. My breath quickens and I close the door
behind me. Dormitory number five has been turned into the new
band room. The beds are gone and the room now looks ten times
bigger. The whole band, with the raised platforms of the brass and
drum sections, faces the entrance door. The sections practice where
they sit as if they were the only ones in the room. How a lad can tell
his sound from anyone else's is a tribute to boxed ears. The band
doesn't sound as loud as it did in the old band room. But it's loud
enough to get rid of any funny stuff that's gumming up my brain like
glue. Almost.

O'Connor's talking to someone in the saxophone section. There's
Itchy, with Patser Lennox's trombone. But wait now! Who's that
sitting beside Ernie Fanning with Itchy's old horn? Don't tell me.

A fire wells up inside. *That's my trombone, ya thief!* I'm exploding as I stagger blindly to the trombone platform. Someone bumps into me very roughly from behind. It's Fatser McBride with his trumpet in hand. His cheeky, ugly face is framed with an evil grin, which disappears when my fist lands smack in the middle of it. He falls and bangs the trumpet on the floor. Jesus, what did I hit *him* for? What's wrong with me? Before he can pick himself up and beat the crap outta me, O'Connor has his leather strap out, beating the crap outta me.

"Ya dirty-looking bowsie. You could have split his lip or broke his teeth. He'd never play the trumpet again." His strap is everywhere. "That's for being a blackguard." Whack! "And that's for being a thief." Whack! Whack! Whack!

"I'm s-sorry, sir. I . . . I . . . didn't mean it. I was m-mad because someone else is playing my trombone." All the lads have stopped blasting and my cries tear through the sudden silence.

"What are ya talking about? Your trombone? And where have you been for the last six months?" he shouts.

I try to answer but I'm choking in tears and snot, gasping for breath while trying to look into his eyes, imploring him.

"Never mind. Just get out of my sight. You're nothing but a thug and a thief. I gave you a chance and you betrayed my trust. I never want to see you within a mile of the band room again, do ya hear?" He's screaming. I'm crying. The lads are staring.

He called me a thief. That I am. But how would he know? And how did I betray his trust?

I somehow find myself outside the band-room door. I'm trying to walk down the iron stairs to the playground. Where's me legs? Some lads pass me coming up and laugh loudly at me. I can't . . . I . . . I want to go to bed. I turn and climb back up the stairs again and find dorm four. You can get yourself murdered for entering the dorm during the day. I don't care. There's me bed. There's Ma's case beneath it. I open it up to breathe in her smell, but it's gone now.

"Who the hell are you?" There's a new brother instead of the Mackerel in class number one. His face is covered in pimples. The lads are all different too, except for Cranny, the squealer.

"I used to be in this class before I had TB and went into hospital."

"What? You had TB?" The brother, who has big glasses, looks disgusted.

"No, sir. I didn't. I . . . I have a cloud . . . I mean . . . the X-rays were wrong . . . me ma had TB so the doctor thought . . . but the nurse said I'm better now . . . but I'm still sick, sir."

"What are ya talking about. Sit down at the back and stop blathering, for God's sake, man. And why don't you walk straight and hold yer head up instead of crawling around bent up like a snake? I thought Saint Patrick banished you and your kind to the sea. Eh, lads? Remember our lesson yesterday?" The lads all laugh, looking at me. I sit down, but I can't stay awake in class. His leather strap soon changes that.

Rasher is aghast. "What? Yer out of the band? Didn't anyone tell O'Connor you were in hospital? Christ! This place is mad. And you punched fat Andy McBride? You're in trouble there, Dano. He won't ever forget that. And you're in Pimpleface's class? That won't be fun. You'll have to start walking properly, pal. The lads will banjax ya if ya keep this shite up."

I'm dizzy with all of this. I can't think straight and I'm cold and weak and stupid and I don't know what to say or do and nothing makes sense any more. Rasher stops talking in mid sentence with a strange look on his face.

"We have to get Black Daniel back on his horse before the Indians scalp his baldy arse." He's thinking about something. He has that look he gets when he's just thought of a new money-making stroke. "I know. You'll join the kitchen. You'll be a Moniumer. That'll smarten your hump. Lots of your old pals are there: Gibbo and O'Reilly and Antho Kelly. Come on, let's find O'Driscoll, ask him if he'll let you be a kitchener. You'll be out of the cold and you can stuff yer face all day long. That'll put some meat back on them bones."

"I'm not hungry," I say angrily. What's wrong with me?

"Come on, stop it. You'll be grand." He drags me off toward the ref.

We find O'Driscoll behind the ref, stoking the huge furnace. With the heat, his face is even redder than usual. He's in a real bad mood. "What's wrong with yez?" His Cork accent is as round as his huge belly.

"Sir, this is Danny Ellis. He's just come out of hospital and he's not himself at all, at all, so he isn't."

"Wait a minute." O'Driscoll is looking at me oddly. "You're that . . . that lad back last Christmas Day . . . you were waiting for your mother . . ." He trails off, remembering that he gave me a cup of tea in the brothers' kitchen.

Rasher jumps in. "Yeah. He wants to work in the kitchen. He'll be okay, sir. I'll teach him everything real quick."

Oh, shite! Tears . . . I can't stop them.

"Good God, man. What's ailing ya?" O'Driscoll snaps back into his usual foul mood.

Rasher nudges me sharply with his elbow. "He's just been thrown out of the band, sir, and he's feeling sad. He's not the full shilling at all at the moment, sir," he says quickly.

"And I'll never play music again as long as I live," I hear myself say in a whining voice that belongs to nobody I know.

"Don't be an *amadon*. You don't need music. That stuff's all pretend. Learn to stand on your own two feet, boy. Strong men don't need that rubbish. Why were you thrown out of the band, anyway?"

Silence.

Rasher is about to invent something creative, but I stop him with a look. What do I care what O'Driscoll thinks?

"I gob-smacked Andy McBride for being a bully."

O'Driscoll bursts out laughing and his belly is rolling like a sack of spuds that fell off a lorry. "That's the spirit. I like a man who stands up to a bully." He stops laughing suddenly as if he's remembered something. "Okay. Okay. Take him to the kitchen and show him what to do," he says to Rasher, who's grinning his head off. He turns to me. "Forget about music and the band. Throw yourself into your work with all your heart and soul and you'll be grand. And don't go punching anyone, ya hear? I don't care what ya do anywhere else, but the kitchen is my domain and I'll not stand for any of that nonsense."

Every brother has his little kingdom, it seems. But still, he doesn't scare me. Looking up at him, I can't help the feeling that I almost like him. Why? Suddenly, I know what it is. He reminds me of Grandah in Green Street. The big fat belly and his trousers falling down. Ah, I remember . . . good ol' Grandah!

Then Grandah—I mean O'Driscoll—sees the look in my eyes and grunts something that's almost good-natured. He turns and barrels off through the door into the kitchen. Rasher laughs and smacks me so hard on the back I nearly fall down. I still miss that trombone, but at least Black Daniel is riding again!

CHAPTER 20

My sisters and I are giddy as poodles to be back together again for the first time in a year. At least Katie and I are. Patricia isn't. I can't understand what's wrong with her.

We're all at my Uncle Matty's house in Whitehall, and we're having a real Sunday dinner. My tongue is so happy with the food, it won't stop talking.

Katie is laughing. Patricia is scowling. I've just done an impression of O'Driscoll with his huge belly and big eyebrows. It was pretty good, considering Patricia never looked at me once. She was busy trying to burn a hole in the plastic tablecloth with a fiery frown. God, but they've grown. Katie's red cheeks are fatter and Patricia's blonde hair is down to her shoulders.

It all started ten days ago, when we'd just finished our drill exercises with Mr. Prout, the drill master. You'd think we're in the army with all the marching and left-turning and standing to attention and falling out and falling in and dressing to the right. Every day it's the same. It's enough to drive you mad. But it keeps us warm and sometimes I'll pretend I'm on my way to war and I'll get the shivers up and down my spine. Prout had just finished one of his lectures on "a fit body serves a fit mind" and all that crap and the Maggot was calling out the names of the lads who'd received letters from home. He does this every few days after our drilling. I hardly ever pay attention—I don't want to hear my name not being called. I was swapping some chestnuts for chewing gum with a new friend from the kitchen, Jack McDonald, when I nearly collapsed with shock.

"Danny Ellis," the Maggot shouted. *A letter from home? It must be Ma. Great! Massive! Mustard! I'm going home.* My knees were shaking as I ran up to collect the envelope. It'd already been opened—like all Artane mail. But wait now . . . it's not from Ma. It's from Uncle Matty, Ma's brother. The disappointment stole the life's blood from me. I couldn't bear to read it. I bit into McDonald's gum till my teeth ground.

After the Maggot dismissed us, I sat down on the shelter wall and forced myself to read the one-page letter. My uncle has received permission to have me come visit him in Whitehall, once a month on Sundays. I can come a week next Sunday and—Mary, Mother of Sorrows—Patricia and Katie will be there too! For the first time in ages, I stopped missing the trombone and Ma. I leapt off the wall, shouting for joy through my tears, nearly knocking over Rasher, who'd run up to me.

"Laughing and crying at the same time, eh? What's up with you?"

"I'm going to visit my uncle and my sisters will be there. It'll be my first time to see them since I got here."

"Great! You'll have to ask the Maggot for the bus fare—there and back. Then you'll have to cadge some money from your uncle to repay him. Remember what happened to O'Reilly?"

Christ! Nothing's simple.

Rasher continued, "Don't be surprised if your uncle doesn't want to cough up. But don't take any shite from him. If you don't bring back your bus fare, the Maggot will skin you alive and you won't be let out again in a hurry."

—◊—

I had to wait a few days to answer my uncle's letter. I can read pretty well, but my handwriting could be mistaken for the winner of a mad monkeys' map-drawing competition, so I had to wait till Saturday.

Every Saturday, in class eleven, some senior lads help the younger boys to write their letters home.

So, on Saturday morning after breakfast, I shuffled into class eleven. Ten or twelve older boys were sitting at desks, each with a younger lad beside him, writing away as the youngsters, delighted to be telling the bigger lads what to do, dictated their letters. In the back, on his own, was Tommy Bonner. He was writing a letter. My heart was thumping as I went over and sat down beside my hero. My tongue had gone on holliers. Where's Black Daniel when you need him? Of course, I see Tommy in church every week, but I've never actually talked to him.

"I . . . I need help to write a l—letter," I stuttered.

He nodded. "I'll be with ya in a sec, soon as I finish this letter to me sister." He finished the letter, stuck it in an envelope, and brought it up to the Maggot, who read it and put it with a pile of other letters in a shoebox on his desk.

When he came back I said, "Is your sister in an orphanage too?"

"No, she's at home with me other sister," he said flatly.

I was speechless. His parents have kept his sisters at home and put Tommy in Artane? Jesus! I've heard the same thing from other lads. How does it feel to be the one that's sent away?

He saw my long face and said matter of factly, "Me ma isn't well and the girls look after her. They can't really afford to keep me, ya know." He shrugged and grinned. "Okay, who's this letter to?" He dipped his nib in the inkwell in the desk, his big hands dwarfing the pen.

"It's my Uncle Matty. I'm going to see him Sunday week." I watched the neatest writing I've ever seen spell out my uncle's name across the blank sheet. We finished the letter and I signed it with a spidery scrawl that made Tommy's writing look like the *Book of Kells*. As he addressed my envelope, I remembered that I'd forgotten to ask my uncle for the bus fare, but I didn't have the heart to make him start all over. He stood up, proud and happy with his work, ruffled my hair, and winked. He was about to turn and walk off when a shout rang out across the crowded classroom.

"Bonner!" It's the Maggot, shouting from behind his desk at the top of the class. "Don't touch the younger lads. You know better than that."

With his back to the Maggot, Tommy's face turned hard. He hissed under his breath, "Filthy minds have filthy thoughts." He walked out the door, completely ignoring the Maggot's evil stare.

What was all that about? Confused, I walked up to the Maggot and handed him my letter and envelope. I turned to walk away, feeling the Maggot's eyes boring into the back of my head. But unlike Tommy's defiant exit, mine faltered, and I was disgusted to hear myself say to the Maggot, "Thank you very much, sir." Christ Almighty, when will I learn to just keep my mouth shut?

—⁓—

Sunday week came soon enough and the sheer glory of the ride on a double-decker bus was almost more joy than I could bear. I always sit upstairs in the front seat. The streets, the houses and gardens with kids playing on the grass with their dogs, and the men and ladies all dressed up after Sunday Mass—the world is a happier place from a bus.

After an hour of stumbling around Whitehall trying to find my uncle's house, I finally asked someone, who led me to it: a tiny terraced corporation house nestled among hundreds and hundreds of the same. The girls were already there. Laughter and tears—from me and Katie—and stories and more stories as I ignored my uncle and his wife, and Patricia's dark looks. Uncle Matty and Aunt Margaret, smiling kindly, didn't seem to mind.

—⁓—

Dinner is over now and the girls are playing with some dolls they've brought from their orphanage, which, I just found out, is across town, by the sea, in Booterstown. For some reason, I'm uncomfortable and short of conversation, but soon I'm busy banging away on the piano in the living room—the only downstairs room besides the tiny kitchen—learning that *Fallon's Do-Re-Mi* notes are on the piano too. They're all over the place—thank God. After a while, I ask my uncle, who's been pretending not to be annoyed as he tries in vain to listen to the radio above my awful din, about Ma.

Everyone goes real quiet all of a sudden. Uncle Matty turns the radio off. Aunt Margaret goes into the kitchen.

"No one has heard from your mother, Danny. Not us, nor your grandparents in America, nor my sister in England. There's not been a single word from her." Uncle Matty's face is very sad behind his kindness.

The girls have stopped playing and we're all looking at the floor. Strange patterns on that linoleum, aren't there?

Then Patricia can stand it no more. "She's just a terrible, terrible person and she can stay away forever if she wants."

That makes me mad but I hold back my anger. "Don't talk about Ma like that. One day she'll get better and take us all home. You'll see. She's just real sick, that's all."

"She can die, for all I care," Patricia says quietly. Jaysus, why can't I say things with that evil, quiet feeling wrapped around them? I'd have a much easier life on the playground.

"Stop it, Patricia. Don't be like that," I say, confused at her cold strength.

Patricia turns and looks me full in the eyes for the first time since I got here. Her eyes are ablaze with an anger I've never seen in her. "And you, Danny Ellis, the *big man of the house*, me arse. Supposed to look after us, weren't ya? You're just a coward—a dirty, filthy coward. You just lay there and did nothing."

An electric shock runs up my spine and suddenly I'm sweating and cold and sick to my stomach.

Patricia comes in for the kill across the waves of nausea. "And you can die, for all I care. You should drop dead right now."

"Don't say that," cries Katie, who's now in tears, looking into Patricia's face.

"You shut your mouth, you silly eejit. What do you know about anything? You were asleep. You know nothing. He's a coward. A coward!" Patricia pushes Katie away. It's a harder push than Patricia intended and she looks sorry—for half a second.

Uncle Matty stands up and tells us all to be quiet. He turns on the radio.

It's time for us all to go back to school.

Rasher was right. When I ask my uncle for the bus fare to pay the Maggot back, he looks at his wife oddly. They both shake their heads and, after some humming and hawing, she finally dips into her purse and hands over the shilling.

We're saying goodbye outside on the street. Patricia is still mad. Katie is all kisses and hugs and tears. Looking into her sweet, blue eyes, I'm suddenly filled with a terrible, hopeless anger I don't understand. I turn around to Patricia. "If you ever hurt Katie in any way, I'll run away from Artane and come and banjax ya, do ya hear?" *Jesus, what are you saying? It's not her fault.* But right now I need a strong enemy and Patricia fits.

She must need an enemy too, but I'm not strong enough for her, cos I nearly cry when she hisses quietly, "Drop dead, ya skinny, ugly-looking coward."

—〰—

For a week I was really upset about what happened with Patricia. I was so looking forward to seeing her. Why did she keep calling me a coward? *I'm not a coward!* I kept saying to myself over and over.

After a year of not seeing each other, I wanted her to be proud of me.

Maybe that's it, right there. Maybe I was showing off too much, acting like the big shot in front of Katie, who's always made me feel confident and strong. That's what it was: Patricia was jealous of me and Katie. That felt better—for ten minutes. But the next day, when I wasn't looking, a tear fell into the dirty water over my knives and forks as I washed them in the trough in the back of the kitchen. Between missing music and this thing with Patricia, I was going bonkers. *Tighten up, ya eejit, ya can't let yourself slip now.*

Over the next few days, I threw myself into the kitchen work like a wild man, cleaning everything in sight that needed it and some things that didn't.

"Slow down, Dano, for Jaysus' sakes," said Rasher one day. "That floor's been swept already. Yer giving the rest of us a bad name."

But I couldn't slow down. Running around like a cat on fire, I exhausted myself doing nothing. And now I lie here awake in the dorm, sleepless again. For the hundredth time in a week, Patricia's words echo around my mind.

You're a coward. You just lay there and did nothing. You were supposed to look after us.

Why didn't I ask her what she meant by that? Forget it. She was just in a bad mood. She didn't mean it. Try to get some sleep.

Think of something else. Think of anything else. Think of a nice, warm day with the sun shining. Maybe a river with fish swimming beneath the shimmering surface. There we are—it's the River Dodder, which I used to run to as I mitched from school in Rathfarnh— Shush . . . don't say that word. Try to sleep. A song to sleep by.

> *Down where the Dodder flows*
> *That's where the lilac grows*
> *That's where my true love sleeps*
> *That's why the lilac weeps.*

Look into the river. The lilac seems to play with its own reflection in the water. The sunlight is dancing with the lilac. The water goes dark as the sunlight disappears. I'm sinking into the water now. Clouds of purple and violet wrap around me. I sink deeper. I can breathe the colors underwater. They come. I go. I fall away. In a fall-away world.

Oh, but it's the weeping.

The whole world is weeping.

Soft and helpless and so piteous.

Patricia. Sweet Patricia.

Stop it, Patricia. I was nearly asleep. You'll wake Katie. Go back to sleep.

But she won't stop.

Something, someone is crushing the lilac.

That's why the lilac weeps.

Why not do it to Danny? He's the oldest.

Her cries are suddenly muffled now.

The darkness itself is crying.

Am I crying too?

The air is fear and filled with a black sorrow.

Everything is black.

Her cries are no longer muffled.

It's over now.

But the lilac still weeps.

The lilac will always weep.

—m—

In the blackness a blacker shape rises. The black shape is moving and its breath is Guinness. It's standing now unsteadily, breathing its rottenness in waves. The bedroom door opens and the landing light explodes the black shape into one of Ma's men friends. He's bending, pulling up his trousers.

A scream from the landing! Long and rent with anguish. It's Ma.

"You filthy bastard!" Her voice is despair itself.

The man rushes out past her. Footsteps down the stairs. The front door crashes open. He falls. Ma is screaming as she runs out into the street past him.

Shouting! The whole street is shouting. Men's voices. Angry. Frightening. Strong. Good.

"I got him!"

"I got the dirty fucker."

"Hold him! Hold the bastard."

Scuffles and sickening sounds of fist and boot, again and again against skin and bone.

Different screams now from a single voice so full of fear that when they stop suddenly the silence is even more frightening.

"Someone phone the police!" The shout is taken up across Loretto Crescent.

"No, please. I fell asleep. It won't happen again." Ma's voice is imploring.

"This has to stop, Mrs. Ellis. This has to stop."

CHAPTER 21

Thank God for the noise. It's like a battle charge—in a battle you can win. Stops you feeling things. The kitchen is nearly as loud as the band room. It's in the same building as the ref, as long but not quite as wide. It's equipped with six large, brass meat-boilers, a huge double-door potato-steamer and a twenty-foot-long trough where we wash the dishes. O'Driscoll runs things like an army barracks. A boy-in-charge serves three tables, seeing to the portioning and laying out of food. Each boy-in-charge has a helper who washes dishes and sweeps up. With a dozen or so lads doing other background chores, such as maintaining the storerooms, fridges, and bread rooms, there must be forty of us here in the kitchen. Maybe a quarter of the kitcheners are over fourteen years of age—as such they are traders, and work here full time from dawn to dusk. The rest of us put in maybe four hours a day, between class, which is fine with me—keeps me out of the cold. The traders do most of the dangerous work: cutting meat or dealing with the hot food in the boilers and the potato steamers. As well as O'Driscoll, we're also overseen by two laymen, who are nearly as cruel as him.

Eight hundred metal plates and knives and forks and spoons make for a grand clamouring. Washing and sorting and laying them out on the forty tables of the ref is a mad rush of sweating lads slipping on greasy concrete, everyone chewing on something out of sight of O'Driscoll, whose pramwheel strap makes itself known to almost everyone, every day. He hasn't hit *me* yet. I don't need anyone else to hit me—I'm beating myself up. *Why?*

O'Driscoll's over there now with a huge ladle in hand, spooning off the dripping—the Monium—from the boiling meat in one of the six big, brass boilers. His farmer's hat is stuck fast to his head, so it doesn't move an inch, even when he bends down to pour the Monium into a metal bucket at his feet. His belly doesn't let him bend completely and he's out of breath as usual. I'm surprised to notice that I'm feeling sorry for the mean old bastard. It's a feeling-sorry kind of time—for myself, for Patricia, for the lads around, and yeah, for O'Driscoll. But I'm careful of the slippery floor as I walk over to him.

"Let me hold the bucket for you, sir, so you don't have to bend down."

He looks at me as if I've gone completely bonkers. "That's . . . that's very nice of you, Ellis. You're a kind lad. I see the way you muck in and help others when it's needed. You have some respect, not like some of these other mopes."

I don't know what the hell he's on about. But something happened a few days ago that changed the way he deals with me—the way we deal with each other.

I was feeling pretty bad about Patricia and just couldn't care less about anything. That seemed to fill me with an insane disregard for everyone. All day, I was ready to give battle. You see, O'Driscoll calls us "mopes" all the time, but nobody seems to know what a mope is.

"Mope this and mope that. What the bloody hell does he mean by a mope?" Rasher said as we marched out of the ref.

"I don't know, but there's one way to find out," I said brazenly. I broke rank and shuffled straight over to O'Driscoll, who was marching us out of the ref. The lads couldn't believe what I was doing. Neither could I—nor O'Driscoll.

"Sir, what's a mope, sir?"

O'Driscoll gaped at me in disbelief.

"Maybe if we knew what it was we could try not be one," I said. As I look at him, I'm turning O'Driscoll into Grandah. "And you wouldn't have to beat us all the time," I added coldly and softly, just like Patricia.

So that's how she does it! It's easy when you don't give a shit about anything any more.

O'Driscoll was speechless. The lads stopped marching. Everyone was holding their breath.

"So, please tell us, what's a mope, sir?"

"A mope is someone who walks around in a daze, feeling sorry for himself and doesn't do his job properly." He sighed.

"Thanks, sir. Now we know what it is, we can try to be better."

The lads were in shock.

O'Driscoll was struggling for words. "Good . . . good . . . very good."

As I joined the ranks marching out of the ref, Rasher was winking at me like he had a wasp in his eye.

Now as I help O'Driscoll with the bucket of Monium, I can feel the lads—Rasher, O'Reilly, Kelly, and McDonald—looking at me, wondering what I'm up to. I'm not up to anything, but I don't mind them thinking I am. As O'Driscoll struggles with the Monium, I wink at the lads, who wink back furiously. *That's it, Dano. Work it for all it's worth.* Let them think what they want. But I'm just surviving here.

Black Daniel is back—with a smarter horse and lots of new ammunition.

—⁓—

Maybe Black Daniel doesn't miss the band; he's too busy pulling fast ones and being a smart Alec. But at night in bed, when there's no one around to impress, he rides off somewhere and lets me cry for the music I miss so much. I can almost feel that trombone at my mouth sometimes and my hand goes out to move the slide beneath the blankets. My body arches in bed as I imagine letting my heart burst in one long, wild blast. Then more tears. Then Black Daniel rides back, just in time. *Stop it! Tighten up!*

I won't talk to Rasher or anyone else about it cos I'm getting known as a bit of a jack the lad and I can't let my aching for music spoil that. But I can talk to my Uncle Matty about it. He understands. He has a lovely collection of Glen Miller records, which he plays sometimes when I visit. Matty is hard to figure out. He looks like he almost totally understands me sometimes and then he goes all quiet and closes off. Maybe I don't care. I can do that as well as anyone.

Here at Matty's again now, I'm listening to Glen Miller, wondering why he, a trombone player, doesn't play more trombone. Patricia and Katie haven't been here with me since that first visit when we were all here together. Apparently they've been taken under the wing of a couple of nice ladies who live near Blackrock. They go there every other Sunday. Lucky things! They're allowed outside to visit every fortnight, instead of every month like me. But they're coming today. In fact, they should be here soon.

Matty's a very kind man but acts strange when I try to talk about Ma; like I said, he likes to disappear inside himself, but I'm not letting him get away with his silences today. Let's see.

"How long does TB last for?" I ask. He's reading his paper and doesn't appear to hear me. To test out his hearing, I go and bang on the piano real loud. He nearly jumps out of his skin. Ah, his ears are fine. I try another approach.

"When you visit Ma in hospital, does she ever ask about me?"

He shakes his head and sighs wearily. "I've told you a dozen times, Danny, I haven't seen nor heard from your mother since she left you in Artane. If I ever do, I promise I'll let you know."

Why won't he look at me? I feel like I'm trying to open a door with no handle.

"If you see her, will you ask her to—" His look stops me. I change direction again. "I mean, if she gets better, will she come and see you? TB can't last for ever, right?"

He goes to say something but stops himself. He looks very sad. Maybe he misses her too. He looks at me kindly. "I think it would do you good to write to your father. Let me give you his address in New York. He's left the army now. He works on the railway in New Jersey." He writes on a piece of notepaper. Just as he's finishing, Patricia and Katie barge in the door.

Excited to see them, I give Katie a hug and a kiss on her curls. Patricia turns away as I try to hug her. Confused and hurt, I blurt out that I'm going to write to Da.

Katie is delighted. "Tell him I love, love, love him."

"What are you writing to Da for?" Patricia says, as if I'd said I planned to kill a kitten. She has a girl's comic in her hand, which she pretends to read.

Of course, I haven't spoken to her since . . . well, since Rathfarnham came back to remind me why I always say I'm from Green Street.

I know I couldn't ever find a way to let her know . . . that . . . I mean, I think I'm sorry for something. Sorry I didn't stop that man from doing . . . from doing . . . I don't know what he was doing to her. But I know it was bad—real bad. I know there's bad things that can happen in the dark. Things that can't happen in the day. I wish I could . . . I don't know what I wish. But I do. That's all.

"What are you writing to Da for?" She asks me again, louder this time.

"Oh, y'know yerself. I just want to write and tell Da what's going on," I say too easily.

"Will you tell him you're a coward?" She chokes back the tears quickly and turns away to look out the front window. Some tiny children are playing ball on the street. A bigger lad is bossing them about.

Nearly in tears, I whisper fiercely from behind her, "I'm not a coward. But I know . . . "

One of the kids on the street cries out loudly, hurt, as the bully throws his weight around more and more. The thought of interfering comes and passes; the bully is much bigger than me. Sick to my stomach at my helplessness, I can't put my words together.

"I know . . . I know I'm afraid of everything." I'm sweating. My knees buckle. "I *am* a coward." There I've said it! My chest is red hot and the wave moves to my face and my feet at the same time. "Everyone in Artane can kick my arse and they all know it. I fight them, but they always win. I always lose. Always."

Silence.

She shifts her weight.

Wait now. Thinking suddenly of Hennessy and Murphy, the lads I beat up by the wood pile, I blurt quickly, "I always lose—except that one time when I was in a real good mood one day when I wasn't scared when I went for O'Connor's matches on my way to the Slasher and Hennessy and Murphy ambushed me and they were falling over each other like eejits and I popped them in the—"

Patricia turns around and her face stops my blathering—for a second. It's not exactly what I would call a smile, but I know I'm on the right track. *Be a hero—that's the way to go.*

"I didn't lose *that* fight. I banjaxed the pair of them. I could've done it with one hand tied behind me back and both legs nailed to the ground."

That gets her.

Her eyes are swimming pools. She looks at me so soft and sweet with understanding that I have to stop the tears by pretending I'm winking. Black Daniels doesn't cry in front of his sisters. He winks—with both eyes, one at a time, real fast.

She's smiling now. She lifts her hand with the comic still in it. She points her finger to a page. "Can you teach me how to read the writing? There's an eejit in here who thinks she's magic. Whaddya make of that old shite?"

I grab the comic. Girls like lads to be heroes.

—◊—

So yes, I wrote Da a long letter—with the help of a big lad in class eleven—telling him my whole life story since he left Ireland. I never expected to get an answer back, so when the Maggot shouted my name at mail-call, I nearly fainted. There was a ten-dollar bill in with the one-page letter. Well, not actually in with the letter, but there was a handwritten "$10" sign on the envelope with the Maggot's initials beside it. God forbid we should be allowed to open our own mail. The money goes into the Book, which the Maggot keeps in his desk in class eleven. Every Saturday I can take out as much as I need. With nearly three dollars to the pound, I'll have about three pounds in the Book. Now, that'll get me . . . let me see . . . about 120 large bottles of lemonade or 300 Rollos or about a gazillion gobstoppers or five contrillion marbles. Or, if I was smart at cards, I could turn it into ten pounds, which would get me—

Oops! The letter blows out of my hand and across the playground. Shite! I haven't read it yet with all my reckoning. I run and get it from under someone's foot. Da's writing is nearly as bad as my own. But I can hear his clear voice and see his strong shoulders as I read:

Dear Son,

I hope this finds you well as it does me. I am sending you 5 dollars for some sweets or toys. I saw your grandparents last weak and they tolled me to tell you they were asking for you. Your Grandah works in an ice cream factory. He keeps busy because the weather hear is very hot at the moment. I hope you can get back in the band again, son. The Artane Boys Band is very famous here in New York. I'm saving up to buy a bike.

I remain
Yours truly
Your Father.

Thanks Da. But wait a minute. Read that again. Jesus, Mary, and Joseph! The Maggot's made a huge mistake. He must be blind as a bat. Or he can't tell a five-dollar bill from a ten. Tell the truth, neither could I probably. I've never seen either. I'm richer than I should be.

—∾—

I just got a great idea! These sausages could be smaller if I squeeze them in the middle and twist them round. Now instead of the 150 that O'Driscoll carefully counted out for each of us four lads to stab with our forks, I've created a half-dozen extra with my squeezing and twisting. No one notices as I stick the newly created sausos into my pocket. I'll cook them later, outside on the huge hinges of the furnace door—which stick out like tiny frying pans, just begging for something to be fried on them—with Rasher and Willie O'Reilly. We finish stabbing the sausos and now O'Driscoll has us spreading margarine on hundreds of slices of bread. We're making ham sandwiches to be eaten at Portmarnock Strand later today.

We've waited all year to see 'Marnock Strand. The long, sunless winter is no friend to fun and play, although to keep warm, play is always very inventive—and very rough. As winter turned to spring and daffodils sprung up around the grounds and playing fields, you could feel everyone's mood gradually change. By the time June came around even the brothers were cheering up, knowing soon they'd be away off somewhere, far from Artane, handing things over to other brothers drafted in for the summer. A blue sky and a warm breeze work wonders on gray buildings and gray faces.

For the last week our prayers have been very sincere: *Dear Holy God, up there in heaven with all your pals, do your very best, try as hard as you can, but please, please, don't let it rain on Thursday.*

Yes, today is Thursday and tanks be ta God, it's not raining. It's the summer holidays, called holliers, and we're off to the beach today. I missed the holliers last year, lying on my back in hospital with not TB. There's only about half of the lads left. The rest have gone home to friends, fosters, and family. Chores have also been cut in half and of course there's no school and no daily Mass. Mass is only held on Sundays during the holliers.

All year long, through the cold, dark evenings of winter and the slow promise of the fickle, damp spring, we looked forward to the summer and the summer sandals they issue us in June. What a relief it is to run through the grass in the soft sandals after limping around the playground all winter long in the prison of the hobnail boots.

> But summer sandals soft and easy
> Will set my feet to fly
> At last I'll feel the grass beneath me
> It springs back as I pass by
> In summer sandals light as paper
> I'll hardly touch the ground
> Ah, now, that's what feet were made for
> Running free and flying round.

We're on our way to 'Marnock and the train is packed: three hundred lads screaming and shouting and singing and throwing toilet rolls out the windows at the locals as the train passes through their backyards. The skeleton staff of younger brothers, brought in for the summer, haven't a clue what they're doing and don't even try to maintain order. So, we let it rip like the steam that drives this old train to Portmarnock Strand. We burst out of the train as it pulls in to the station. Breathless with excitement, we walk the mile to the strand. With each step, the smell of the sea gets stronger and the sand is already in our sandals as we walk along. We're barely able to stop ourselves from running over the sandy path. We pour over the strand and climb the tall silver dunes to look over the top and catch our first glimpse of the gray majesty of the Irish Sea. We don't care how many flies are in our lemonade. We don't care how much sand is in our ham sandwiches. And we certainly don't care how cold the Irish Sea is, cos it's Thursday in the summer and it didn't rain and we're going swimming.

In the delirium of sea, sand, and sun, everything is forgiven. Old grudges are forgotten.

> *Thank God the summer's nearly here*
> *Most are off to friends and families*
> *The rest of us stay right here*
> *Making friends of bitter enemies*
> *We fight on dunes of silver sand*
> *Errol Flynns and Marlon Brandos*
> *They line us up like knights of old*
> *And when that silver whistle blows*
> *We rush to sea like it was gold*
> *And hold our breath against the cold.*

CHAPTER 22

Holidays or no, there's still a special feeling about a Sunday. Today is one of the nicest days I ever remember. Balmy breezes blow across the fields from the south and it seems the whole world has stopped biting itself for the moment. A bunch of us have gotten together and are running around the perimeter of the fifty acres of open fields behind the handball alleys. Every now and then Brother Cumming—a new brother, easy-going and clueless—will blow his whistle and warn us not to run out of bounds. We run and we run. Nice and easy does it—it's not a race. After half an hour of this, it feels like my breath is coming from somewhere that hasn't ever breathed before.

I wave at Antho Kelly as we pass him by. He's walking along by the western edge of the fields, looking pretty miserable. Poor Kelly! He was caught laughing in Mass this morning by the Maggot, who told him to report to him in the boot room after lights out tonight. That's put paid to his day. How can you eat or play when all you have to look forward to is the leather strap?

"Come on, Antho. Join in, for Jaysus' sakes. Don't let it get you down." I should talk. The thought of the boot room would probably paralyze me for a month.

Kelly shakes his head and we run on. About fifteen minutes later, we're turning left by the gate to the fields when we're stopped by the sight of a crowd of lads gathered around Brother Cummings. Everyone's talking at once. Something is obviously going on. I've cramped my calf slightly in the run, so I leave my group and limp over, curious.

"Yeah, he was sitting there one minute and the next he was gone," some lad is shouting breathlessly.

Someone's done a runner!

Cummings blows his whistle four or five times to get the attention of the hundreds of lads running about the playing fields. He's shouting now. "Gather round here, lads. Everyone over here immediately."

Gather round? Christ! *We can tell you're a new one,* we're thinking. The proper term should be "fall in," ya eejit.

So, instead of falling into orderly ranks as usual, three hundred lads are pushing and shoving one another to get close to the action, which is an inch from Cummings's face.

"Is everyone here present?" he asks stupidly, then corrects himself. "I mean, Anthony Kelly, if you're present, please make yourself known," Cummings shouts, trying to push back the teeming hundreds.

Crikey! Kelly's run. He's not waiting for the boot room; he's probably halfway to Galway, which is where he's from. The lads all take up the cry, making fun—"Kelly, are ya here? Where are ya, Kelly?"

Cummings screams above the tomfoolery, "Okay, okay, it looks like Kelly's gone missin', doesn't it? Did anyone see where he went?" Very stupid question.

Dozens of hands shoot up in the air. "Please, sir . . . Yes, sir, I did . . . Me, me, me, sir, I did, sir . . . Please—I saw him."

Cummings throws his hands up in despair and points hopelessly to Sean O'Mara, a weaver lad who's making the most noise. O'Mara is taken completely by surprise and stutters, "Y-yes, yes, I . . . I saw where he went, sir. I did. Yes. He went . . . " He looks around the fields for inspiration. "He went . . . he went that-a-way, sir." He's settled on north, almost certainly not where Kelly would have run.

But Cummings is caught up in the moment. He pulls himself up into what he imagines is his most gallant and military pose and shouts heroically, "Well, by God, lads! Let's go get him!"

A roar erupts from the mob and before Cummings can intervene, three hundred lads are running north at a breathless gallop, spreading out across the fields like cavalry or Indians or buffalo or whatever imagination can conjure up in this wild wave of lawlessness that has nothing whatsoever to do with poor Antho Kelly.

Cummings sees his mistake. But it's too late. The herd has reached the north hedges, beyond which no Artane toe has ever ventured, and the boundaries are falling like soldiers in Custard's Last Stand. Cummings, red in the face from blowing his whistle, is almost in tears. I'm frozen to the spot, my cramped calf preventing me from joining the fun.

There's a brief silence as the lads are now out of earshot. I hear Cummings mutter under his breath, "Jesus, Mary, and Joseph, I'm in big trouble."

Then the din picks up again in the distance. The mob has turned back—stopped by the large hedge by Kilmore Road, probably. The thrill of seeing the stampede rushing toward me disappears as I'm knocked over on the grass. Some lads have turned west with shouts of "There he is! He's over here!" Another splintering runs south. "No, he's over there, honest!"

Never was a lad seen in more places by more people with more conviction. When they catch him—or more likely, when his parents send him back, as happens with most runners—he's in more trouble than when he started.

Lads seldom run. The punishment is too severe. After they've been skinned alive by the brothers, most times they're sent to an even worse orphanage (hard to imagine) in the countryside—Letterfrack or Daingean. I've seriously considered it myself a time or two. But where would I run to?

Kelly's gone missing
Now what was he thinking
His mother and father

Will just send him back again
Four other brothers
Five other sisters·
Not one of them working
They just can't afford him.

CHAPTER 23

I'm sweeping up in the ref, alone. If I don't get this floor clean, I'll be here all bloody night. But singing makes the time pass right quick.

Do-Re-Mi. Mi-Re-Do. Mi-Fa-So. So-Fa-Mi.

It's funny—over a year of kitchen work has hardened my hands and knees, but no matter how much singing I do, my voice just gets softer and sweeter. That's music for ya! I sing the *Do-Re-Mi* notes all day long. Fallon has taken his Tonic Sol-fa to a whole new level in class: rebel marches and beautiful, slow Irish airs. Through the clear light of the *Do-Re-Mi* notes, music reveals her soft secrets and contours like a mountain to moonlight.

But Jaysus wept, I miss that bloody trombone. I'd give up playing cards forever if I could just blast away at it for five minutes. *Don't think about it now, too painful, just mop the floor and get yer arse off to bed.* It's half past nine and I'm alone in the kitchen except for one or two other lads: Antho Kelly, who was caught in August by the Gardai, hitchhiking to Galway—the Maggot beat him stupid in front of the whole school—and Gibbo, who are doing odd chores. I finish up wearily and hang my apron on its hook.

I'm outside the ref. It's freezing. *God, what are you doing to us?* O'Driscoll is always telling us to ask God for stuff. The whole world and everything in it is praying to Almighty God, he says. Okay. So, November must be praying for July, and brass monkeys must be praying for warmer balls. And I'm still praying for Ma to get better and come and take me home.

It's too dark to see where I'm going so I take a short cut across the football field. It's forbidden, but I'd rather fall on grass than concrete. *Oh, Sweet Jesus, what's that white thing?* Ah, it's only the goal post. I shudder and make the sign of the cross quickly as I pass by the church. Still a bit shaky from mistaking the goal post for a banshee, I look up at the sky over the churchyard. A world full of stars shines down on me. A few days back, O'Driscoll told us that the Russians had sent a dog up to space and he's floating around up there somewhere. *Hello, Laika, how are ya? I hope yer warm up there.* In the cold light, my breath is like cigarette smoke. I send one breath upward to see how far it rises before it disappears. That's nice. Now I'm lying on the ground sending my breaths up to the shimmering gazillions and I'm not cold or scared anymore. All there is is sky and light and my eyes are wide as the heavens.

> *Suddenly all of the stars in the sky*
> *Came alive in a blaze*
> *And I'm lost in a trance*
> *And it's then that I hear them—singing to me*
> *Heartbreaking melodies above*
> *Down from the stars out of this world*

The stars are music: every melody I've ever heard, all blended up into one sacred chorus of beautiful, impossible harmony. My breath has stopped. I could lay in this . . . this Star Song forever. I'm dissolving into light and music. My eyes widen and widen. My heart gladdens and gladdens. A growing smile threatens to crack my skull wide open.

I'm being pulled into the sky by my own smile. I have to fight real hard to get my eyes out of this expanding feeling. I hear the lads coming from the kitchen and in a second I come out of my trance. I feel cleaned out from head to toe and that smile still lingers through my body, in my eyes, in my chest, on my face. Something about that smile, the feeling that it could keep growing forever, is trying to remind me of something. I can't get a grip on what it is. It's too vague.

I'd better not tell anyone about this. Especially Rasher. He'd think I'm mad. But if this is madness, then please, God, let me go stark raving bonkers. Something just happened to me that I won't ever forget. I know something that I don't need words to explain. I am the sky. I am the music.

I have the sky for a home, and I have music for a friend.

—⁓—

I can peel spuds faster than anyone. Actually, it's only the eyes that I peel. That big potato-scouring machine in the corner does the rest. Sometimes I'll leave a spud in the machine, spinning and spinning till it's smaller than a marble. O'Driscoll caught me yesterday turning spuds into marbles and before I could turn him into Grandah, he had his pram-wheel strap out and whipped me viciously around the legs. Then he looked sorry he'd hit me. *Don't make me beat ya, lad.* It's impossible to understand this man—or any of the brothers, for that matter. One minute they're almost kind and the next they're almost . . . well, something happened the other day that reminded me that madness can spring from the same heart as kindness.

The kitcheners were getting lunch ready. Jack McDonald was fed up, dragging his feet as he carried a big pot of pea soup through the ref. O'Driscoll, who looked dead on his feet, was in a terrible mood, trying to keep the small army of kitcheners running smoothly. He picked on Jack, whipping him viciously across the legs with his pram tire.

"Smarten up, ya mope! Get going!" he growled.

McDonald's legs gave out beneath him, but he desperately tried to hold on to the pot of soup. As he hit the ground, the pot went flying through the air to land with a clatter. Pea soup flew everywhere. McDonald moved like lightning to steady the pot, which had landed right side up and was wobbling. O'Driscoll went wild, lashing out at Jack as he held on to the pot.

"You did that on purpose, ya blasted idiot. Eat it up!" O'Driscoll grabbed a spoon from a table near by. "Eat it up, or I'll murder you!" he screamed at Jack who was hanging on to the pot for dear life. "Eat it up, ya hear!" He shoved the spoon in Jack's hand.

On his knees, McDonald bent down and scooped up a spoonful of soup from the dirty floor and hesitated. O'Driscoll whipped him across the back. "Eat!"

Jack swallowed the goo and immediately spewed it up again in a shower that carried his breakfast with it. Again and again he vomited till it seemed last night's supper joined the breakfast and soup.

There was barely a sound except Jack's endless retching. Every one of the dozens of lads serving and cleaning and setting tables had stopped, riveted by the madness.

"Get back to work!" O'Driscoll screamed hoarsely. "Get back to work, or I'll skin every one of you alive."

Like an invader, like the devil that the brothers tell us can come and take over a person's body and soul, the madness takes over the brothers. They spend a lot of time warning us about being possessed by the devil. I'm beginning to see why. They seem to know what they're talking about.

And yet yesterday, when I turned the spud into a marble, he was almost begging me to behave.

"I don't enjoy this, ya know. So don't make me do it. Do your work properly and pray to God for guidance," he'd said.

"I will, sir, I will." I've heard O'Driscoll praying under his breath a few times. He needs to pray harder.

I'm not sure if what I do is called praying or not, but ever since the stars sang to me a couple of weeks back, I've been feeling closer to God, or heaven, or something. Feeling like I'm kind of looked after. I pop into the chapel now and then—if I get too cold. There, Columbus told me one day that God looks out for us. *But hold it right there, partner*—Black Daniel doesn't like that stuff. *Tighten it up.* He leaves when I get that looked after feeling. But still, he comes back quickly enough when I need him. Between God and Black Daniel, I do all right.

Now, if only I could get my hands on a trombone now and then . . .

I stop peeling spuds, thinking about the band. There's some band lads in my new classroom: Fran Dunne, who became my friend after we had a fight, and Michael Farley, who plays clarinet. (I was moved up a class when Pimpleface found out I could read and add and subtract better than most lads in class one. Thanks to the nurses—and the cards!) Farley and Dunne are always talking about music. I find myself hanging around them, rubbing shoulders with them in the hope something might wear off on me. When I see them on a Sunday, marching around the parade ground with the band, it's all I can do not to run over and grab a trombone and start blasting.

But O'Connor never gives anybody a second chance. Every time I pass him anywhere on the grounds, his eyes cut through me like razor blades. Strange, how even hate from someone you respect can almost make you feel good. No hopes of getting back in the band though, so I'll have to be happy with singing. Fallon singles me out to sing in class sometimes, along with Michael Farley, who's a bit annoying as he's a genius at everything. But he's not the kind of lad you'd be jealous of cos he's really funny too. He's not shy either, and he sings well. Not as good as Tommy Bonner, but he might be as good as me when he's on form.

But I've a million more spuds to eye so I'd better stop thinking and start peeling. Singing makes it easy. I'll give Fallon's new Tonic Sol-fa song a bash. I've been practicing like mad so I'm getting real good at it. It's called "The Irish Washerwoman." It goes:

SFMDDSDDMDMSFM
FRRTRRFRFLSF
MDDSDDMDMSFM
FMFRSFMDDD

Grand! How about a bit faster? There we are. The notes fall off my tongue like raindrops from a tree, free and easy. Why isn't everything as smooth as this cascading eloquence? God, if you can put your delight and freedom here in this music, why have you hidden it everywhere else?

Yeah, but I couldn't be happier if I was a pig knee deep in mud. Faster and faster I sing.

What's that noise?

I turn around sharply to find O'Driscoll bending down behind me, listening to me sing. He's probably crept in, trying to catch me turning spuds into marbles. Instead, he's caught me turning notes into raindrops. But he has the strangest look on his face. Wait now . . . that couldn't be kindness, could it? Mother of God! It took me a second to recognize it, beneath the eternal bad-tempered frown that pulls his bushy eyebrows almost down to his unshaven chin. It *is* kindness. And I wasn't even trying to turn him into Grandah. He shoves a fat finger under his little farmer's hat and scratches his thinning hair.

"'The Irish Washerwoman,'" he says very slowly. "By God, she's never been in fitter form. You're daft, Ellis. Daft as eggs. But that kind of madness never did anyone any harm. I'm going to speak to Brother O'Connor over the weekend. I know yer heart is still with the band, me lad, and I'll put a good word in for ya. I can't promise anything, but I'll do my very best. You can be sure of that. You can be certain of that." He nods his head as his lips purse tightly, like a man whose mind is made up.

Music is reaching out for me again.

> Now I know that
> God gives these melodies to us
> It's almost like He dresses up
> Puts on a suit we'll understand
> So we can have music for a friend.

—m—

O'Driscoll embodied the paradox present in so many of the brothers of Artane: on the one hand, he was cruel and callous, with one of the most violent tempers I've ever seen; and on the other, he was a deeply pious man, capable of real empathy and kindness. The madness of Artane was such that we never knew when the viciousness would explode, which should have made us distrustful of even genuine warmth, but when the tiniest spark of humanity was revealed by the brothers, we clung to it for dear life, sensing it was real and the cruelty an aberration. Who can say?

Later that night, after O'Driscoll caught me singing, just before bedtime the brothers had us throw hundreds of pails of water down the slight slope of the playground toward the dormitory buildings and the drinking fountains.

"It's going to be a cold one tonight, lads," the Maggot had said, rubbing his hands. "By morning we'll have an acre of ice and the craic will be ninety! Let's hope."

—m—

Yeah, but why does hope feel so bad? I'd more or less given up all idea of ever playing in the band again, but now, after O'Driscoll's promise to have a word with O'Connor over the weekend, I'm lying in bed awake and afraid that he'll say no. I eventually slip into a restless sleep, dreaming of golden trombones.

As we come down the iron stairs to the seven-thirty Mass, the sight of the playground thrills me silly. I've heard about the "skating rink" before from older lads, but this is my first time seeing it. And what a sight it is. The playground is a shining lake of ice in the dawn's gray light. The rivers of water have frozen into one solid mass, making it almost impossible to walk without falling.

After breakfast the fun begins. Hundreds of lads—almost the whole school—are lined up by the shelter wall, banging their feet and clapping their hands to keep warm. Most of the brothers have come out to watch. The Maggot's divided us into ten or twelve lines about ten feet apart. Rasher and I are near the back of a line in the middle of the shelter wall. Everyone is breathless with excitement.

The Maggot blows his whistle for silence. He gets it. You can hear the ice waiting for us.

He blows again. Then the whole bloody place goes screaming mad!

The lads at the front of the lines start to run like crazy down the iced playground. How can they run on ice? They're followed by the ones lined up behind them. After running ten yards, the skating begins. The sight of it! Six or seven hundred lads in twelve straight lines, slipping and sliding, calling and falling, pushing and shoving, banging into each other. When they reach the drinking fountains, the lads dash back up the playground to line up and slide back down again.

Lads on the way back up the slope are slipping into the lads sliding down and soon there are heaps of bodies all over the place. But the fun—the red cheeks, the screams, the laughter—even after falling a hundred times, it's the best craic I've ever had in my life. I soon get the hang of it. I'm not famous for my athletic skills in football or hurling or boxing, but I can skate these bloody hobnail boots into the ground as good as anyone.

Christ! I take that back! Rasher's dropped to his knees in front of me and is sliding backward! Backward!

"Pick this up, Dano!" he shouts as he drops one of his woolen mittens on the ice. Ten feet behind, I drop to my knees, surprised that I don't fall on me arse. I grab his mitten and I throw it to him as he turns to the front, just in time to jump over someone who's fallen. I jump over the body too and run smack into Rasher. But we've started something; soon everyone's dropping hats and gloves and toys on the ice for lads behind to bend and grab. Delirious with these new found skills, I'm whooping and yelping, bending and turning till my head is spinning and my heart is a hammer and my breath is a train.

Then my legs slip out in front of me and my head hits the ground with a sickening thud.

I somehow crawl out of the sliding line and lie on the ice on my belly, propped up by my elbows, watching the spectacle in a daze. Something's happened to my ears, and I can't hear.

In silence, the flying boots pass me like black battleships on the sea of ice. Above them, the bloodied knees rise to red-white thighs, which float in ill-fitting, rough tweed pants that chafe the cold flesh raw. A small boy falls beside me, his face twisting in pain for a brief moment till his eyes light up again with that impossible mixture of fear and joy I've seen a thousand times in playground games.

My ears clear suddenly. The noise is deafening. My head is splitting.

I pick myself up shakily as the Angelus bell strikes twelve o'clock. The Maggot's whistle blows and the tableau freezes. We all stand in silence, contemplating the Angel Gabriel's appearance to an astonished Mary, announcing the coming birth of Jesus.

At least that's what we're supposed to be doing. But I steal a glance around at the silent, standing hundreds. There's another angel present in everyone's eyes and it's not Gabriel. Although there isn't a lad who's not bleeding somewhere—hands, knees, foreheads, noses, cheeks—there isn't a face that's not grinning.

> *And a cobbler's curse on hobnail boots*
> *Leather buckets round yer ankles*
> *You'll hear them coming, that's the truth*
> *Metal heels all jingle-jangle*
> *But pails of water we had tossed*
> *Like a river down the playground*
> *Have frozen in last night's frost*
> *And now the boots are great to skate on*
> *We'll slide the damn things into the ground*
> *And hold our breath as we fall down.*

Chapter 24

It's Monday morning and I belong back in the band and that's where I'm headed. Out of the ref door, down by the classrooms, across the playground, up the iron staircase, turn right at the top, up the few wooden steps past the washroom, and I'm in the door of the band room, quiet as a mouse in the shadow of a cat, cos O'Connor is standing with his back to me on the conductor's platform, in the middle of one of his long sentences.

O'Driscoll told me he spoke to Joe Boy about me last night. I should go and ask O'Connor for another chance, he said. Even with O'Driscoll's "good word" I'm still nervous. My legs are putty and my heart is a riderless horse. Black Daniel has fallen off it somewhere and the looked-after feeling isn't feeling itself at all.

O'Connor finishes talking and the band lads start up with individual practice. It's a beautiful noise. I can't believe it's been a year and a half since I last stood in this room and punched Fatser McBride like an eejit and lost everything. O'Driscoll's always talking about humility. Here it is.

Joe Boy steps off the platform and sees me standing by the door. He walks toward me, veering off to a little room at the back of dorm five—I mean the band room, where the Whistler used to sleep. Must be O'Connor's office now. He jerks his thumb toward it. *In there.* We are. There's his desk. The vision of his money-box hidden behind the left-hand drawer crosses my mind in a flash. I banish the thought. I have more important things to deal with: O'Connor's fiery glare, for starters.

I look up at him, trying to turn him into somebody kind. But instead, my eyes tear up and I've lost control of my legs completely.

"What are you doing here? I thought I told you I never wanted to see your face again."

Sobs and more tears. "O'Dris—I mean Brother O'Driscoll said he'd put a good word in for me, sir. I . . . I want another chance to play in the band."

Those hard eyes of his rip through me like the potato machine rips through a spud. He's trying to turn me into a marble. I don't care. Turn me into a pinhead if you want, just let me back in the band, won't ya? I don't care what trombone I play.

"'The Irish Washerwoman,' is it?" he growls. Is that a glint in his eye behind the scouring machine?

"I . . . I don't know what you mean, sir."

"Let me hear it. Go on now. Sing it."

Jesus! I can't believe it. I have a chance. Now I know where I am. This is my home turf. Don't even need Black Daniel on this prairie. I'm feeling looked after again.

"Sing it, lad, before I change my mind."

I cough and clear my throat. The Irish Washerwoman takes off her shawl.

God is hiding beneath it.

—⁂—

"God, when I think of the confluence of events that got me back in the band," I say to Liz, "the mind boggles. If I hadn't turned the spuds into marbles with the scouring machine; if O'Driscoll hadn't been spying on me to catch me at it; if Fallon hadn't taught me Tonic Sol-Fa—a million *ifs*. But when I got in front of O'Connor and sang, the music carried me, the clouds parted, the sun danced, and the angels sang. I can feel the relief of that moment as if it were yesterday."

"Why didn't you just ask him earlier?" Liz asks, puzzled.

"Like I told you before, ever since I came out of hospital, O'Connor looked at me like he wanted to murder me. So, I kept my distance."

"I don't like the sound of this man at all. I can't understand why you still have so much respect for him."

"He left a big impression, not all of it good. But in a battle, if someone saves your life, the fact that he's also a jerk is gloriously irrelevant."

"Yes, but when the battle's over you move on."

"I needed heroes. I hadn't a single adult role model I could relate to. O'Connor simply filled that slot."

"Some hero. He must have known how much music meant to you. He could have cut you some slack when you punched Andy McBride."

I laughed. "Ah, but me punching fat Andy Mcbride was only the half of it."

"Yeah? And the other half?"

"Rasher! It took me ages to find out, but my best friend betrayed me. Or, at least, I think it was him. It put me in O'Connor's bad books for years."

Liz looks puzzled.

"Remember my conversation with Rasher just before I went into hospital, when I told him where O'Connor kept his money?"

CHAPTER 25

The Artane Boys Band! With music to smooth the way, the last year has moved quicker than spit on a stove. But even apart from missing my kitchen friends—Rasher, Kelly, Gibbo, and McDonald—it hasn't all been easy sailing. In fact, I thought I was sinking for a while. Band Two practices beneath the dorms in a large, beautiful room beside the Long Hall. I'd only been back a week when I realized I was in real trouble—from two sources. The first was my old enemy, Fatser McBride, and the second was, of all things, music herself.

I'll get to Fatser, the mad terrier, later, but music, God bless her! I still couldn't read her to save my life. The other trombonists, Smasher and Itchy, could read better than me. The other fellah, the Belcher Ryan, who played Itchy's old horn—well, I wasn't sure if he could read or not. But feck it, I could play louder than any of them, and once I learn something in my head, it's there forever; I played the music by heart and I was damn sure it sounded better than Ryan's farty attempts as he stared at the sheet music. But heart only takes you so far. Whenever Mr. Crean brought out a new piece, I was lost. My heart was fine, but my eyes wouldn't see the music on paper. *I'm missing something. I can't keep bluffing forever.*

But one day, after a month mixed with joy and frustration and Crean's encouragement and patient tut-tutting, something happened that changed everything.

Smasher was trying to help me out with my reading when it hit me like the Flattener's leather strap across the arse. When I hear a piece of music, even once, my mind immediately turns it into Tonic Sol-fa notes. *Wait a minute,* I thought. *I can read Do-Re-Mi notes on a blackboard when Fallon writes them and I can turn any music I hear into Do-Re-Mi in seconds. I'm missing a step—what is it?* Jesus, hold on there! What if I could read the notes on the page as if they were Tonic Sol-fa? Then I'd be away like a midget on a pig's back.

So, I put all my time into training my mind to say *Do-Re-Mi*, and so forth, when I saw the notes on paper, instead of B flat, C, D, and so on.

I'd cracked it!

It just got easier and easier to read till one day, a month later, Old George Crean came into the practice room and said to the Belcher Ryan, "Okay, lad. You've had yer chance. Give it to Ellis."

"What, sir?" Ryan asked in surprise.

"The trombone. Give it over to him and take his old one." Itchy and Smasher winked at me, delighted. Poor Ryan was devastated. But his heart had never really been in the band. He left us a few weeks later to belch in the brothers' kitchen. My old battered war horse of a horn went to a bright new lad, James Egan. At last, as if this was meant to be, I had my hands on Itchy's old trombone. The difference is impossible to describe. With the new instrument, the *Do-Re-Mi* conversion trick, and the vote of confidence from Crean, my playing and reading went through the roof.

A few months later, Crean moved me up to the first chair in Band Two. Itchy liked to play bass trombone, so it made no difference to him, and Smasher, as easy-going a lad as you could hope to meet, was glad to hand over that responsibility to me.

O'Connor seemed pleased too, although he still acted like he detested me. Or, at least, he did until my final encounter with my tormentor, Fatser McBride.

The only one who wasn't happy about my progress was Fatser. For ages, while I was in the kitchen, with our different schedules I managed to avoid him. But the minute I got back in the band he was all over me: standing in front of me in the corridors, not letting me pass, staring coldly at me. He wouldn't dare do anything physical to get his own back because O'Connor knew he hated me and had warned him to stay away from me. But McBride was hell bent on scaring the shit out of me at least once every day.

Usually whenever things got very hot between two lads, the brothers would make them both put on boxing gloves and go three rounds together. Dozens of other lads would stand around in a circle cheering them on. It had happened with me and Fran Dunne, back before we both joined the band. Neither of us got in a decent punch and finally, totally exhausted, we shook hands and became friends.

Some months back, I saw one fight on the playground that wasn't a boxing match: it was a free-for-all. No brother was around to stop it. It involved Willie O'Reilly. Poor O'Reilly was putting up a brave effort but he was getting pretty badly beaten up by some overgrown bowsie. Lads were shouting them on like they were Roman gladiators. Suddenly O'Reilly's right boot came flying off in the scuffle.

"Me boot! Oh, me boot!" O'Reilly's pathetic cry rose above the shouting, which stopped suddenly, as did the fight. "Oh, me boot," he said again, running over to it and sitting on the ground to put it on. His big opponent stood by, scratching his head as O'Reilly laced the boot very carefully. Willie jumped up in a minute and ripped into the fight again like a madman.

I don't know why, but the sound of his voice as he lamented the loss of his stupid boot, the studied concern with which he laced it up, and the way he then gathered himself and came back fighting, it all filled me with a deep sadness for every one of us lost lunatics and the circumstances that united and divided us.

But back to Fatser McBride: O'Connor won't have his lads involved in boxing matches or fights of any kind, so I knew I was safe from Fatser's huge fists. But just by looking at me, he could still turn me into Gabby Hayes. After months of daily intimidation, I'd had it.

I knew I was going to have to call on someone a bit tougher than Black Daniel. But who?

I didn't really know Tommy Bonner at all . . . how about Kelly? No. He was smart, but not very tough. Rasher? No. Although fast as lightning on his feet, Rasher wouldn't last long against Fatser's heavier weight. Think. Wait now . . . a broken nose beneath a spiky red head jumped into my mind; the infirmary and the thermometer on the radiator—Jimmy Redmond. *Redser!* Just the man for the job.

A few days later: "What happened to you, McBride?" O'Connor asked Fatser, who'd just limped into the band room with a lovely big, black eye.

"I got into some trouble playing ball on the playground, sir. It won't happen again."

But Fatser was wrong. A week later he couldn't play the trumpet with his gorgeous, thick lip.

O'Connor was livid. "If you can't keep out of trouble, boy, the band is no place for you. This is your last chance, ya hear?"

Afterward, I approached Fatser as we were going down the iron staircase for supper. "Look, McBride, I know I punched you for nothing, and I'm sorry. I was just out of hospital and I wasn't myself . . . "

"I couldn't give a fuck whether you're sorry or not. So piss off, ya scrawny shitehawk."

"Look, I know you've made an enemy out of Redser Redmond. He's a good pal of mine and I can tell him to go easy on ya, if ya like."

Fatser looked as if he was going to rip me apart.

"Okay, okay," I blurted hastily. "Forget I mentioned it. You obviously can deal with Redser Redmond without my help. I'll tell him you said so." I walked off humming, banging my rolled-up Superman comic against my thigh. *We'll see.*

Suddenly Fatser grabbed me by the back of my jacket, almost ripping it off. "Why would you fucking help me? You hate my guts."

"No I don't." We'd come to a halt at the bottom of the stairs. Band lads pushed past us impatiently. Itchy stopped and looked at me intently. *Need help?* I wink and shake my head. He ran off. I turned back to Fatser. I realized, for the first time, that he looked very like my Green Street friend John O'Shea. Suddenly, it wasn't hard to be sincere.

"To tell you the truth, McBride, all I wanna do is play my trombone and enjoy meself. I can't do that with you looking like you'd like to murder me all the time," said I, but he wasn't turning into John O.

"Well, I do wanna murder ya, ya stupid bastard, and I won't let you forget it either—not ever."

I was nearly in tears. I'd had enough of that shite. "Well, go on then, do it! Get it over with, for fuck's sake." I stuck out my chin for him to punch. "Go on, hit me. There's no one here." All the band lads had gone and we were alone.

"You'll just run and go squealing to Joe Boy, won't ya?"

"No, I won't, I swear. Do it, will ya?" I shouted, in tears.

"You won't tell O'Connor?"

Before I'd finished shaking my head, my guts exploded as his fist tore into them, just beneath my ribs. His fist seemed to reach all the way to my spine. My breath had gone away somewhere on holiday and I was on the ground—where's all the fucking oxygen gone? It wasn't to be found in my lungs or the evening air around or anywhere else. I lay there for what felt like a year or two, gasping and thinking I'd never breathe again. I looked up to see Fatser's open hand above me. I winced and braced myself for more. Then I realized he was offering his hand to help me rise. I took it and he jerked me up to my feet like I was a rag doll. He held on to my hand tightly and shook it hard, up and down.

"Okay. We're quits. All right?" His nose was touching mine his thick lip quivering. "Now tell your thick pal Redser Redmond to leave me the fuck alone. I haven't a fucking clue why he picked on me in the first pl—"

My face must've given the game away for he stopped suddenly. His mouth dropped open and his brow furrowed. Then he threw his head back and laughed. "You jammy bastard! You put him up to it, didn't ya? Well, fuck me pink, Ellis. You couldn't fight your way out of a paper bag, but yer one canny fucker, that's for sure." He tapped me playfully under the chin with his knuckle. "If you could fight as well as you can play, we'd all be in trouble."

I dearly wish.

"Tell Redser we're quits now, okay?" He stuck out his hand, grinning, and I shook it again, genuinely glad to be done with it. He took off toward the ref and I bent down to pick up my Superman comic, which had fallen in the scrap. As I was straightening up, I looked up to see O'Connor standing at the top of the iron stairs with his hands on his hips. How long was he there? How much did he hear? I dunno. But from that moment on, O'Connor treated me with a wee bit more respect. He still seemed not to like me, but at least it wasn't total hatred.

—m—

Ever since that evening, ten months ago, Fatser has left me alone. We're not exactly friends, but when I needed a break last winter and "caught" a very high fever—thanks to the thermometer on the infirmary's radiator—he welcomed me back to the band when I was "better," saying with a grin, "He's back! Nail down the roof, for Jaysus' sake." I took that as a compliment from a fellow roof-blaster—he can play pretty loud himself. He's not so fat any more, or so aggressive. That and the fact that he's a really good musician have earned him the right in my mind to be called by his proper name. *Hi Andy, how's she cutting?*

—m—

George Crean is always a gentleman, but he's been extra kind to me today for some reason. He's taken some time to go over a beautiful

Bach chorale, which I think I play pretty well already. But I can always learn something new, right? Over and over it we go as the other lads in Band Two practice individually. After half an hour or so, Crean is well pleased. "Good man, Danny. You'll be fine."

Yeah? Confused, I thank him and ask permission to go for a leak.

When I come back, O'Connor is here, talking to Crean. Everyone's on their toes. One word from O'Connor to Crean and you're out of the band before you can blink. I grab my trombone from atop one of the six grand pianos that surround the room and take my place in the section.

"Let's hear it," grunts O'Connor, looking at me. Crean walks over and opens the chorale we'd been working on. He nods at me, motioning me to play.

I play that little piece like it was the only music ever written. When I'm done, Crean looks at O'Connor proudly, clapping me heartily on the back.

O'Connor looks pleased. He nods at Crean and turns to me. "Okay, Ellis, put your trombone away. Go up to the main band room and find Dessie Tate. He'll give you his trombone."

Oh, my God! Dessie Tate's big, beautiful golden horn.

"Dessie leaves Artane on Monday. He's expecting you, and he'll show you how to take good care of it. It's an expensive instrument, and I expect you to give it the respect it deserves. Once a month I'll be checking it for dents and I better not find any, ya hear me? You'll be sharing second chair with Patser Lennox, okay?"

I nod feverishly, speechless.

O'Connor continues: "Band Number One is no place for thieves, cheats, and liars, and I expect you to mend your ways. Your playground friends won't help you if I hear any more about your blackguarding, got it?"

"Yes, sir. I do, sir. Thank you, sir. I'll—"

O'Connor interrupts me impatiently, but there's a hint of a glint in those steely eyes. "And if Redser Redmond even looks crooked at anyone in the band, you and he will be hearing from me." Christ! For nearly a year he never mentioned it, but he must have heard every word of my conversation with Andy at the bottom of the iron stairs. O'Connor's a deep one all right.

For the last time, with lads congratulating me on all sides, I pack Itchy's old trombone away.

"Well done, Dano." Itchy grins. "We're gonna miss yer skinny arse."

"It'll be your turn soon enough," says I. Ernie Fanning, on bass trombone in Band One, is getting long in the tooth.

"Yeah, I know," say Itchy wistfully. "Sometimes I think I'll be in Band Two forever."

You're wrong, pal, I think to myself. *Nothing's forever. At least not for long.*

—~~—

We're marching. We're playing. There's nothing else. No time for lonely wishing—not for Ma, nor my sisters, nor my old pals on Green Street. I put it all down the end of my trombone and into the marching and the music. Left, right, left, right. The trumpeter behind me, his bell only inches away from my ear, is Tommy Phelan. His sound tears through me like a saw. I can almost feel the hot air of his breath on the back of my head. In front of me is a big lad, his tuba swings with impossible ease to the music. He's Martin Cullen. His broad back sends my own sound back to me like a ball thrown hard at a stone wall. I catch it and throw it back again, harder. To my left, Itchy Reynolds—now in Band One, doubling on bass trombone—and Patser Lennox move their slides wildly, like me, missing the lads in front by the grace of God and inches. Further up to the front, the drummers, six of them, pull us all forward like a train through this gray day on this green field in front of the main buildings. Behind the trumpets, Garret Nesbit and Paul Gates coax a warm easiness from their saxophones that blends the harsh brass and the soft woodwind together like molten chocolate. Michael Farley, his clarinet swinging a foot to either side of him, encourages his section; Fran Dunne, Seamus Roche, and Jack Whelan try to keep up with the French horns: here we go now, lads, a bit more. Up there, in front of us all, Barney Duggan, the Drum Major, is waving his mace like he'd flatten anyone who came near us. With determined, deliberate flourishes he urges us forward. Come on, lads. Blow it all out now. That's it. Our sound echoes off the low-lying clouds above, falling back down on us like rain on a desert. Music, mercy's mantle, wraps around us. We know something special. We know we have the band for shelter and music for a friend.

—∞—

I'm busy deleting emails from my inbox. Far too many are from friends still valiantly alerting me to the fuss in the Irish press: abuses in the industrial schools in the fifties and sixties. It seems the Irish Christian Brothers—the Congregation, as they like to call themselves—are in danger of extinction. *Well, it couldn't happen to a nicer bunch,* I think to myself.

I've often joked with Irish friends over the years. We'd imagine a scenario in a typical Irish family with a clatter of kids; the mother and father, alone by the turf fire at night, are discussing their children's future.

"Mary has a huge, caring heart in her, she could be very happy as a nurse," the father says proudly. "And Siobhan, a great head she has on her shoulders—probably an office job, with her brains. Patrick, strong as an ox! He'll stay here with us on the farm and work the land like my father and grandfather before. Conor has the hands of a craftsman: a carpenter or a cabinetmaker maybe. But Ronan . . . what are we to do with that crazy eejit? Thick as a brick and a temper to match. Now where on God's earth is he going to fit in?"

The house goes quiet as Ronan's talents occupy the minds of his parents. The turf fire hisses in the night.

The mother sits up suddenly, excited. "I just had a grand idea," she says. "How about the Irish Christian Brothers? Brother Ronan! Now that has a nice ring to it."

I laugh at the memory. So many young men were forced by their parents to join the Brotherhood that the joke is universally understood. Maybe there's a bigger story there than I care to look at. But there's no excuse for inhuman treatment of children, so I put my altruism aside; I'll leave that for historians and people who didn't suffer through it. I continue deleting any emails with the words *Artane* or *abuse* or *Industrial School* in the subject line. I don't even read them any more. Oops! Undo that delete! That one's from Liz. I open it. There's no text and I click straight on the link she's sent. In seconds my mouth dries so quickly I can't swallow. From the center of the web page the words tear at me like claws:

"Brother Joseph O'Connor accused of raping Artane boy."

CHAPTER 26

Now that's the worst bloody thing I ever heard in my life. Mr. Hickey, the conductor, has us playing a long, slow, dreary march that must have been written by a very sad man with one leg. It'll take all day to get to the end of this dirge. Hickey says it'll give us tone and subtlety. All it's giving me is a headache. I've been in Band One over a year and up until today it's been great.

A week or so before every outside band engagement, O'Connor, after his usual long speech, calls out a list of the lads who'll be playing. There are many more lads in the band than actually play at outside engagements. There's usually a couple of lads in each section who double. Me, I'm doubling on second trombone. Itchy is doubling on bass or third trombone. Andy McBride, who joined a few months after me, is doubling on third trumpet. Us doublers are not always called, and if we are, it's usually to get us "warmed up" to playing outside and to see how we do under pressure. How soon a doubler gets to play out depends on how old the lad in the main chair is. If he's old enough to leave Artane soon, the doubler will play out all the time. I've been doubling with Patser Lennox and he's fourteen and not leaving anytime soon. So let's just say I'm not famous for my patience. I'd waited for months, before every outing—holding my breath as O'Connor would go down the list. No, no, and no, again and again. Torture of the worst kind. It'd taken so much of my mind that there wasn't any room to think about anything else. *Sorry, Ma. I still miss ya.* Ah, that's better.

Then shortly before my twelfth birthday, after months of figure marching in front of the main buildings, my name was called. Ellis! I nearly crapped my trousers on the spot because the outing was to Croke Park—the All Ireland football final, between Kerry and Galway.

The welcoming roar of seventy thousand football fans when we marched out of that tunnel under the Hogan Stand was like nothing I'd ever heard or felt. "The biggest little band in the world," they called us. With both teams marching behind us, even dwarfed by the mountainous, tiered stands, I felt ten feet tall. I'd been to *Croker* before, with my uncle Pat, shivering and scared in the cheaper terraces as a five-year-old. But marching on the field itself, mesmerized by the giant stadium—thank God I knew all the music by heart—the shivers running through me weren't from the cold. And I wasn't scared either, I felt I could take on the devil himself and kick his scorched arse over the tall wall and into the Royal Canal. Warm waves of genuine love flowed from the crowd, down across the field and through our ranks, filling us with warrior abandon. They, like football and hurling fans across Ireland, had seen the Artane Boys Band march at the major GAA—Gaelic Athletic Association—games for years. They all knew about Artane too—many of them as children were warned by their parents, "You'll end up in Artane if you're not careful, me bucko!" Their shouts and claps let us know we weren't alone; they knew, or at least thought they knew, what we were going through. That was enough to make me fight like blazes to hold back the tears as I played so loud my swollen lips nearly reached my chin.

> *Loved by everybody*
> *Welcomed 'cross the land*
> *How could you be lonely*
> *In the Artane Boys Band.*

—⁂—

More and more outings included me—fundraisers in town halls, churches, and such—as I realized that I wasn't being tested out any more, I was becoming a real part of the band. Martin Cullen, marching in front of me, has had plenty to say to O'Connor about me, and O'Connor himself has complained when I've taken a day off "sick"—with my magic thermometer trick. I may have to give up those days relaxing in the infirmary. I don't mind. It's not the band I need a break from, it's—well, it's everything else.

But nothing stops the music. Not the constant, paralyzing fear of the leather strap; not the beatings themselves; not the wheeling and dealing on the playground; not the friends who turn into enemies; not Rasher and our card cheating; not my helpless sympathy for the other lads who are not as lucky as us band lads; not the brothers who feel it necessary to come down extra hard on the band lads because of that; not the trips to my Uncle Matty's house every month, hoping Patricia and Katie will be there too; not the aching for Ma. Nothing stops the music.

—⚬⚬⚬—

It's April, but thinks it's December. It's Sunday Mass and it's freezing. Not to worry—Tommy Bonner will sing in a minute and warm us all up. George Crean is wailing away on his organ like Ron Chaney, Jack McDonald is reading a comic, and Willie O'Reilly is starting to snore. Me, I've gotten into the habit of following the Mass in the little prayer books. It helps to pass the time. Black Daniel doesn't like it, but I don't need him in Mass.

From behind us a voice starts to sing the Kyrie. Jesus! It's awful! I risk a quick look around. It's not Tommy Bonner; it's some other skinny git with glasses. Tommy must have the flu. Hundreds of lads have had it over the last week. The infirmary is overflowing and sick lads have been put to bed in their dorms, with brothers walking around smoking cigarettes to "kill the germs." The Kyrie is not feeling too good either. It's being slaughtered. The noise of it has woken O'Reilly. He's making faces and raising his eyes up to heaven. God have mercy. Jack McDonald has stopped reading his comic in protest and is shaking his curly head. On goes the torture.

Mass is over. We're outside, lining up for breakfast. Someone chirps up, "I'm bloody freezing. I hope the grub is warm. Although I'm so hungry, I could eat lumpy porridge off a scabby dog. But who told that fellah he could sing?"

"I know," says I. Poor old George Crean must be going deaf. "Tommy Bonner must have flu or something. Jesus! I hope he gets better soon."

"Tommy's not a bit sick at all. I'd say he's feeling pretty good," says Jack McDonald with a grin. "He turned sixteen the other day and he's skedaddled. Lucky bastard! I've got four more years to go."

I stop marching suddenly, like I've hit a brick wall. Someone bumps into me from behind and pushes me forward roughly. I move again, but my feet are like lead. Tears are trying to form in my eyes. It must be the bloody cold. I turn away so no one can see me. We march toward the ref. Someone is talking away to me but I can't hear a word. Suddenly, I've no appetite for breakfast and can't eat a thing. The lads don't mind. They gobble it up. We march out of the ref. Everyone's laughing and joking.

Don't they know? Don't they know that they'll never hear Tommy Bonner sing again as long as they live? No more sweet tones to cheer your heart and help you find strength, even as they give you permission to feel the ache in your soul that you can't feel on the playground cos someone would notice and kick your arse for it. No, they don't know that Tommy's gone.

Lads are leaving every day. Pat Murphy and Gibbo left in quick succession about a year back. Parents find their feet again and fight in court against the brothers, who hold on to the lads in their "care" as if they were gold. We are gold. The brothers receive a nice sum of money for every lad here. But still, lads leave, or run away to

England, or turn sixteen and get a job. You get used to finding a good friend suddenly not here any more.

But I'll not get used to finding Tommy gone. When he sang, somewhere in his dark, sad, strong voice, Ma was there. I could feel her coming through him like the light through the stained-glass windows in church. *Snap out of it, man. Tommy would laugh to see you like this.* I run and catch up with the lads quickly, burying my thoughts. *He's gone, get over it.*

For the umpteenth time, I type "Tommy Bonner" into the Google search line. No luck. Maybe I'm spelling or remembering his name wrong. Maybe it was Bonney? No luck there either. Thomas Bonner? No. Oh, well. I'd love to know what he's up to, let him know how much he meant to us. Rasher, too, but no luck there either. I've met many lads from Artane over the years; half of them have never driven a car. Most never married. An Artane "education" left many ashamed of their lack of skills and afraid of anything that highlighted or challenged that lack. So it's not a stretch to imagine they'd shy away from using computers, email, or the Internet all together.

I think of the impact Tommy has had on my singing and I smile. There's another verse brewing for the song I thought was finished. I've recorded it and six or seven of the other Artane songs. But this keeps happening—I think a song is finished and the subject matter screams at me, *Wait a minute, what about this?* I make a note of my feelings about Tommy's leaving Artane.

Liz, who is infinitely more practical than I, is mildly concerned about this dynamic of revising. *If you keep going back and redoing every song it'll take forever.* It's an old fight with us; I'm eternally tweaking, and she's always pushing me toward the finish line.

But she's got a more compelling objection today.

The allegations on the Internet about Brother Joseph O'Connor are very serious and deeply disturbing. The whole of the Irish press, in the links sent by Liz and my friends, is ablaze with outrage. Liz has printed them out; pages and pages.

She's adamant. "You've got to take him out of the songs, sweetie. It's all gone crazy. You can't dignify him with your music."

My mind races. Liz is looking hard at me, waiting for my response. But this is my story and I'm going to tell it like I remember it. I'll let the present unfold any way it wants to, but the past is mine. It's what I remember. Not some posting on a website.

I avoid Liz's pointed stare. She waves the printed web postings urgently. "There's some stuff on here about O'Driscoll too. Have you even bothered to read what I sent you?"

"Yes. I've read it all—many times. But I'm not going to read any more of it. I'm going to let my memories unfold as I remember them—unencumbered by the Internet."

I pick up the list of my newest songs from my music stand. O'Connor has crept into three of them so far. O'Driscoll's made it into one. I point to my list. "This is what's real to me. There's not a shadow of doubt in my mind that many, if not most of the brothers, including O'Driscoll—and maybe even O'Connor—were criminally psychopathic and much more. But the songs are true to my remembering."

Liz says quietly, "Maybe there's something wrong with your remembering." She turns and leaves.

Distraught, I return to my handwritten notes on Tommy Bonner's leaving Artane. Past and present. His sudden departure affected me more than I admitted at the time. I couldn't face it then. I can now. I open my word processor and after a few minutes, out it comes.

> At first I felt again abandoned
> Deserted and betrayed
> It seemed that everything I loved

Would run and leave me here
Lonely and afraid
But there and then a seed was planted
And I wish I'd felt back then
Just a small taste of the joy I'd find
Tryna sing like Tommy sang.

—⁂—

Yeah, as hard as I try in Fallon's singing class, I can't get near Tommy's lovely dark sound. But I sure as hell can play this trombone and that's all I need. But here now with the band at the Irish Hospital Sweepstake in Ballsbridge, I think I'm going to need a stretcher. We just finished eating in a large marquee tent; the most amazing display of food I've never seen in my life.

"Don't eat too much," O'Connor said earlier. "You have to play in a minute." Too late! I'm gonna need carrying to get me on to the stage. But I'm not alone in my gluttony. The band lads around me are stuffing their faces as if the Irish Famine was coming up the road on a bike.

Itchy looks like a hamster with both cheeks full. He's my newest best pal. I'm spending less and less time with Rasher because of band practice. I've tried to teach Itchy how to cheat at cards, but he's too honest. Still, we look out for each other.

This is my first real, true engagement with the band. Not some fundraiser in some musty old town hall. Not marching around a football field in the rain. No, the Irish Hospital Sweepstakes is one of the best events of the year. Or so Itchy told me. And he's right. They make such a fuss of us it's almost embarrassing. Here comes Hickey, the conductor. "Finish up eating lads, it's time for the concert." We'll be playing a Celtic medley, a collection of the most beautiful Irish airs imaginable, and some swinging Glen Miller song called "In The Mood"—which we have some trouble getting right. God, I love this music, every little bit of every kind with its wild variety: classical, Irish rebel, and American marches, hymns, ballads, and, of course, Broadway.

Thank goodness we'll be playing sitting down. I couldn't march to save my life. My belly is so full I'm afraid the sherry trifle is gonna come down the bell of the trombone, followed by the mash and roast beef and turnips and the—*Oh, God, don't think about grub.*

In our scarlet and blue uniforms—tunics with gold belt and gold embroidered pockets, tasseled hats, and buckled shoes—we're a sight to stop traffic as we walk to the bandstand. Even though the sun, believe it or not, is shining, there's a breeze blowing and I'm freezing. I can't get used to these short trousers of the band uniform. In dorm three, they gave me long trousers a few months back. What a difference! No more chafing at the thighs with the tweed and no more sore knees in church. In the last year I've shot up. I'm bigger than Itchy now and Smasher Magee too. Smasher sits beside me now, sharing the second trombone seat. Patser Lennox has been moved up to first chair and Itchy is on bass as usual. I squirm in my chair with gas in my tummy.

Hickey fixes me with a stony stare over his glasses. *Concentrate, Ellis, or I'll burst ya.* He's right. This is not an easy piece. It's in the key of A. I have to do some mental gymnastics to get the *Do-Re-Mi* to work for me in this key. But I've got it—if I focus.

CHAPTER 27

Brother Columbus is dead. The brothers have decided he was a saint and should be honored. The whole school is lined up to view his corpse.

He's been laid out in a casket in one of the downstairs rooms in the brothers' quarters. As the line slowly moves forward some of the lads are acting like eejits.

"He had a good run at it," says Rasher. "He's as old as God."

"He's dead, Rasher. That's as old as ya get." Antho Kelly laughs.

"Quiet, you lads," hisses the Maggot, who's trying to look holy with his rosary beads out. "Have some respect for the dead." The Maggot moves along the line.

"I hope to Jaysus Columbus has some respect for the living," sniggers Rasher. "If he starts praying out loud all of a sudden, I'll crap meself."

But I'm very quiet. The only other dead person I ever saw was the Gas Man on Granny Ellis's street. I still have those bloody nightmares with him and his bulging eyes. It's always the same dream: him waiting at the top of a staircase, grinning at me. I shudder in the waiting line and make the sign of the cross. I hope they've closed Columbus's eyes.

We turn a corner and now we're in the room with the body. I feel a deep sense of loss. He's always been a light on in a dark room for me, a guardian angel among devils.

I remember one cold, dark winter's evening a couple of years back, just before I joined the band, I'd sneaked into the chapel to warm my icy hands on the radiators. That causes chilblains, they say, but I didn't care. Barely able to see, I made my way through the gloom of the empty church to the pipes by a side wall. I was just thawing out when I heard a sound that made my hair stand on end. I nearly ran out of the place. It was coming from the front of the chapel. It sounded like a wounded animal calling for its own kind. As my eyes got used to the dark, I saw a black shape bent over by the altar rails. Remembering another black shape, in a Rathfarnham nightmare, I shook from head to toe. Then the shape let out another wail, one so hopeless and heart wrenching that all fear vanished as a wave of pity washed over me. Unable to stop myself, I crept forward cautiously, holding my breath. The shape turned around to see me.

"Come here, child. Don't be afraid." It was Columbus.

I was still hesitant. He beckoned me forward. He didn't recognize me. He took my hand with both of his.

"I thought I was alone with God," he whispered hoarsely. "I'm sure my prayers put the heart crossways in you. But let me tell you a little secret, child." He patted my hand gently. "Our Almighty Father loves to hear the cries of His children's woe. It's music to His ears."

I have some music I'm sure God would love, I was thinking. If I felt any discomfort with Columbus holding my hand, it was disappearing by the second.

"Not many people know how to pray. They say the words like a parrot: *Hail Mary, Holy Mary, Hail Mary, Holy Mary.*" I laugh at his nasal mimicking.

"God doesn't know what to do with that kind of prayer. If you want Him to hear your prayer, you have to mean it from the bottom of your heart."

He raised his hands and started to pray. "Oh, Dearest Father, King of heaven and earth, I'm so lost and alone in this cruel world. I can find no rest here any more. I'm tired and weary and oh, so lonely." There was a cry in his voice that touched my heart deeply. He continued as if I didn't exist: "Can't you teach me, won't you show me how to live in your love. I . . . I keep drifting away from you. Please, Holy Father, please hold on to me." I was thunderstruck by the depth of emotion welling up from the depths of his soul. If I was God, I'd answer that one.

Exhausted, he finished, noticing with mild surprise that I was still there. "Ah, there you are. Do you have a prayer, son?" His voice was kindness itself. "One that will bring tears to your eyes as you pray and tears to God's eyes as He listens?"

"I'm . . . I'm not sure I do, sir." But thinking of Ma, my heart broke in two.

He saw my thought. "Go on, lad. Don't pretend to be strong. Not in front of the King of Heaven. Let it all go, son. God will put you back together again. He answers every sincere prayer. Kneel here by the altar and open your heart to your Heavenly Father."

Before my knees touched the long, velvet cushion that ran along the altar rails, I was praying aloud: "Dear Holy God, I miss me ma. I miss her an awful, awful lot. Please make her better so she can come and take me home. I miss me sisters too. Please put us all back together in our house in Green Street, I mean Ratherfarn . . . I mean in a house somewhere nice." The realization that I, too, didn't have a place to call home, even in a prayer, broke me apart in deepest sobs.

Columbus was kneeling beside me with his hands folded in prayer. He dropped his hands to his sides abruptly, whispering, "Wait, now. You're the boy at the gate! Christmas Day, last year. Waiting for your mother?" His whole attitude has changed. He's suddenly very alert.

"Oh, you need a different kind of prayer, son. I think you . . . I spoke to your mother that day she came to visit. She's not . . . well, you need to ask God for strength, son. That's a better kind of prayer. Strength. That's something He can help you with."

"I thought you said God answers every sincere prayer. Wasn't I sincere enough?"

"Of course you were, son. But some things . . . your mother . . . I mean, God wants . . . He wants what's best for everybody."

He was very, very sad. But I was feeling pretty good. I felt God would answer my prayer. Or, at least it felt good to pray like that. Columbus had shown me something. Something that I'd always remember. The prayer itself is the thing. Maybe knowing that God is hearing it is enough.

There he is now in that cold casket. His face is ashen but has a look of deep peace. O'Connor and the new Brother Superior, Flannigan, are there behind the casket, overlooking the parade of lads. It's my turn. "Goodbye," I whisper under my breath, and go red in the face as I look up to see that O'Connor has heard me. Grim as the gray corpse, he nods his head slowly.

—⁓—

It's my turn to teach new lads who have just joined the band to read music. I've tried to teach the *Do-Re-Mi* to some fellahs, including Smasher and Itchy, but I've learned to keep it to meself. It causes more problems than it solves. *Let people find their own way, stupid.*

I pop a piece of chewing gum in my mouth. O'Connor doesn't like us to chew gum in the band room. It mucks the horns up, he says. Makes sense, but with teaching, I won't be playing trombone today. Still, better be careful.

I'm writing out the minims and the crotchets and quavers on the blackboard behind the drum stand. My reading of regular music is as good as anyone's now, but the band takes up so much time, I've been having trouble with my lessons in class. Not that anyone's noticed. The brothers are changed around so fast—the Slasher's gone, so have the Mackerel and the Whistler—it's impossible for anyone to know what's happening to anyone's school progress, or lack of it. But I'm not complaining. Music is the only progress I'm interested in. Especially after Tralee!

The band had an outing to Tralee, in Kerry, last June. It was a
stay-over trip. We stayed for a few nights with families from the school
who sponsored the band trip. My host family was a young couple with
two children: a two-year-old girl and four-year-old boy. God Almighty!
The way they cared for those kids; the patience and tender little
corrections, the sweet talk and total attention as the mother allowed
them to take all the pots and pans out of a kitchen cupboard, then
followed them around the house, laughing as they created a mad mess.
It all just about . . . well, it made me think of Ma, with her cigarettes
and screaming tantrums and the nights she'd come home real late and
Guinness kisses and the food she wouldn't share and the—

Stop it! Don't ever, ever think about Ma like that.

The band had a night off and the parents got a babysitter. . . .
They didn't leave their kids alone and afraid in the dark . . . *I told ya
to stop it, didn't I! Stop thinking about Ma.*

They read a story to their kids and tucked them in as the
sixteen-year-old babysitter turned the lights out. *No, Mammy, leave
it on, please. Of course, darling.* We piled into their Morris Minor
and they took me to a dance hall downtown.

We pushed our way into the dance hall, past the crowd at the
door, and Holy Mother of God and the gold lame jackets! The band!

If I ever had any doubts about a life in music, they were blasted
away forever that night. The band was called The Blue Roses:
guitar, electric bass, drums, and three-piece brass section. The
music electrified me. It was loud and fast and mad with an energy
I'd never known. The steaming heat of the smoky dance hall, the
shouts from the sweating dancers sliding on the beer-covered floor,
the lads throwing the lasses around like spinning tops, the hoarse
voice of the lead singer—it all filled me with a joy I'd never even
dreamed of.

So, I'm not worried about my education. I know how I'll make
my living when I leave Artane School behind me, thank you very
much all the same.

We've been on a dozen stay-overs since, and every chance I get I try to persuade the family to take me to a dance hall. Sometimes it's a *ceilidh*: Irish music with accordions and fiddles. It's nice enough, but after hearing The Blue Roses playing "Rock Around The Clock," I know where my heart is.

Watch it! With all my remembering, I've put a stem on a whole note on the blackboard. Eejit! I correct it just in time, cos here comes O'Connor. He's got a new lad beside him I've never seen before.

Take out that gum! Too late!

"Ellis, I want you to meet a new boy. This is Michael."

I shake his hand, mumbling some words past the gum. O'Connor looks behind him impatiently—he's always in a hurry. "Where's your brother?" he asks Michael.

Michael points. A lad comes running up, buttoning his fly.

O'Connor continues, "And this is his brother, Timothy." Surnames are too much information.

"I'm pleathed to meeth you thoo." My tongue is struggling to keep the gum from flying into Timothy's tiny, sad face.

O'Connor frowns at my garbled words. "They've just come from the nuns in Rathdrum. You'll teach them their notes till they're ready to play an instrument."

The brothers are about eight years old and look totally lost. They stand close to each other, touching shoulders. They look very alike.

O'Connor leaves abruptly.

Michael takes off one of his boots and rubs his ankle. I can see his bed and dorm number stamped on the boot: 4–38; dorm four, bed number thirty-eight. That's all we are here, a bunch of numbers. He'll get used to that—and the sore ankles and chafed thighs—soon enough.

I say, "The nuns, eh? What were they like?" Uncle Matty took me out to visit Patricia and Katie in their orphanage in Booterstown once and I know right well what nuns are like. But I'm just trying to be friendly.

I'm wasting my time. Michael shrugs and Timothy looks confused.

"Well, you'll get to know the bold Christian Brothers soon enough. They're stark raving mad, most of them." I laugh. They look really scared now.

For some reason, I feel sorry for these two and I hurry to put them at ease. "But you're in the band now and we have the life of Reilly here. Band lads have it cushy." I wink at them.

"I don't want to be a band lad," says Michael, cool as cabbage. What's wrong with this fellah?

"Don't be stupid. Everyone wants to be a band lad."

"Well, I don't and neither does Timothy." He points to O'Connor, who's over there with a lad with a sax, looking at the instrument's pads. "We were told by that brother that we had to join the band, whether we like it or not." Michael nudges his brother. "Isn't that right, Timothy? We hate music and we hate bands."

Timothy nods.

I can see why O'Connor would love to have two brothers in the band. Things like that are very important to him. He's a showman and a real crowd-pleaser, I can just hear the old ladies at the concerts; "Ah, would ya look at the pair of them. Aren't they beeootiful?"

Michael puts his boot back on. "We're going out to play. Music is a load of old bollox. It's for sissies and silly, stupid people." Michael starts to walk off, pulling Timothy.

I grab them. O'Connor will murder us all if I let them go.

"Let me go. You can keep your stupid music," say Michael.

I'm mad now. No one speaks about music like that. "Music can save your life in this shithole. It . . . it . . . " I've never had to convince anyone before. "It can lift you up when you're flat on yer arse. It holds me like . . . like . . . "

I'm about to say *like my ma*, but recently I've been remembering she never really held me much and . . . well, I've been working real hard on not thinking bad stuff—or any stuff about Ma.

I continue as the brothers stare at me, waiting: "Music doesn't care who you are or what you've done. It's just . . . it's just massive, that's what it is. It's mustard."

They look at me like I've gone mad.

I give up. But O'Connor told me to teach them their notes and that's what I'm gonna do. I take my chalk and draw a line under the first note on the blackboard.

"Repeat after me: A semibreve is a white note with no stem, count four."

No answer. This is going to take a while.

—⁓—

Liz and I, like all married couples, have had our ups and downs. But the last few days have been tougher than anything we've known. I never know who's more stubborn. But it doesn't seem unreasonable to me to want to tell my story like I remember it. I'm drawing a line in the sand here. I just hope the line falls somewhere in the middle.

Liz has been very quiet. I've been busy recording the album and gigging. She's been at work all day and is asleep when I get home. Irene has said a few times, "Are you and Mom okay?"

It's time to talk.

I wait for Liz to come home and before she can get out of the car I get in. I don't want Irene to hear this—whatever *this* is going to be. Liz is extremely tense.

I kiss her cheek. She doesn't respond. "Okay, babes, what's going on? It's been three days and we've not had a single meaningful exchange," I say softly.

"I'm sorry." She's very sad.

"Is that it? Nothing to say about this . . . this wall of silence?"

Nothing.

I look out across the vegetable garden to the meadow under the trees, where last year, when we first rented the cabin, we both picked weeds for hours without gloves, resulting in Liz's whole body being covered in a roaring, red-raw poison ivy rash.

I take Liz's hand. She squeezes. "Well? I'm happy to stay here holding hands, if that's all it takes." I laugh.

She takes her hand away. "You know I've been thinking a lot recently about you and O'Connor. I appreciate this is a very sensitive subject, maybe even none of my business. But I need you to be absolutely honest with me." I've never seen her so serious. I'm a little unnerved.

"You know I've been doing a lot of research and you've point blank refused to read the information I've found on the Internet." She hesitates for a moment, then continues. "I have to ask you something about O'Connor."

I know where this is going. I tense up. I fumble with the radio knobs distractedly.

"Please, I need you to look at me, Danny." Her eyes flood with tears as she struggles to frame her question.

CHAPTER 28

Willie O'Reilly is the kind of a fellah who gets everything wrong. But in this particular case, we're hoping that for once he knows what he's talking about, because we don't. But the subject matter is such that we're more than willing to give him the benefit of the doubt.

It's a subject that remains a deep mystery for all of us—even Rasher, who's fifteen and will leave Artane soon. He and Kelly and I look at O'Reilly with new respect, stunned at this outpouring of secret knowledge. I don't know where he got it cos every book in every dorm library—and I've read almost every one of them—has been combed through by the brothers for anything even remotely concerned with . . . well, they call it "badness." The forbidden pleasures of the flesh.

For years I've felt the waking promise in my loins. I've felt the softness harden in the dark of the theatre—seconds before the brothers turn the projector off in panic—as the hero and his lady lock themselves in passionate embraces and hungry kisses. And yes, recently I've felt that hardness explode as every fiber of my being united in a starburst of pleasure-pain that set my tortured breath free. The crippling shame that followed, although not enough to discourage further investigation, dogged my days and nights till, pursued by the devil himself, I ran to the confessional in search of God's forgiveness.

In his last lectures, Father Moore, the school chaplain—as kind a man as you could hope to meet—had droned on vaguely about marriage and babies, and even more vaguely about how men and women help God perform his greatest miracle. Clouded in Moore's mysterious language, the subject passed over our heads like incense. We couldn't have been less interested.

But O'Reilly's put that horse in a different race altogether. Amazing how a man who knows what he's talking about can give ears to the deaf.

"Sex! That's what Father Moore was talking about," he says, flattered at our rapt attention. "A man's what-you-may-call-it is like a key and a woman's thingamajig is like a lock. The man sticks his key in the woman's lock and out comes a baby. Plock! Like an egg from a hen."

Speechlessness! Jaysus! It makes perfect sense!

O'Reilly darts a quick look around the playground. The Flattener is hovering nearby. O'Reilly's got us and he doesn't want to let go. He continues in a mock-whisper, "It doesn't look like a baby to start with. It's a bit like a monkey, or a . . . a goat."

"A goat?" says me and Kelly in disbelief.

"Yeah, except it doesn't have any horns or hooves or beard or anything like that."

"So, how does it look like a goat then?" asks Rasher, shooting me a look.

O'Reilly sees us grinning at each other. His pace quickens. "It just does, okay? That's what it looks like. A monkey or a goat. I won't tell yez any more if you don't stop making fun of me. Yez are just jealous cos I know more about it than—"

"Go on, for Jaysus' sakes," says Kelly, raising his eyes to heaven. "Tell us more."

O'Reilly is sulking. I'm caught between wanting to know more about the real "lock and key" business and making fun of O'Reilly's obviously made-up bits. For the moment, science wins.

"Come on, O'Reilly. Tell us how the key turns the lock and how long it takes before the baby comes out." I'm trying to be very sincere.

"Oh, it's not long at all, at all. Just a few turns of the key and out it pops. Bob's yer uncle, quick as a flash. There ya go. A brand-new baby." O'Reilly's back on the horse.

"How do they make it into a boy or a girl?" Rasher is keen again. The quest for knowledge is a grand thing.

O'Reilly looks stumped for a second, then he blurts quickly, "It's the key. Yeah, it's the key. Ya just give it a few more turns for a boy. Less for a girl." He grins at us in triumph. *Top that!*

"And I suppose the boy looks like a monkey and the girl looks like a goat, eh?" says I, thinking that'll be the end of it.

But O'Reilly runs with the ball. "That's it. That's right. That's why the goat doesn't have a beard or horns, cos girls don't have 'em. Right?"

Makes sense. "How do you know all this?" I ask in awe or disbelief, I'm not sure which.

"I heard me big brother and his girlfriend talking about it when I was visiting me ma's last Sunday. I was under his bed robbing his comics when they came in and sat on the bed talking. They started fooling around and I giggled and they heard me. My brother gave me a smack on the head, but not before I heard one last bit."

"What's that?"

"If you don't want to have a baby at all, ya have to pull the key out at the last minute, real quick. Pop! That shuts the lock up tight and that's the end of it."

Rasher's heard enough. "If your da could've known they were going to have you, he would have pulled his key out before he put it in."

Everyone except O'Reilly erupts in fits of laughter. The Flattener, who's been watching from about fifty yards away, blows his whistle and raises his finger at us, curling it. *Come here, you lot.*

It's amazing how fast a laugh can turn into a bellyache.

The Flattener points with his leather strap. "Rasher, face the wall by the drinking fountain. O'Reilly and Kelly, you face the wall by the dorm doors, ten feet apart. If you even as much as look at one another I'll skin you both alive. Okay? Ellis, come over here."

Jesus. I know what he's up to. It's a dirty little trick he uses to catch lads out. He's going to ask me what we were talking about and then he'll ask the others separately. Our stories won't match up and he'll tear our arses up.

"Not playing our usual cards today, are we? Now what's so amusing, Mr. Ellis. There was something funny in the way you buckos were laughing. What was it?"

"Oh, we were just laughing about locks and keys, sir," I blurt before I can think.

"Is that a fact now? And what's so funny about locks and keys?"

I look at his ugly, hard eyes and his tight lips and know that I can't win this. Rasher, Kelly, and O'Reilly will tell different lies and . . . . Wait now. Jesus! I got it!

"Well, sir." I blink my eyes like Katie and take a deep breath, knowing I've got nothing to lose. A lie is always sinful, the brothers tell us. Tell the truth and trust in God. All right, God, here we go— I'm trusting.

"We were talking about how God makes babies, sir," I say innocently.

The Flattener looks like I hit him with a hurley stick. Before he can say a word, I continue. "Father Moore has been talking to us about how God makes babies and the blessing that he gives mankind is to help him out in that department, sir. O'Reilly was saying that a man is like a key and a woman is like a lock. And God's miracle is to put the key and lock together and make a beautiful little baby, sir. The greatest miracle of all, Father Moore calls it."

The Flattener is beetroot-red and his mouth is opening and closing, but nothing is coming out.

I can feel Father Moore's exact words running through me like hot tea. "Isn't it amazing how God uses us to perform His holy will, sir? He could do it all by Himself, but He uses mankind to help Him out. That's how much He loves us."

Moore had finished off his lecture with something that I didn't understand at the time. But I understand it now as I repeat it. And just for good measure, I make the sign of the cross.

"In this holy work, sir, God asks man to join him as co-creators." I'm about to genuflect but that might overdo it.

The Flattener, who has been holding his breath, lets it out with a long sigh. He blows his whistle at Rasher and O'Reilly, motioning them to go and play. *Get lost, you bowsies.*

"You too, Ellis, scoot!"

I turn to run after the lads when I'm stopped by the Flattener's shout.

"Wait! You haven't told me what was so funny, Ellis. Why were you laughing so hard?" He looks like he's got me this time.

"Well, sir, Rasher was saying that if O'Reilly's parents had only known the trouble they were in for when he was born, they mightn't have been so happy to help God out in his holy work, sir." I blink earnestly.

That did it! The Flattener doesn't know whether to laugh or cry. Caught between murder and God's work, he crumbles.

"Get out of my sight, Ellis. There's something fishy about you and sooner or later you'll get what's coming to you. I pray to God it'll be from me."

Nothing like a nice little prayer to finish it all off.

I catch up with the lads, who had stopped dead when the Flattener called me back.

"What the fuck did you tell him?" Rasher pants. We're running now, putting distance between us and the Flattener.

"The truth." I laugh. "Well, kinda. Keep running. Don't look back."

We've lost sight of the Flattener among the hundreds of lads running around. We stop behind the north wall of the handball alleys, breathless and weak with relief. I tell them everything. Kelly whistles and blesses me like a priest. "Father Moore would be proud of you, my son."

O'Reilly says, "Ellis, I'm working late in the kitchen tonight. I'll have the key to the bread room. I'm bringing you the biggest bloody loaf of bread I can nick."

"Just make sure you don't leave the key in the lock." Rasher giggles.

—៣—

In evening class, I'm still congratulating myself on my run-in with the Flattener when a lad bursts in the door. He's been sent by O'Connor, who's called an immediate meeting with the band lads—*make it snappy,* he'd said. Running, almost racing, Michael Farley, Fran Dunne, and I stop at the drinking fountains to catch our breath. We watch half a dozen lads from other classrooms run across the playground toward us excitedly. Smasher Magee and Eddie Cavanagh join us and we rub our hands together, knowing something big is up.

"What do you think is going on?" Farley asks.

"Haven't the foggiest," says Smasher.

Fran Dunne knows something. He has a smug smile on his face. He's very close to O'Connor.

"Come on, Dunne, what's going on?" Cavanagh pushes him playfully.

"I can't say a word. Joe Boy would kill me. But don't be surprised if we'll be taking a long flight some time next year." Dunne winks.

America? Da? Oh, my God. There's been whispers for weeks that O'Connor was working on something.

In the band room, the traders—lads who work at a trade as well as the band—are already seated as we enter. O'Connor, on the conductor's podium, shouts for us to be quiet. Everyone's talking at once and he claps his hands loudly.

"Lads, I have great news. Great news indeed! I'm proud and happy to announce that the Artane Boys Band have been invited to play in the United States." Cheers and whistles. "There are many details to work out, but it's already been confirmed, for May of next year."

Christ! That's over a year away. But still, it'll give me plenty of time to write and tell Da. He was right—the Artane Boys Band *are* famous in America. My mind is dizzy with the possibilities. I wonder if Da will let me . . . *don't* . . . *stop dreaming, ya eejit.*

We're all laughing and joking, delirious with the news. After a while, the band-room door opens and in rush the other band lads who are not part of Band One. They soon hear about America and are mad jealous. *Ya just have to do your time, lads, like we all did.*

Band Two is now full of really young fellahs because so many from Band One have left recently. Lads barely here a wet week are suddenly thrown into Band Two before they've even learned their note names. The new youngsters I've been teaching, Timothy and his brother Michael, have been designated to sax and trumpet, respectively, and are bravely trying to make a fist of it. O'Connor, anxious for them to be in Band One, pushes them mercilessly. Most boys thrive in the band, but these brothers, forced into music, hate it. O'Connor likes to think of himself as a fair sort, but he's dead wrong here. He must know it. I feel sorry for the two brothers, but it's none of my business.

—◊◊—

My chest is on fire. The heat from my suppressed laughter is threatening to set my blankets ablaze. I peek out from beneath them. I can hear the same muffled giggles and snorts from all around me. It's half past ten at night and the dorm has gone completely bonkers. We're all killing ourselves laughing and screaming. For the last five minutes, McCarty, the night watchman, has been losing his sanity and he hasn't a single clue what's going on. We're breaking all the rules here, but we couldn't stop it if we wanted to. Let me back up a wee bit.

It all started with O'Reilly coming up from working late in the kitchen. I'd been waiting for him, my mouth watering in anticipation of the promised loaf of bread. His bed is a few rows to my right, near the wall. McCarty, as usual, was fast asleep while still sitting bolt upright. He grunted in his chair as O'Reilly crept by him in the dim light, a single bulb in the middle of the dorm—left on all night. O'Reilly made his way to his bed, halfway down the rows. "I've got yer loaf, Dano," said he in a screaming whisper, pointing to a lump under his jacket.

"Smashing!" said I, licking my lips.

"It's a corner loaf, Dano. It's hard as a rock, but it's the best I could do," O'Reilly croaked. "O'Driscoll was watching me like a hawk so I grabbed the first thing I could."

A corner loaf! Loaves are baked by the hundreds in batches of sixteen. With kind, old Joe Goulding in charge of a dozen sleepy lads, things could go very wrong in the bakers. A corner loaf, exposed to the heat of the oven from all sides, was the first casualty.

"I don't care what kind of loaf it is," I whispered back. "Just chuck it over, will ya, before I die of the hunger." Twenty or so lads in the nearby bed rows were listening enviously. Always hungry.

Like the born eejit he is, O'Reilly threw the loaf with tons more force than needed. It flew out of my hands and hit the floor with a God Almighty bang.

Silence. No one breathed.

> *Up jumps McCarty droopy as a drake*
> *Famous as an idiot when fully wide awake*
> *Twenty years a watchman, sixty years a fool*
> *As tough as he was stupid and as stubborn as a mule*
> *And then he said the funniest thing I ever heard—*

"Okayeee," said McCarty slowly, with the air of someone who knows exactly what's going on. "Who threw the bloody boot?"

Well, if I never laugh again . . . I've laughed enough tonight to last a lifetime. The lads nearby who knew what was going on erupted uncontrollably. McCarty couldn't have gotten it more wrong if he'd mistaken a fart for a song. As word of his stupid misunderstanding spread around the dorm like wild fire, things just got worse and worse. And it's not over yet.

There he goes now, out of breath and out of what little mind God cursed him with. "I'll find that blasted boot if it's the last thing I do," he shouts.

More howls from everyone.

"And when I do, I'll have your bed number and by Christ, you'll get it from me." This sends us into hopeless roars again under our blankets. McCarty runs around the dorm again, whacking beds with his leather strap. Like a perfectly orchestrated symphony, different parts of the dorm take turns to burst out in helpless laughter. Lads are now laughing from a far corner of the dorm. He runs over there, only to find it quiet as another corner erupts. He runs to the new source of laughter to find it, too, has gone quiet.

"Shut bloody well up and go to sleep." More laughs at this nonsense. Sleep? Some chance! Somehow, the comic miracle of us all knowing something he doesn't has reduced the feared bully McCarty to a member of the Three Stooges and for a mad minute we're all free of the tyranny of Artane.

The giggles fade and we go quiet. He's down on his knees again, searching for the. . . . No, don't say that word . . . don't say it. . . . He's inches from my bed. But I can't stop myself from saying it. . . .

The boot!

He, he, he.

"Okay, lads, I'll give yez all one more chance. If you own up like a man, I'll go easy on ya. But make no mistake, I'll find that boot, and

when I do. . . . I'm only going to ask one more time. Who—trew—
da—boot?"

Sweet tears and hot laughter, pure joy and total freedom, I'm in
heaven! My stomach is sore and my jaw is locked open forever. For
Christ's sakes, hobnail boots must weigh five pounds with all the
studs and the metal heel tip and heavy leather. Just the thought of it,
the blessed irony of mistaking a loaf of bread for a boot, says all that
ever needs to be said about this place.

> *Who trew da boot?*
> *I laughed till I was hoarse*
> *We're underneath the blankets*
> *Stifling the roars.*
> *Who trew da boot?*
> *We howl again some more*
> *The night O'Reilly's loaf of bread*
> *Nearly broke the floor.*

CHAPTER 29

The band is just back from a weekend stay-over in Ballyhaunis, County Mayo. I love the band lads, but I always enjoy getting back to my rougher, dirtier old playground friends. After unpacking my overnight case and putting everything back into my band-room locker, I hare down the iron stairs to find my pals.

There's Antho Kelly playing handball in the alleys. My friends are dear to me for different reasons. Kelly is a smart, solid pal with an honest, down-to-earth way of talking. If you want to know the simple truth of things, Kelly's your man. Rasher, now he's great if you need to find a way out of trouble or need someone to watch your back. Willie O'Reilly is just a howl. If you're feeling bad about yourself, spend ten minutes with O'Reilly and you'll feel like you're a genius. He gets more things mixed up than anyone I know, but his innocence is always a breath of fresh air.

I try to catch Kelly's attention, but he waves me off impatiently. "I have a shilling riding on this game, Dano. Buzz off! I'll see ya in the ref at supper."

The traders have just come up from the shops. Here comes O'Reilly. He's playing with a new cloth ball. He's a tailor now and they make those things by the dozen—when the man in charge isn't looking.

"Hey Willie, how's she cutting?" I shout through the rush of the traders as they break ranks.

"Ah, sure she's cutting rightly. Catch!" He throws me the cloth ball, which is hard and heavy. Sometimes the tailor lads will place a small stone in the first rolls of cloth to give it weight, like the

Flattener's leather strap. O'Reilly runs towards the shelter and I throw the ball high to him. He runs with it, turning suddenly in mid stride, and lobbing it back to me.

But I'm eager to play some cards before supper. "Come on, let's find Rasher and see if we can play a couple of hands before the whistle blows."

"Rasher's gone, Dano. He left on Saturday morning, while you were away with the band."

—⁓—

"We're going to America. I'll be seeing Da," I say excitedly.

"Danny, I'm delighted for you." Katie is never anything else but delighted. She makes an envious little pout, but she still manages to look delighted. Patricia is not as impressed, although she's happy for me. We're together again at Uncle Matty's, which seems to happen about once or twice a year. How beautiful they've grown.

"I bet Da won't even know you," says Patricia as Uncle Matty writes down the address of his parents, my grandparents, who also live in New York.

"You're not staying there, are ya?" Katie's voice is suddenly full of concern. I ignore her and change the subject. Patricia raises her chin and looks at me funny. I ignore her too.

Uncle Matty hands me my grandparents' address. "Let them know as soon as possible. I'll be writing soon meself, but they'll be delighted to hear it from you personally."

"Yes, delighted," says Patricia in a mock English accent, grinning at me. "Everyone is absolutely delighted. I'd be delighted myself if it wasn't for the fact that I don't remember a thing about our dad except the bloody smell of Guinness." She holds her nose comically and we all laugh.

"No. That was years ago. I'm sure things are different now," I say quietly.

—∞—

I'm on the iron stairs leading down to the Long Hall with a dozen lads from Band One. We've been polishing our band shoes and shining the silver buckles, and are making our way to the band room. I'm walking along in a bit of a daze, daydreaming about America again, when O'Connor's shout snaps me out of it.

"Okay, that's it. Come here, you brazen lump of misery." He's after Michael. He and his brother Timothy are on their way down the stairs to Band Two. Michael's been dragging his feet around for weeks, shooting sulky looks at O'Connor every chance he gets. Joe Boy's had enough. Timothy hangs back timidly, fingering his sax. I notice the boys' skinny thighs are badly chafed inside and out from the rough tweed of their short trousers and the cold October weather.

O'Connor is not used to being treated rudely. But Michael has the strength of a lad who has right on his side. He walks cockily over to O'Connor, who looks ready to kill him.

"I've warned you before about your attitude, haven't I? Most lads would give their right hand to be where you are, do you know that?" O'Connor snarls.

"I'd give my right hand to be anywhere else," says Michael icily.

The leather strap appears in a flash of black and explodes on Michael's chafed thigh like a thunderclap. Again it lands in exactly the same place.

"Into the office! Get in there this second." He points with his strap and whacks Michael again.

Michael limps into O'Connor's office, crying. He's had the presence of mind to hold on tightly to his rusty old trumpet as O'Connor whipped him. I don't know why, but that little detail breaks my heart.

O'Connor grabs the trumpet and shoves it into someone's hand. The door slams behind them.

"Take your trousers down," we hear O'Connor scream. The sound of the leather on bare flesh, again and again and again and again and again, is sickening. Timothy is crying silently as his brother's muffled cries echo around the band room. The door opens and Michael comes flying out, holding up his pants, pushed by O'Connor, who is still shouting.

"You will stay in this band till you leave Artane and you will like it!" All he cares about is having two handsome little brothers in his band to parade before a doting audience.

CHAPTER 30

It's New Year's Eve, 1961, and it's the same old feeling. The biggest little band in the world has been chosen to bring in the New Year at the Gresham Hotel, Dublin's finest, and to celebrate the inauguration of Ireland's very first national television station, RTÉ. O'Connor has told us that tonight is a historic occasion. We're going to be a part of history, he said proudly.

We've finished the rehearsals and have got some time to relax before they ring in the New Year. Watching all the preparations—the Radio Eireann Orchestra, the pipers, the big cameras, the balloons, all the revelers in tuxedos and evening gowns—makes me feel I should be happier than I am. Or at least historic. But it's the same old feeling. It creeps in now and then when least expected and for no real reason. It's not fear of the strap or a brother or a bully. I'd almost rather be afraid of something real than feel this vague emptiness. Maybe I can turn it into fear. Let's see. There's Andy McBride sipping lemonade by the drink stand. But he doesn't scare me any more, we're almost friends. There's O'Connor, talking to the floor manager. Am I scared of him? Not anymore. Not since the Monaco Royals. I'm almost sorry I'm not scared of O'Connor or Andy anymore. Fear is miles better than this same old nothingness. *Where are ya, fear? Come back, all is forgiven.*

—⁓—

Up until the Royal Reception, neither the Flattener, nor the Maggot, nor any other brother for that matter scared me as much as O'Connor did. Not that O'Connor whipped me more than them. In fact, he's hardly ever beaten me at all. He doesn't have to. I stay out of his way . . . those eyes can peel skin. It's just that I can't *get* to him like I can most of the others. But he always knows how to get to *me*—not just to frighten me. He's always made me feel like he knows something about me that I don't; almost like I have something coming to me for my sins. He's always praising me in front of others for my music and then he'll look at me like I deserve a hiding. But the last time he whipped me, I didn't deserve it.

It was Grace Kelly's fault. Which is terrible, because I've been in love with her for ages, ever since *High Noon,* when it was obvious she didn't really like Gary Cooper at all.

It was last May. By the time O'Connor had finished one of his long speeches, we were all aware how honored we were to be picked to play for Prince Rainier and Princess Grace, who would visit Ireland in a few days, and we all needed to be spick and span and have our instruments polished with Duraglit till he could see his face in them, or we'd be in big trouble.

I've plenty of time to clean my trombone, I thought. I was wrong. The very day of the Royal Reception, Itchy Reynolds, who'd held on to the Duraglit for days, finally used it all up. I was left to clean my trombone with soap and water. I hadn't finished polishing it with my chamois when O'Connor barged in, all panting and sweating.

"That's it, lads, pack your instruments away immediately. We've just heard from the Gardai that the band instruments need to be over there hours before we do," said he feverishly.

In a panic, we all ran around getting our cases from the back room behind the drum stand and packing away our instruments. O'Connor marched up and down, looking at the brass critically. He stopped by me as I was closing my case.

"Wait now, Ellis. What's this?" He lifts my bell out of the case and there's a big, long streak left by dried, soapy water along the top. Jesus, where did that come from?

Without a word, O'Connor lashes me about my thighs with his leather strap, just high enough for the blows to land on my short pants. Mustn't mark the band lads on the legs. Princess Grace might notice. *Well ffffuck Princess Grace and her bad-weather husband. And ffffuck you, O'Connor, and ffffuck the Gardai for not giving me time to clean my horn properly.*

We played for the royal couple as my thighs burned their way through the marches and the ballads. Everybody loved us, including the princess. O'Connor was over the moon, smiling at everyone and shaking the lads' hands. I think he'd had a whiskey or two at the reception. He's a bit fond of the hard stuff. He glanced over at me a few times as we rode back on the bus, but I ignored him, scowling. When we got back to the band room he approached me, obviously pleased with our performance.

"Good work, Ellis, but for God's sake, stop sulking. You need to take your medicine like a big man."

Ma's expression "big man" must have ruptured a pipe in my brain because the words burst out of my mouth before I could stop them.

"I'm not a big man and it's not medicine. It's not fair, that's what it is. Itchy Reynolds had the Duraglit for days and used it all up and before I could clean my instrument properly, you were rushing us around like cattle while you were all nervous and bad-tempered. You're just as mean as the rest of the brothers here."

O'Connor threw back his head and laughed for a full minute. Then he motioned me to follow him into his office. *Christ! I'm in for it now.*

In the office, instead of his leather strap, O'Connor offered me his hand. He was a bit tipsy. "Well, good man yourself! In nearly four years, that's the biggest mouthful I've ever heard you say. I thought the cat got your tongue." He shook my hand vigorously.

It's true. I'd never said more than two or three words to him. For the first time, I realized my awe of him confused him as much as it did me.

"That's the way to do it. Speak yer mind, no matter what. You're a bit of a genius, Ellis, in a sly, sideways sort of a way, but you need to walk straight. Find some spunk and stand up for yourself."

Unable to meet his stern gaze, I turned my eyes away, and before I could catch them they wandered over to the drawer in his desk where he keeps his money. Old habits die hard.

He saw my glance. "Ah, yes. I'm sure your conscience is still bothering you about that."

"About what, sir?" I was totally lost.

"Don't play games with me, Ellis. You know very well what I'm talking about. Or you've even less scruples that I thought and you've forgotten it."

"Forgotten what, sir?" I still hadn't a clue what he was on about.

He reached over to his desk, pulled out the drawer, and pointed to his money box behind it. "That!" His eyes were burning through my puzzlement. "The money you stole from me a week after I let you know it was there."

"I never stole any money. Sir, I swear to God, I didn't."

O'Connor grabbed me by my lapels. "Don't insult my intelligence, man. I can stand anything but a liar. I trusted you. Tell the truth and shame the devil."

I was crying, desperately trying to remember back. Jesus! Wait, now. The day I came out of hospital and punched Andy McBride, O'Connor said I was a thief, that I'd betrayed him.

"It couldn't have been me, sir, I was in hospital a week after you showed me . . . . It must have been someone else . . . . It must've . . . " Suddenly the blood rushed to my head and my mouth dropped open as the truth came pouring out of it before I could stop it.

"Rasher!" I cried hoarsely. I immediately put my hand to my mouth, but I was too late, the cat was out of the bag. Then I remembered Rasher had left the week before.

O'Connor put his palm flat on his face in genuine shock—the most human gesture I'd ever seen him make. "So, it was Rasher.

Good God above! For years I thought it was you. I never mentioned it after you joined the band. You seemed to have turned over a new leaf."

"I did, sir. I really did."

He looked very sad suddenly. "I'm so . . . I'm . . . " He's not about to apologize, is he? No chance! He just can't do it.

He tightened up. "It's yer own fault! You told him, didn't you? You told Rasher and he stole the money." Blame feels better than shame.

"I never thought he'd—"

He gestured impatiently. "All right then. All right! You brought it all upon yourself. Anyway, punching Andy McBride was crime enough and you deserved out of the band for that alone."

I felt like I'd been shredded! *My best pal . . . I might never have gotten back into the band. Who knows how different things might have been if he hadn't . . . ? Hey, maybe it wasn't Rasher at all. Maybe he told O'Reilly or Kelly and—*

O'Connor interrupted my meanderings. "It's all water under the bridge. Let's both shake hands like men and forget it."

He shook my hand hard, but his voice was soft. "I know I've treated you unfairly. I blamed you. You're a good lad, Ellis. I'm glad to finally see I wasn't wrong in my first assessment. But you have to get a grip on your moods. Make more friends. The whole world isn't going to run after you just because you can blow a trombone louder than God's thunder." His eyes bored into my soul with fierce purpose and he said emphatically, "Grow up, lad. You have a great future ahead if you can stop feeling sorry for yourself."

—ᴡ—

"What?" I say, sideswiped by Liz's question. I was expecting something totally different.

"Did O'Connor sexually molest you?"

I laugh so hard that every ounce of tension disappears from Liz's face. She's so relieved, the gathering tears she's been fighting come streaming down her face. I'm relieved too. For days I've been thinking she was digging her heels in, wanting me to take O'Connor out of the songs again.

"Sexually abuse me? Don't you think that's something I would have told you about? The only abusing he ever did on me was with his leather strap. Now if I'd had the choice between the two . . . " I crack up laughing again.

"It's not funny." But she's laughing herself now.

"I think it's hilarious. Except when I think of you believing that I'd held something like that back from you. No secrets, remember? Remember that night on the beach in Torremolinos, when the car got stuck in the sand? As we dug ourselves out with our hands we found some big rocks to give the wheels traction and we made a promise to each other: *No major rocks, no minor fooling around / no more serious sand stopping our wheels going round.*" I sing the line of the song I wrote about our second night together.

She's crying again. "I'm so sorry, baby. I thought you might have been so traumatized you couldn't speak about it. Or worse—you'd buried the memory." She looks coyly at me and grins impishly. "It would have explained a lot."

"Well, thank you very much, Mrs. Ellis. 'Mad musician's inexplicable behavior traced to buried memories of sexual abuse.' I wish it were as simple as that. The nearest I came to being molested was a comical groping by an older brother while I sat heating my thermometer on the infirmary radiator. He saw me idly fingering some chestnuts in my pocket and said with a filthy grin, 'Let's see what you're fiddling with there, lad.' He put his hand in my pocket and grabbed a hold of my tiny manhood. His look of disappointment turned to terror when I let out a yelp that should have woken the dead in the cemetery next door and brought the nurse running." I laugh, remembering my mad dive to grab the thermometer off the radiator before she noticed.

"That's not funny, baby. That's sexual molestation. You can't trivialize it like that. That's a serious violation of his vows and . . . and . . . ordinary human propriety."

I sober up. "Well, ordinary human propriety wasn't very prevalent in Artane."

"Did you know if other boys were molested?"

I scratch my head. "You know, there were always whisperings and nods and winks, some jokes about the boot room and such. But I never heard of anything specific. I know the Internet is afire with reports of sexual abuse, and when I left the orphanage, I heard some ex-Artane lads speak of it vaguely. I believe now for sure that it happened. But by whom and to whom or to what extent, I can't say. But I honestly never came across it while I was there. Maybe I was too ugly—even for the Christian Brothers."

—⁓—

It'll be midnight soon. The RTÉ cameramen are nervous. So is O'Connor. Not me.

"Fifteen minutes to countdown," shouts the floor manager. I couldn't care less.

It's been many months since O'Connor and I shook hands. But as the days rolled by like backyards seen from a seaside train, as the kaleidoscope of school and band engagements and holidays blurred into each other, O'Connor's last words to me that night still resonate.

When someone speaks to you with that intensity, with eyes that feel as if they're burning through you, you have to believe they're right. *Grow up. Stop feeling sorry for yourself.*

I'm trying real hard, for Christ's sakes. *Try harder.*

We're lining up now. Jack Whelan, our conductor, is up front, trying to catch the section leaders' eyes. I ignore him. *Stop feeling sorry for yourself.*

I am. I'm putting it all behind me, aren't I? I've put Rasher and his busy fingers—or big mouth, I don't know which—out of my mind. I can't blame him really. I'd have done the same had our roles been reversed. And I haven't . . . I mean, I've hardly thought about Ma for ages . . . and as soon as I do, I grab my horn and practice something really difficult. She's making me a better trombone player, for God's sakes.

Jack Whelan raises his baton and glares at me.

I raise my horn. No matter how good I get at this trombone or how many games of cards I win, it's still there. I can't even say it's Ma any more. It's all turned into a feeling with no name or shape. All I know is it feels awful and it's always been there in the background like a shadow.

It was there when my essay on Irish shellfish won me a place in the finals of the Shell nationwide writing competition. It was there when I got sick—really sick—and couldn't go to the competition finals.

It was there at the cobblers, where they put me to work in July, when I turned fourteen, where the din of fifteen lads hammering and scouring leather and metal would echo in my head till I heard it in my sleep.

It was there in the summer holidays when the Fennessy family—in Listowel, County Kerry, with eight young children of their own—opened up their doors to me for the month of August. It was there as they hugged me goodbye at the station. It was there through their smiles, their tears, and, lastly, their dismay when they found I hadn't the train fare back to Dublin.

It was there when Bing Crosby stood at the top of the steps to his plane in Dublin airport, his long trench coat blowing in the September wind. When he joined us, singing along as the band played his signature song, *"Where the blue of the night meets the gold of the day, someone waits for me,"* my tears fell like his on the tarmac.

It was there at a band stay-over last month, after I got my first kiss from a red-haired, sixteen-year-old lass backstage, her sweet lips changing my heart and my world, till I later found she'd kissed half a dozen other band lads.

And it's here now at the inauguration of RTÉ, Irish television, as they count down to midnight and 1962. We play "Auld Land Syne," bullied by the floor manager into swinging our instruments side to side like eejits. As the revelers sing, *"Should auld acquaintance be forgot,"* and I wish it could, I get the same old feeling.

CHAPTER 31

The Artane Boys Band is here in New York City! It's May 1962.

We're in a bus on our way to play at a Gaelic football match. Da is going to be there, and I can hardly breathe with anticipation. As I look out the window, dazzled by the endless traffic, the buildings that touch the sky, the neon signs, and the sheer energy of the city, I'm a little punch drunk by it all—I have been for days.

It's been a rollercoaster of nonstop excitement since we boarded the plane in Shannon a week ago. My first airplane flight! The sight of Shannon and the coast of Clare from the air nearly stopped my heart. When the pilot banked the plane steeply to give us a panoramic view of the fields, roads, and tiny houses, the lads let up a shout of amazement that had the other passengers laughing and clapping their hands. The passengers soon lost their tolerance as our excited laughter and constant chatter woke them from their naps time and time again. The flight passed in a delirious haze and before we knew it, we were landing. Our delight at the beauty of the city of Boston at night and our hushed gasps of awe at the landing had the other passengers back in a good mood again.

As we staggered through customs in Boston airport, O'Connor had us loaded up like camels: in addition to our personal luggage, each lad carried five liters of Irish whiskey! *Multiply that by fifty and someone in Boston will be drinking a lot of the hard stuff,* I thought to myself. O'Connor said it was for the American Irish Committee. *Sláinte!* A delegation from the Christian Brothers of the Catholic Memorial High School was there to meet us. After months of preparation, rehearsals, lectures from O'Connor about the band being ambassadors of Irish culture, and letters back and forth to Da, we were finally here in the USA. The excitement was almost too much to bear. The lads were like drunken soldiers, laughing and clapping one another on the back. I was a little more subdued, tired maybe, and wishing we were in New York and Da was here. I couldn't wait to see him and give him the present I'd bought him, with money I'd saved from folks at band stay-overs—a really cool, battery-powered electric razor.

Somewhere in the back of my mind, ever since O'Connor announced we were bound for America, I'd carried the vaguest idea that maybe, just maybe, Da might let me stay here with him in America. *Wait now, hold on there, pal. That's enough of that.* But God, I thought, as I buried my wishful thinking for the hundredth time, I can't believe it. We're actually here! The United States of America—home of Roy Rogers and Gary Cooper and cowboys and Indians and red sunsets behind huge mountains.

But whatever happened to Technicolor? Somehow I'd expected America to be shaded in the glorious reds and blues of the movies. It was a shock to see that everyone and everything was the same color as back home. But that vague disappointment vanished as, one by one, my senses were overwhelmed by the country that had filled my family's dreams for as far back as I could remember. I know Ma had dreamed of us all joining Da here, and my own dreams were never far from the Land of Plenty. But it was hard to take it all in. We drove through the city in a luxurious coach bus with freezing-cold air blowing at us from above. How do they get the air so cold? "Ice in the ceiling," Itchy said, winking wisely. He knows stuff. But the sight of it all: the cops on motor bikes . . . the size of them! The size of everything! With the huge cars and lorries—I mean trucks—and the turnpikes and skyscrapers and Coca Cola signs everywhere, I soon lost my sleepiness from the long flight and the extra waking hours. Before long, we got to the high school where we were assigned

to the parents who would put us up till we left for New York the
following week.

The family I stayed with had three children. They lived in the
suburbs, in a house five times as big as Uncle Matty's. They were
beyond kind. Over the week, they showered me with love, money,
food, and clothes, till I was totally depressed. How can people have
so much and be so kind and carry such light in their eyes and hearts.

The breakfast table wasn't half as big as those in the ref, but ten
times as much food was spread on it in embarrassing abundance:
eggs, scrambled and fried, sausages, home fries—their version of
pan-fried spuds—yogurt, cereal, milk, orange juice, apple juice,
lemonade, prunes, toast—brown, white, and one in the middle with
a funny taste called rye—and God bless us and save us, real butter.

We played for the high school students and their band played
for us. They were a thousand miles better than us, which sent me
into a sulk until the Glee Club sang, which made me want to slit my
wrists. Every lad sounded as good as Tommy Bonner and the girls
all looked and sounded like Doris Day. The biggest little band in
the world was feeling smaller by the second. The jealousy turned to
nausea as the roast lamb, mint sauce, and spuds tried to make room
for the downpour of ice cream and soda that followed. Afterward
I crawled into a spotless bed, to be woken at dawn to go to the beach
with the family. I knew I was in a different country when I got badly
sunburned on a cloudy day.

After a couple of sold out public concerts—at the high school
and a beautiful venue in the city—we played for Cardinal Cushing
at his residence. In my mind, he was as far from a cardinal as Bing
Crosby was from a priest. He walked and talked like someone who'd
been in a few fistfights in his life, and we were very comfortable in
his huge presence. He really seemed a good fellah and was genuinely
interested in how Artane School worked. He pretended not to be
surprised at our stony silences in the face of some of his questions

about the history of the orphanage. But his sharp, intelligent eyes missed nothing. He seemed to know more about Artane than we did. We played for him in his beautiful garden, the Massachusetts spring bursting out all around. I looked at him as a kind of hero—a John Wayne or Spencer Tracy. *Why don't we have clergy like him in Ireland?* I thought, as we watched him move among us, relaxed and making jokes. He gave us all a signed photo of himself, which, although I really liked him, I promptly lost. He made a donation of five hundred dollars to O'Connor for the band fund.

Then we flew to Mansfield, Massachusetts, for a day and night. As we climbed down the plane's steps, the Mansfield High School Band was there to meet us on the tarmac. Blackest jealousy tore through me again as they marched and danced and flung their horns about like jugglers, all while playing the wildest version of "The Saints Go Marching In" imaginable. How did they learn to play like that? Who taught them? The only music lesson I ever got in my life was from a fellah next to me in the band whose only goal was to keep me from learning more than him. These lads—I mean guys—were massive, mustard, and mean as hell.

I was sent to a local family, who again showered me with love and grub, and I, in turn—in the most embarrassing moment of my life—showered them with carrots and peas as an unstoppable sneeze sent my dinner spraying over them. The silence that followed was as long as my red face. They cleaned themselves off and drove me to the high school, where the band played a concert. Afterward they taught me to do the Twist, and the next day they sent me off with a pocketful of dollars and half a dozen records—LPs of Chubby Checker, Joey Dee and the Starlighters, and Glen Miller, which I didn't lose.

The flight to New York was barely long enough for me to check that the batteries in Da's electric razor were working. I unwrapped it carefully so I could wrap it back up again. Unlike most of the lads my age in Artane, I didn't have even a ghost of a beard. Lads teased me in the washroom sometimes about my hairless legs, arms, and face.

But the razor worked fine—Itchy let me try it out on his arm. He was full of high spirits. But then he always is. He was almost as excited as I was to meet Da.

Absorbed by thoughts of Da, I held back a wee bit from the joyful shouts and excitement of the band lads on the plane. They didn't miss me, all sunburned and laughing, full of the dizzy freedom of the American, well, the American happiness, I suppose, bursting out of everyone everywhere. Although New York City looked gray and dirty from the plane, still the sight thrilled us all. *My da is down there somewhere,* I thought as the plane circled and circled the city.

Over the long months of preparation before coming to the US and since we've arrived, I've been able to think of nothing but seeing my father. His memory has always shone like gold in my mind. How well I remember those last moments in Green Street before he left. Jesus! Was it really eight years ago? Strong and tall, so brave in his army uniform, the memory of that last salute has thrilled me ever since. I miss him. I've always missed my da. God, I missed him even while he was there with us in Green Street. And now, he'll be here in a moment to meet me when this bus arrives at the football stadium in New York where we'll play and march.

As the bus pulls up, hundreds of people are lining up for tickets. Except for the tiny stadium and smaller crowds, we could be at Croke Park in Dublin—you can take an Irishman out of Ireland, but you can't take Ireland out of an Irishman. Even from behind, I can tell my countryman from any other nationality, just by the way he puts his hand into his pocket or the way he scratches his head. There's something casual and sure about him—he's comfortable in his clothes and he doesn't mind if they don't fit. I can pick out the Americans too. They're more perky and self-conscious, more aware of their surroundings; happier, too, but nervous, like racehorses that have to win something to be satisfied. Looking out of the bus window with pounding heart, I search the crowds for Da's golden hair, those piercing blue eyes. *No. That's not him. Wait now . . . Maybe . . . No.*

"Move Dano, will ya?" Smasher Magee prods me in the back with a Coke bottle. Coke is everywhere.

We grab our instrument cases from the storage spaces under the bus and line them up by a wall. O'Connor is shouting orders. I'm jerking my head around so much, looking for Da, that I get a crick in my neck. *Stop it, ya eejit. He'll be here soon enough.* We're taken to a tent where they serve us Coke and chicken sandwiches. I've never had chicken before and am not sure I like it either, but the Coke sends it down easy enough. Everyone is shaking everyone else's hands and the atmosphere is festive, but I've got a funny feeling in my tummy.

Twenty nervous minutes pass. No sign of Da.

We're lined up now at attention, ready to march around the pitch with the teams behind us. I straighten my music on my marching stand and suddenly I see him walking toward us from the alcohol stand and—*please God, no*—he's got a bottle of Guinness in his hand, swigging it as he ambles along. People get bigger as a rule when they come nearer, but he seems to get smaller the closer he gets. I start to wave my hand to get his attention, but I don't know what's wrong . . . my hand won't move. *Move, ya bastard. There we go. Da, here I am!* He grins and waves back, changing direction awkwardly toward me. Smaller and smaller he gets till the top of his head is barely above my left shoulder. He's standing next to me, grinning crookedly. Christ, he's tipsy—and sad. A tipsy, sad, little old man. Those piercing blue, blue eyes are dull and unfocused and ringed with dark circles; those strong, erect shoulders are slumped and unsure. My da? How long I've waited for this. How many times I've pictured this as I lay awake at night.

"Would ya look at him? Dressed up like the cat's pajamas. Ya look smashing," he says as he shakes my hand feebly.

I blurt something and smile tightly. He slaps my shoulder and winks.

The drums start up. We're playing now. Suddenly Da straightens up proudly, like a soldier on parade, sticks out his chest, and marches alongside us. I'm mortally embarrassed—the hot blood rushes to my head and over every inch of my body. He's swinging his free arm stiffly as the Guinness hangs loosely from the other like a guilty thing. Out of the corner of my eye I sense him watching me proudly. Some forgotten anger from the back streets of Dublin surges up inside me and I blow louder than I've ever blown in my life. Itchy, to my right, shoots me a look and he too takes it up a bit. As if they feel my heart, the whole band blasts the bejaysus out of their horns as we march around the field.

The football match is over. Da shakes my hand again with a little more gusto this time.

"I'm proud of ya, son. That's a grand noise ya make on that trumpet of yours."

"It's a trombone, Da."

"Ah, but you've made something of yourself. Look at the size of you. I don't know who you take after with the height of ya."

"Ma's family are all very tall," I say lamely.

Da's face goes dark. He turns his head to look at the band lads putting their instruments away. I'm trying to take him in, behind his cloud of cigarette smoke, trying to see past the wrinkles and the sleepy eyes, past the tired resignation and the shuffling uncertainty, to my hero of a thousand daydreams. But I can't get there. How many times I've asked myself in troubled moments, *What would Da do?* Now I know what he'd do. He'd reach for another Guinness or another cigarette. Uncle Joe, his brother, once said to me, *You're not half the man your da is.* As Da's trembling hand lights another cigarette with the old one, I hear myself whisper, *You're not half the man my da was.*

O'Connor, who's been directing the packing of the bus with urgency and vigor, comes over to us.

"Mr. Ellis, I'm Brother Joseph O'Connor. I'm very pleased to meet you." He shakes Da's hand firmly. O'Connor is much older than Da, but his manner, his body movements, his strength of character

all seem to make Da shrink into himself. Looking at them both—
the man who deserted me and the man who gave me music, this
broken alcoholic and this fierce warrior—I'm lost in confusion as my
world seems to turn itself upside down. Cherished notions of a loving
family chafe against the hard edges of tyrannical authority, and I'm
aghast and ashamed at which one I'm most attracted to. Any thoughts
of staying here in America vanish like fog.

"You should be very proud of your son, Mr. Ellis. He's very
talented musically. You should be very proud." O'Connor walks off
abruptly as if he has better things to do.

While Da wanders off for another Guinness, I board the bus
to change out of my band uniform. I climb into a new outfit the
Boston family bought me: long pants, cotton shirt, sneakers, and
a windcheater jacket. I'm to spend two nights with Da. He'll take
me back on the subway before our next concert in New York. *Two
nights, Jaysus!* Tomorrow, I know the lads will visit Saint Patrick's
Cathedral and have lunch later at Jack Dempsey's restaurant. I know
they'll be taken on a tour of the city and have a steak dinner and go
to a movie. I know *they're* going to have a great time. *Stop it!*

Da comes back and we watch the lads board the bus. I avoid their
eyes, especially Itchy's, who really wants to meet Da. *No chance, pal,
sorry.*

I watch the band bus drive off. I'm alone with my father for the
first time in my life.

—w—

Da fumbles about making breakfast. I've just told him I need to go
back to the hotel where the band is staying.

"But I thought we were going to spend two nights together?" He's
mildly upset. The amount of whiskey he drank last night should've
given him other things to worry about.

"Yeah, I know. But I just remembered that there's a new piece of music we have to learn for the concert and I'll have to practice it for most of today," I lie coldly as I pack away my toothbrush and comb in the plastic bag I brought with me. From the bottom of the bag his present, the electric razor, looks up at me, waiting. The time hasn't felt right to give it to him yet. The presents he gave me kinda overshadowed mine: the transistor radio, the tape recorder, and the gun.

Yeah, the gun: a huge, black replica of an American army forty-five. A BB gun, he said it was. Lying on the floor of his neat little one bedroom flat, I'd spent much of yesterday evening shooting it at the padded target that came with it. Later, playing with the transistor radio, I marveled at the size of it, thinking, *I can listen to this in the dorm all night long and no one will ever know.* I recorded some *Do-Re-Mi* songs on the tape recorder. The magic of hearing myself back in seconds was mind-boggling. We watched the end of a game of baseball on TV till it was time to go to the pub to meet my mother's parents, my grandparents Maher.

My grandfather was a tall, gentle man from Donegal. My grandmother, a short, abrupt Scot, showered me with wet kisses till I blew a bubble with my gum every time she came near. At least they weren't Guinness kisses. Her poison was, of course, Scotch. I noticed that everyone called her what sounded like Mrs. *Marr.* I know her name is Maher, but I like Marr better. It's cool and American. Marr it is! With a good part of my family around, I'm sure I must have expected to feel something more than I did. But as I stood by the slot machine alone, looking across the pub at my father and grandparents, I knew I didn't belong in their world of drink, cigarettes, and loud— too loud—cackling. If, somewhere deep inside, I had any tears, or emotional resonance to give to the reunion, they were quickly banished by the almost laughable indifference of everyone. *Thank God for music,* I thought more than once.

But the pub was full of Da's friends, all eager to meet me and give me money, which I accepted eagerly. No one noticed my bad manners toward my family as everyone flocked around making a fuss and buying me soda after soda. It was ten o'clock before I noticed I was starving. I hadn't eaten since one o'clock—in the tent at the football match. A couple of ham sandwiches and a few more sodas later and I was almost ready to face them all again.

Someone brought out a deck of cards. Massive! It was great to be back in control, with the cards in my hands, as all my ideas of family and home scattered like marbles on the Artane playground. It was pontoon—or blackjack as they call it here. *Now I know where I am.* Ignoring some raised eyebrows at my dealing techniques, I fleeced them for all I could get. *They're all drunk, loud, and rich, and I'll never see any of them again, so what do I care?* Later, as Da passed out on the sofa, I crawled into his bed to count my hard-earned money. Eighty-five dollars! A good night's work.

Now it's breakfast—a runny egg and some burnt toast, no orange or apple juice, no cereal or yogurt, as I'd become used to with the various American families. As I eat, I allow myself to feel the disappointment I've been burying about Da's flat; it's a tiny, drab, two-room excuse for an apartment that is as depressing as it is tidy. I don't know what I was expecting, but Uncle Matty told me Da makes good money working for the Lackawanna Railroad. I address his mail to Prospect Avenue, Brooklyn, which has always sounded pretty posh to my ears. But if the amount of money Da spent in the pub last night is a regular occurrence, I'm thinking this is probably all he can afford. But I'm getting good at burying disappointment and I do it again here. Thinking of disappointments, I decide to risk it and ask Da about Ma.

"Have you heard from Ma at all, Da?"

"No." He sticks his knife roughly into his toast, which breaks, sending pieces flying round the room in all directions.

Silence.

"Did she get ever get better?"

"What are ya talking about?"

"She had TB and went into hospital. That's why she put us all into the orphanages." I'm feeling sick suddenly.

"Ha! Is that what she told ya?" He stands, looking down at me. My stomach turns again.

"She put you into Artane because she was too fond of a good time to be a mother or a wife."

I'm standing now, clenching fists, shouting. "She was a great mother! And what kind of a father were you anyway? Always away off somewhere."

"That's what ya do when there's no work at home. YOU GO TO WHERE THE WORK IS ."

"The work? The work? What about us? You broke the family up with your bloody work."

Da's voice cracks. "Your mother broke us up when she . . . she took another man into my bed. You were there. You must have seen it, eh? Eh?"

I can't look at him.

Da takes a deep breath. "Yer ma didn't have TB when she put you in Artane. She had it years before and it had cleared up by then."

The words echo around the little flat for a full minute. Cold heat. Up from my stomach to my head.

"Oh, she was sick all right. Sick in the head. You have it all arse about face, kid." He lights a cigarette, his hands trembling. "She didn't have TB when she dumped you all," he says slowly, "and she never went into hospital either."

I sit down. He sits, too, trying vainly to hold my eyes.

"She got rid of yez all and caught the first boat to England to be with some shitehawk that meant more to her than either of us." His anger can't hide his hurt, nor banish mine.

I notice my fingernails are dirty. O'Connor will have a fit. *Stop it!*

My hand wanders over to the tape recorder on the table. I fumble with it. *Face it.*

The batteries are worn out on the tape recorder. I left it on all night. It won't play. *It's over.*

I've known it for seven long, lying-to-myself years. I knew it on that cold Christmas Day, in 1955, as I watched that refectory clock, listening to Brother Columbus tell me basically what Da has just said. But I couldn't face it then. I ran back to the gate, waiting for her. I've been running back to that gate ever since.

It's time.

Face it now.

Then bury it.

Beneath the cold comprehension, a slow clarity creeps over me. *Thank you. Thank you very much.*

I feel Da sense my returning strength. It gives him leave to return to his normal state. Bent over the table, his head almost touching the salt cellar, he looks over at me like a puppy. For the first time, I feel a distant pang of pity for the man who was never my father.

I stand and look out the window. "I think I need a breath of fresh air. I'll be back in a minute."

"Prospect Park is only a few blocks away. Here, I'll go with ya." Da reaches for his jacket, which hangs on the door of the flat.

"Thanks, but think I need to be alone for a while."

He looks so downcast I almost change my mind. I don't. I get the transistor radio from my plastic bag. Da mutters some directions, and I leave.

—~~—

I'm in the park, walking on the new spring grass. It's Monday and I'm alone except for some mothers playing with their preschool toddlers. The sun peeks out from behind a cloud and suddenly it's warmer than an Irish August. By the lake, a lone old man plays with a tiny sailboat. His childlike delight is beyond my understanding. I envy it. He waves at me as I pass. His languid movements seem to say, *It's all just a dream. Slow down. Enjoy your life.*

Remembering the radio, I turn it on. A song I know from our band repertoire, "You'll Never Walk Alone," is playing. I turn it off quickly. Turn off that stupid lie.

That's all you ever do. You walk alone. There's nothing surer. That's fine. I'm good company.

Alone, you know where you're going. Alone, you don't have to ask anyone for anything. *She lied to me. Stop it!* Alone, you don't have to look behind. *She knew from the very beginning she was never coming back. I said bury it!* You walk alone and always have. You just didn't know it. Nothing's changed.

Nothing's changed. That gets to me. In all the years of hoping, there was never any hope. I never gave up on her, but that faithful, never-giveup business was all a meaningless waste of time. That was the cruelest thing about her lie; I believed it. But Jesus Christ, what else was I supposed to do?

The sun, which had gone behind a cloud, suddenly comes out again in a blinding blaze. I turn my face up to the golden warmth. *That's it, face the sun.* You've been overtaken by the wrong voice in your head—the going-back voice. *Don't go back—ever!* Quicken up. Get away from it. Get back to the . . . the going-forward one. *There ya are, Black Daniel. What took ya so long? Keep moving. You'll be grand. Giddy up!*

—⁘—

I'm back at the flat before I realize it. Da is running around me, fussing. I'd been walking for over an hour. It's time to go. Suddenly, I'm the adult. The big man of the house. It's time for Da's present.

"Oh, I nearly forgot. I got you something from Ireland."

"What's that, son?" His eyes light up.

I give him the present. He opens it like a child.

Standing real close to him as he unwraps the package, I notice he doesn't have a beard. Not even stubble. Wait, I know he didn't shave this morning. Jesus, he's just like me. No facial, arm, or leg

hair. Not even baby fluff. Nothing. My present is useless as boots
to a cat.

He laughs when he sees the razor. He turns it on, running it
across his jaw and chin, backward and forward. When he's done he
rubs his hand over his face, nodding approvingly. He winks. "Smooth
as a baby's arse."

—⁓—

As the songs are finished and recorded, one by one, my voice has
been changing in a startling way. I'm recording the vocal on the
Tommy Bonner song. These lyrics, I can climb inside them. I'm
feeling something I've never felt. It's been the same with all the new
songs.

Some years back, I read about something that I never understood
till this moment. Italian university researchers were interviewing
peasant singers throughout the Italian countryside. They were trying
to ascertain why many peasant singers, without any vocal schooling,
had an extraordinary emotional depth and authenticity of expression.
Almost to a man, the singers were very reluctant to talk about what
they were accessing emotionally as they sang; most wouldn't even
talk about it at all. Now I know why; one may go there, but one
can't easily tell others what's going on. I realize I'm going to have
to acclimatize my body to holding this amount of emotion without
caving in. Now I know why Tommy Bonner held himself so nobly
erect when he sang.

Years of rocking out in smoky pubs and clubs grafted layers of
bluff and bravado to my natural vocal sound. Maybe in those rough
and ready environments, those crusty layers were necessary.

But not here. Not now. Not in this song. An aching, a longing,
seems to create a wider, darker space in the back of my throat as
I allow myself to feel more deeply.

Let the broken heart sing. Let the frozen part breathe. For the first time, sing your mother, sing your father, sing the child you never were. Sing the lost hundreds.

I look out of the studio's window as I'm singing and recording. Liz is looking in at me, smiling. Ashamed of my vulnerability, my whole being quickly morphs into my usual tough, rock 'n' roll stance. Black Daniel is singing again.

That's OK, something inside says cockily, *I'm a group, it's all part of me.* But beneath, a quiet longing seeps up; *you've just buried something sacred.* Overwhelming anguish for my fractured, splintered soul washes over both those parts of me and then I get it! Suddenly, I'm laughing like drunken sailor.

All of the voices are okay! The Cocky, the Sacred, the Poet, the Rebel, Gabby Hayes, Black Daniel. They're all part of me; *800 voices.* Ah! That's more like it!

CHAPTER 32

Yeah, but right now, singing along with Dion's "The Wanderer" on Da's transistor radio, I'm a rebel. Da's revelations about Ma have changed everything. It's a pity the brothers took my da's pellet gun present from me for safekeeping, because it's open season on rules. Everything is fair game. After seven years in this place—one more to go—I know every trick in the book. If fact, I wrote the bloody book. If you want to know how to get sick properly, or sneak over the wall and go for a swim downtown in Tara Street Baths, or make some money, or get out of a fix, then I'm your man! Tell the truth, I don't share my secrets with many any more. Or my radio. The speaker turns itself off when I stick in the ear-plug and that's how I want it. This is my world, and I'm the only one living in it. The tiny radio is the secret door to this new world. On the other side are Elvis, Dion, Ricky Nelson, Kenny Ball, and Chris Barber. I open the secret door and *See ya later, alligator!* I'll be fifteen in a few days and in a year I'll be out of this madhouse, playing music like this every night.

Uncle Matty has picked up on my new couldn't-care-less attitude. In fact, on my last visit two weeks ago, he had plenty to say about it.

"Danny, you're getting too wild, son. If you don't get a grip on yourself, you're headed for an almighty comeuppance."

I banged away at his piano as if he was singing and I was accompanying him. *Let's see how much patience you really have.*

Plonk! "Danny, I was thinking . . . " *Plonk!* "Maybe next time you visit . . . " *Plonk!* "We can all go . . . " *Plonk!* " . . . to twelve o'clock Mass together." *Plonk! Plonk! Plonk! Plonk! Plonk! Bloody well plonk!*

Silence.

"It'd do you good to see a Mass outside of Artane and watch the sincere devotion of the congregation in the prayers."

"Why?" *Plonk!*

"You need a good example, and there's no better way than to enjoy the Mass with family and friends."

I have no family and no friends and Mass . . . well, it's okay, but not twice on the same day.

But Matty insisted and in his last letter, the other day, he reminded me we'd be going to Mass if his flu is better. I'm sorry Patricia and Katie weren't there. Patricia would have let him know what she thought of his stupid idea. But I've never stood up to Matty, for some reason.

Now, as I walk down the avenue to the quarry pond with a trash can full of nothing, I'm thinking of ways to avoid visiting my uncle on Sunday. The empty-dustbin trick is my latest stroke of genius. Close to the end of the avenue, there's a small pond about sixty feet across. About a year ago, one of the senior brothers—only God knows who—got the brilliant idea of filling it in, just to fuck over the wildlife for miles around—the frogs, rabbits, birds, and geese who've been using it for decades. The genius who came up with the idea started the process by dumping in five or six beautiful old baby grand pianos that had graced the Long Hall for nearly a hundred years. My contribution to the reclamation was to grab any dustbin in sight—any empty one, that is, no sense in straining—and carry it down the avenue, and the brothers, one and all, would assume I was on some official dumping errand in the noble cause of clawing back nature from those stupid creatures who don't know what to do with it. *Good man, Dan, well done lad, off ya go now.*

It's a beautiful summer's day. The quarry is teeming with life. Sometimes I'll spend an hour rowing myself around the pond on one of the floating pianos. But today, I'm off to Tara Street Baths for a swim. The 42 bus takes me most of the way.

I'll be back in a few hours and no one at the cobblers will be any the wiser. This morning I told Mr. Mullen, the man in charge of the cobblers, that I was sick and needed to go to the infirmary. That way he wouldn't report me missing when the lad doing roll-call duty came around at two o'clock. I know more ways to get sick than could fill a hospital. Mr. Mullen is a decent man who couldn't care less what I do.

Brother Mooney—believe it or not, a really cool new brother—caught me here a few weeks ago. He shouldn't have been there himself. He should've been at prayers, but he was off wandering the fields, smoking and wasting time properly. If a fellow rebel can't keep a secret then the whole world's fucked. But all he was interested in was how I managed to pull it off; how I managed to avoid being challenged as I left the grounds or was reported absent at roll call. When I told him about the empty dustbin and the roll-call trick, he laughed so hard he nearly fell into the pond. He took a Crunchie bar from his pocket and we sat there munching in the afternoon sun, listening to my radio. Then he offered me a cigarette—Sweet Afton. Better than the Woodbines I buy, two at a time, on my romps outside.

But today, it's a swim for me. I slip over the long gray wall that runs up the Malahide Road, encircling Artane School, and catch the bus to town. I always sit upstairs, right up front. The baths are a mad hour of screaming and diving and swimming underwater till my eyes are sore from the chlorine. A Woodbine upstairs on the bus back calms me down.

I'm climbing back over the gray wall behind the quarry when I see him. Shite! It's the Flattener. He sees me too. He looks like he's been waiting for me. My heart is racing. I'm in for it now. He's sitting on a fallen tree, whistling and playing my empty dustbin with his leather strap like a drum. I drop heavily over the wall in front of him.

"Ah, Mr. Ellis. Just the man I want to see. Or should I say spider?"

I frown, confused.

"Have you ever heard of the spider who got caught in its own web? Too clever by far, Mr. Ellis. Too clever indeed. But not clever enough. When I first saw you traipsing down the avenue with the dustbin a month back, I didn't think much of it. But after three times . . . do ya think we're all stupid here or what?" He's working himself into a rage so I decline to answer. *I've been doing this for months and it's more like my tenth time. Yeah, ya are stupid!*

"Well, we'll see how clever you are in the boot room tonight after lights out, won't we?"

I can't stop myself. "Why don't you beat me now? It's not fair to make me wait all day."

"That's exactly the right medicine for your sort, Ellis. You think you can go around breaking every rule in sight, don't you?" He's breaking a few rules here himself. For this kind of infringement, he should report me to the Maggot, the playground disciplinarian, instead of punishing me himself.

"No, sir. I was just—"

"Not another word, ya hear?" He beckons me to follow him as he starts to walk toward the traders' workshops. "Let's go." I walk behind him in silence with lead for feet.

After a few yards he says in a mock-friendly voice, "How is your father in America doing? And your grandfather?"

Puzzled, I say, "They're doing grand, sir."

"And your Uncle Matty? How is his flu doing?" The bastard is rubbing in the fact that he's been reading my incoming mail. He's been keeping a close watch on me, all right. But he's just given me an idea; anything is better than waiting in fear of the boot room all day.

"I'm sure my uncle's on the mend, sir. I'm looking forward to going to Mass with him this Sunday. Afterward he's throwing a big birthday party for me to celebrate my fifteenth birthday." A good lie is a thing of great beauty.

The Flattener couldn't look less interested. He grunts and lights a cigarette.

"Yeah, and that's why I'm glad you're going to punish me yourself instead of reporting me to the disciplinarian like you're supposed to, sir," I say very sincerely. I sincerely hope he buys it.

He stops dead. He looks like he could tear me apart right there on the grass. But he restrains himself. "And why is that?"

"Well, if you report me to the disciplinarian, he'll stop me from going to Uncle Matty's on Sunday for my birthday party. That's his usual punishment. My sisters will be there and all my aunts and uncles and cousins, and I'm going to get lots of presents. That's why I'm glad you're taking the matter into your own hands, sir."

He walks on ahead in silence. But I can feel his ugly mind working this one over.

Then he stops abruptly. He turns to me with a frown, scratching his chin. "And why didn't your uncle mention the party in his letter?"

I almost choke. I start blathering away before I know what I'm going to say. "Ah . . . now that's the very terrible thing about it all, sir." *Think, for Christ's sake.* "I suppose . . . that . . . he thinks it's going to be a . . . a *surprise* party for me." I try to look guilty.

"Oh?" says he dubiously.

Stalling for time. "Yes, sir. But my second cousin, Frances— well, she's not really a cousin. She's a cousin by marriage. Her mother's sister is my Aunt Margaret, who's married to my Uncle Matty." God is in the details.

"Get on with it, man." The Flattener is losing his patience. But I've made enough time for the rest of my story to catch up with me.

"Well, last time I was at me uncle's, Frances accidentally let me in on the secret. She won't be there herself, and in apologizing to me about that, she let the cat out of the bag, sir. I'll just have to try hard to look surprised."

He's deep in thought. I decide to add a little more wood to the fire.

"She told me my cousin, Mary, my grandah's niece from Donegal, is coming down on the train, specially for the party. And she's making a huge ice cream cake just for me. Chocolate and cherry. My favorite." Hope I didn't overdo it. I don't want him to actually feel sorry for me.

But no chance. He's nodding his head as he sticks his bottom lip up above his top one in a sudden-decision kind of way. *Gotcha!* He's thinking. Trying desperately hard not to think the very same thing myself, I say, as if I've lost interest in the subject, "I think it's going to rain, sir. Can I run to the cobbler's shop? I have to finish up before supper. I'll see you in the boot room tonight, sir."

"Not so fast, Ellis. Hold out your hand."

What? After a minute's gaping surprise, I hold it out, gritting my teeth.

"Never mind about the boot room tonight. I've got a much better idea. This'll hold you till Sunday, when you'll be cleaning the dorms all day instead of going to your birthday party at your uncle's."

He brings his leather strap down with all his might.

"And again . . . And again." Christ! Four more times. Harder and harder the leather falls till my tears well up. *Tighten up! Don't give him the satisfaction.* A couple of cracks to my legs complete his "better idea." I didn't plan on this.

"Now, get going. I'll be speaking to Disciplinarian about your visit, or lack of, to your uncle." He used the Maggot's proper name.

Blowing on my hands, I limp to the cobblers. That's the worst beating I've had in a couple of years. But better a half-dozen whacks now than waiting all day for a hiding in the boot room tonight—with nothing between me and the Flattener but my thin cotton nightshirt. I grin through the pain, thinking of Matty's imagined party. Kind as he is, he wouldn't remember my birthday if it was the same day as his own.

Later, as we're on our way to supper, the Maggot calls me over.

"I have some very bad news for you, Ellis," says he, with an evil grin. I have to bite my lip, trying not to grin back at him. Every now and then the cards fall your way, especially if you deal from the bottom of the deck.

CHAPTER 33

The summer holidays are over. Shorter and shorter they've gotten as the years have passed. I spent August in Waterford with a wonderful family near the Tramore Road. I'd met them in April when I was assigned to them on a stay-over with the band, just before we went to America. Years back, I'd learnt the trick, from older band lads, to casually—but oh, so wistfully—mention to families who take us in at a band stay-over, "Oh, yes, we're allowed to spend the holidays outside Artane, if we can find someone kind enough to foster us." The ensuing silence would remain unbroken by me till they either changed the subject or looked at each other sadly, eventually asking, "Have you found anyone who'll take you in this summer?" The Waterford family was more than kind, but for some strange reason, my da's pellet gun, which I was allowed to take on holliers, disappeared after I accidentally shot out one of their windows.

Back in the band room, it took a few days to get my lip back in shape after the month away. Most band lads had spent the holliers with families or fosters. As usual, nobody was happy to be back. For me, the memories—the sunny blur of my vacation, the delirious abandon of hitchhiking to Tramore Beach, diving off the pier all day and going to dances at night—served only to depress me. Over the next day or two, lads drifted back reluctantly from their families. But there was no sign of Itchy. He'd gone to High Wycombe, England, to spend the holliers with his mother, who had married again. He'd become very quiet since coming back from America. It seemed that America had changed us all. Itchy had always been contained and sure of himself, but this new calm of his was like a magnet to me. I'd seek him out for advice when disturbed by some contentious encounter with someone—there had been many for me since America. His measured counsel, had I ever taken it, probably would have saved me a whole lot of trouble. I missed him.

You'd think you'd get used to missing lads. But you don't. Every friend who leaves Artane reminds you that, in the long run, you're on your own. *On your own!* What does that mean, really? With hundreds of lads running around you all day, it's easy to mistake company for friendship and a roof over your head for shelter. But the only shelter I feel is music. More and more, as friends leave and things change, I rely on music's refuge. Especially since my meeting with Da, and his angry words about Ma. I've never allowed myself any anger for Ma, but Da's words still echo in my sleep and waking hours: *She caught the first boat to England to be with some shitehawk that meant more to her than either of us.* Anger is good sometimes; better than loneliness, especially when you can put that anger into music. My trombone never sounded as loud or as clear as those days after coming back from holidays. Maybe Beethoven was angry.

With our new conductor, Commandant Browne, at the baton, we started to ease back into rehearsals, though the trombone section continued to miss Itchy's strong bass. A week passed as the routine of cobbling and band practice slowly reset itself. O'Connor came over to me one day as I was practicing my horn.

"Danny, Jack Whelan is leaving soon and I want you to train to be the new drum major. What do ya think of that?" he asks, expecting me to be delighted.

"I . . . I'm not sure, sir. I like playing trombone." A drum major has a lot of responsibility.

"Oh, you'll still play the trombone, except at marching events. Then you'll lead the band as drum major." He's not asking any more.

So, Jack Whelan has been training me and James Egan to be drum majors in the Long Hall. Joe is a great musician and a really good lad. James is a joker who never stops clowning around. He plays trombone too. We're all friends, so we have a bit of a laugh marching up and down the hall, lifting our legs high like show horses.

But Itchy's chair remains empty. Devastated by his absence and the fact that he never confided in me, I let myself drift into an old familiar melancholy for a week or so. Then, little by little, I come to my senses. He couldn't have taken a chance on me or anyone else. The slightest hint of his plans and the brothers would have clamped down on him like a bear trap. Come to think of it, he did shake my hand pretty heartily before we both left for the holliers. Looking back, I like to think he gave me a clue in that last, long wink.

—⁓—

The album is finished at last. With the help of John Doyle—to my mind, the best Irish guitarist in the world—and Duncan Wickel, a teenage prodigy who plays fiddle, pipes, and whistle as good as anyone I've ever heard, I've mixed, mastered, and sent it to Guy Fletcher, my publisher/manager in England. He's organized a CD release concert in Union Chapel, a popular acoustic venue in South London. Guy was the first person, twenty-five years ago, to suggest I write about my orphanage experience. "No way, I'm not going back to that hellhole—even in a song," I'd said.

It had taken half a century, but now I'm ready to brave that journey. First through my songs, at my concert in England, and later, the real thing.

"While we're at it, let's pop across the pond and visit the old country," I say to Liz, as we're organizing our trip. In all our years together, mostly because of time constraints, I've never taken Liz to Ireland. She's ecstatic at first, then she goes very quiet.

"If you feel up to it, sweetie," she says, after a long moment, "we could go and see the orphanage."

"I've been dragged back in my dreams for decades." I grin ruefully.

"Maybe it's time to do it willingly—and wide awake."

CHAPTER 34

Paddy Kierans' trumpet is ripping through the dance hall like a hot knife through Monium. The sweat is pouring from his brow as he blasts his way through the Kenny Ball hit "Midnight In Moscow." The crowd is going wild and his band, the Boyne Valley Stompers, are wailing away behind him as if it was their last hurrah. His clarinetist is weaving in and out of Paddy's phrases and his trombone player is blaring away between them both. I'm about to crap myself with nerves—I'm on next.

The Artane Boys Band is in Ballybunion, County Kerry. Last night we played a sold out concert in this very dance hall. Earlier today, with me as drum major, we marched around the little seaside town with every man, woman, and child from miles around marching alongside us. It was a glorious autumn day and spirits were high. We did a short stint at a park, where I was featured playing a tune called "Seventy-Six Trombones."

Itchy and I both loved that piece. This was our first outing without him and I blew loud enough for him to hear it in England, or wherever he'd ended up. Afterward, I was packing my trombone away when someone tapped me on the shoulder.

"Are you trying to knock over a double-decker bus with the noise of that bloody trombone of yours?"

I looked up to see a grinning face behind the broad Dublin accent. He was a smartly dressed man in his mid-thirties.

"I do the best I can, sir," I said.

He laughed. "Don't call me 'sir,' for Jaysus' sakes. I'm not a bloody Christian Brother." He made a face. I liked this fellah.

"My name is Paddy Kierans. I'm a trumpet player." I'd heard his name before. We shook hands as I introduced myself. He lit a cigarette. "I'm the bandleader of the Boyne Valley Stompers from Dublin. We're playing at the dance hall tonight." Okay, that's who he is. I'd seen the posters there last night and all around town.

"Do you know 'The Saints Go Marching In'?" he asked.

My heart skipped a beat; I knew where this was going. "Yes, sir. I do."

"Great! How would you like to join me onstage tonight as a special guest?"

"I . . . I think that'd be grand, sir."

He put his hands on his hips. "Relax. I'm not going to bite your head off, man. For the love of God, can't you stop calling me 'sir'?" He laughed.

"N-no, sir. I can't help it at all, sir." I was more embarrassed than I should've been and I didn't know why. His easy manner, his casual speech, and his way of . . . his way of treating me like an equal was more unnerving than any Christian Brother's scowl. In front of this loose-limbed man of music, I felt very exposed. I could feel my face telling him, *I'm an orphanage boy, and I don't know how to be with ordinary people.*

It's something I'd been noticing more and more over the last two years. As the band stay-overs became more frequent, I'd become more sensitive in the presence of "outsiders," as we called them. At first, my heart would open to their warmth and then, in almost every instance, it would bang shut again at some minor slight or look of surprise at my Artane weirdness. We all have trouble woven into our cloth and sooner or later someone scratches it the wrong way and the fabric flies apart.

> *And when you look at me*
> *The tall strong lad is barely half the truth*
> *You see the cloth but not the weave*

The warp and weft of history
Look close and see
The twist within the tweed.

Poor Willie O'Reilly must have run into the same thing. He left Artane in the spring and was sent back again after two weeks. After they turn sixteen and leave, lads are often sent back—a deeply shameful thing for anyone to suffer—for various reasons, often violent ones. Working as a tailor, his trade learned in Artane, Willie apparently punched his boss, who was trying to teach him to use a thimble properly. As Willie shuffled around the playground, deeply depressed, I tried to sympathize with him. "Probably served the shitehawk right, eh?"

"No," said O'Reilly very softly. "He was a really kind old man. I just lost it."

We know how to connive and lie or punch our way out of trouble, but when faced with ordinary humanity, with love and tolerance—and certain kinds of humor—our facade falls apart and the raw orphan emotion takes over.

Feeling the fire course through my body as Paddy Kierans joked with me over me calling him "sir," I realized, not for the first time, that I was a ticking bomb.

But Paddy didn't seem to notice. Or pretended not to. "Don't worry, Danny. You can call me anything you bloody well want, as long as you don't call me before noon." He grinned again and punched me gently on the chest. "I'll see you tonight at the gig. Bring your horn and as many band friends as you want."

—⁂—

Now in the dance hall, I blow air down my trombone as I wait by the side of the stage to play. There's a bunch of Artane band lads giving me the thumbs up from front of stage: Fran Dunne, Eddie Cavanagh,

Michael Farley. The Stompers finish as Paddy brings his horn down with a flourish and I'm shaking like a jelly on a tractor.

Paddy grabs the microphone. "Ladies and gentlemen, I'd like to bring on a very special guest to join us in the next number. He's a fine young musician with a great future ahead of him. From the Artane Boys Band, I'd like you all to give a warm Kerry welcome to—Danny Ellis."

The crowd applauds. The lights onstage aren't red enough to hide my blush. Paddy tears into "The Saints" and I jump in with some wild riffs that have more fire than accuracy, more confidence than skill. But nobody cares, it seems. I'm in heaven. I throw myself into it. There's nothing else going on in the whole wide world except this mad abandon. I've never felt or heard anything like this before. Never even imagined it. The roars from the audience spur me on; louder and louder I play till my lips feel like they're exploding. I barely make it to the end, crescendoing on one last suicidal blare that'll finish my playing for a week. When we're finished, the crowd goes bananas. Paddy shouts for me to bow and I do it awkwardly, nearly losing my balance.

Afterward, in the dressing room, everyone is clapping me on the back, congratulating me. Everyone except Paddy, that is. He's changing his shirt, looking in the long mirror. I walk over to him, flushed with flattery, fishing for more. "Thanks, Paddy, for the chance to play with you. It was massive!"

"You're welcome, Danny," he says flatly, without looking at me.

My self-assurance evaporates. Confused, I ask, "How did I do? The crowd seemed to like it."

He stops and looks at me full on. "Flattery is like pouring water in your ear—it doesn't quench your thirst for more. The punters will like anything from a fifteen-year-old member of the Artane Boys Band, Danny. You won't get by on that for long."

"What do you mean?"

"In the real world of music you'll have to do better than blasting her head off till your lip bursts. You can't have it balls to the walls from start to finish."

I'm speechless.

He combs his hair and turns to me again. "There's such a thing as sensitivity and good taste. And there's a little thing you'll need to learn called restraint. It's the space between the notes that gives the music its meaning. Space!"

Somewhere behind the heat of anger and the cold of rejection I know he's right. I'm burning up inside and out with shame, knowing a minute ago I was strutting around like a peacock. For a second, I have to control the urge to tell him to fuck off, to explode and bring the whole thing down to something I understand very well—open warfare.

> *With each blessed breath we breathe*
> *We fight like hell so no one sees*
> *The anger and the need*
> *The wound too deep to bleed*
> *The twist within the tweed.*

Paddy's watching me keenly, waiting for my response. My whole life looms up in front of me. This is a choice that will affect me forever. My heart breaks as a big tear rolls down my red face.

"I'm sorry. I was just having some fun. I didn't mean to show off," I croak.

Paddy lets out a whoop and holds out his hand to shake mine. "That's the way to do it! Put it there, lad. You have what it takes to make a great trombone player and you can take correcting too. That's a rare combination these days."

I'm lost. Lost and found. In front of this fine musical force, I feel my shattered ego regroup and take heart as his straight talking fills me with the courage to keep trying, no matter what. I hear Columbus's words echo somewhere in my soul. *Let it all go, son. God will put you back together again.*

As I'm silently giving thanks to the grace that kept my mouth shut and allowed me to take the blow full on the chin without argument, Paddy is writing something on a piece of paper.

"Here's my phone number and address, Danny. When you get shut of the Christian Brothers, look me up. I'll find work for you. We'll knock you into shape and have you jamming along with the best of them in no time."

—◊—

I'm at my Uncle Matty's. He's been keeping the records I brought back from America and enjoys them too, especially Glen Miller. But right now, I'm playing Joey Dee and the Starliters' "Peppermint Twist"—too loudly. Matty is a patient man and has trouble expressing even the mildest disapproval, but I see the look on his face and turn down the record player—just a tad.

"You think that's loud!" I laugh. "You should hear Paddy Kierans' band, they'd blow the hair off your head." I've been telling my uncle about Paddy and his offer of work when I leave Artane and he approves. He's heard of Paddy, who's a wee bit famous in Dublin.

"That reminds me, Danny," he says as he turns the music down further. "You need to make sure that whoever you stay with when you leave Artane, they understand you'll be coming home very late sometimes, after the gigs."

Before I can stop myself, I blurt, "But I thought I was going to stay with you and Aunt Margaret." Hot tears rush to my eyes but I shake them off angrily.

Uncle Matty looks like he's seen a ghost. He stands up and throws his hands in the air, totally at a loss. Aunt Margaret, who's been knitting by the table, puts her work down and stares at Matty, who holds her eyes as if I wasn't in the room. They look at each other with the longest, saddest stare I've ever seen. I don't even exist.

Jesus! It's like someone kicked me in the stomach. I don't know why I never caught on before. All these years I took it for granted. Never, not even for a second, did I ever doubt I would stay with them after Artane. What a stupid fool I've been! They've never even invited me out for summer holidays, so where on earth did I get that crazy idea?

Matty coughs and looks away from Margaret. With the intensity of their gaze broken, they too look broken now, and don't know what to do with their eyes. I almost feel sorry for them, but I grit my teeth and fight the feeling off. Margaret looks like she's about to cry for a second, then she too pulls back control with a tight little shake of her head. "I'm sorry, Danny. I really am," she whispers.

"Danny, we've no room here," my mother's brother says lamely. "And we can't be held responsible for you. You're a good lad, but you're . . . well, you're wild as winter and we're getting old now. We don't . . . we don't . . . " He turns to Aunt Margaret for help.

"We don't have any money, Danny," Margaret says and immediately recognizes how stupid that sounds. But she continues stubbornly, "We barely make ends meet as it is."

"But I'll have a cobbler's job and I'll be in Paddy Kierans' band too. I'll have plenty of money." Christ! I wish I hadn't said that. They've obviously made up their minds.

"It's not just . . . there's a lot of reasons, Danny," Matty says.

I'm torn between anger and hurt. For the first time ever with them, anger wins.

"Bollox! Why didn't you say so before?" I shout. "Why did you let me believe I could move in?" I've never raised my voice to them. I don't care. I really don't care. But I can feel Black Daniel back off as tears well up. I look at the man whose gentle kindness has buoyed the last eight years of my life, whose stony silences confused them. "And why did you let me believe Ma went into hospital with TB? For years . . . why didn't you tell me? Why?"

Silence.

"I'm going back to the school." It's only three o'clock in the afternoon. I'm not supposed to be back in Artane till six.

I grab my coat from behind the door and open it too hard, knocking a picture off the wall.

Matty picks it up as Margaret comes forward with her purse. She hands me two crisp pound notes. The best part of a week's wages for Matty.

"We've saved up something to help you get started. We want you to put this toward your new trombone."

—⁓—

Liz and I are in a hotel in London. The concert is tomorrow. It promises to be a great night. Rehearsals have been going well, but I'm so tired. I really must sleep tonight. Liz, as usual, is fast asleep before me. In waves of anticipation and trepidation about the concert, I drift off in a dream.

It's the Artane dormitory building. I try to turn around, but I'm being dragged forward by an invisible force. I'm pulled through the doors to where the iron stairs should be, but they're not there. I'm inside a huge castle now, with chandeliers and statues and mirrors everywhere. In front of me there's a huge winding staircase with marble steps and ornate banisters, and there he is—the Gas Man! I knew it! As usual, I could feel him long before I saw him. And as usual, he's standing at the top of the staircase, grinning that crazy grin of his. For some reason, I'm not as scared as I usually am. Then, while keeping his eyes riveted on me, he climbs on to the banisters and folds his arms very slowly across his chest. Now I'm scared; that deliberate folding of his arms while gazing at me intently chills me to my soul—a fear like I've never felt, a dread so cold that hope itself freezes in the conviction that nothing good exists anywhere in this universe. His bulging eyes light up with a sinister inner glow and slowly he starts to slide down the banisters toward me. *Jesus! He's coming to get me!* He picks up speed, his mouth opens, and, Mother of God, he starts to laugh. A laugh that starts slow and low, and as he glides faster toward me, the cackles get quicker and higher. I try to move but my feet have sunk ankle-deep into the marble floor. If I live to be a hundred, I'll never forget the horror of that ghastly grin coming toward me, faster and faster. I brace myself for impact, thinking he means to devour me. But instead, he shoots off the end of the banister and out of the castle doors into the starry night, laughing like a child on a playground. Higher and higher he goes, up into the night sky, to melt into the ghostly luminescence of the Milky Way— which is singing!

I wake up in a cold sweat but I'm not scared any more. Suddenly, I know . . . .

I know why the Gas Man grins.

That grin—I felt it myself. It tried to tell me something, that night nearly fifty years ago. After working late in the kitchen, I heard the stars singing to me. As I lay on the cold of the churchyard concrete, hypnotized by the blazing starlight, my own gaze opened into a spreading smile that threatened to annihilate my body as it sucked me into its own light. *I am light! My gaze is light. All there is is light.*

But I had some choice in my gazing. The Gas Man didn't.

Up until that moment, he could make little plans or schemes. At every crossroad, he could try—however feebly—to influence the course of events for his own benefit. But as the life left his body, as he went screaming into eternity, no conniving, no finagling, no shenanigans, excuses, or wheeling and dealing could sway that final covenant with the infinite. He took the only option available to him: he welcomed it. He let it take him like a child on a slide. This wasn't a closing down of a life force. This was an opening up to it.

The Gas Man's grin had been trying to tell me for five decades, *Let it go, ya eejit! There's nothing to be afraid of. The very worst thing that can happen to you is this thing called Death, and watch me ride it like a bronco.*

CHAPTER 35

Yeah, but Black Daniel's riding outta here! Today is my birthday. The first one I'll celebrate in eight years. I'm sixteen! At last, I'm leaving Artane forever. I polish up my trombone and pack it away for the last time. It's already been assigned to some upcoming lad eager to get his hands on it.

It's been a whirlwind couple of months. O'Connor, ever in charge of things, sent me downtown to Jerry Rafferty's musical instrument shop; he'd found me a trombone within my budget. His shrewd eyes narrowing, O'Connor had cautioned, "Whatever you do, Ellis, don't give Rafferty all the money. At most, give him a fiver deposit. That'll hold it for you till you collect it later when you leave."

The trombone couldn't hold a candle to my trusty old Boosey & Hawkes. But it would do till I could afford better, and anyway, as O'Connor—and Jerry Rafferty—had said, "It's a poor workman that blames his tool." That tool will cost me thirty quid—almost every penny I've saved from Da's money and my band outings. Still, music is more important than food or clothes, and I can always nick some grub here and there if necessary. On various trips downtown, I'd learned to wait outside the Rainbow Café in O'Connell Street till folks had paid their bills and left. I'd rush to the leftover fish and chips on their plates and gobble that up before the waitress chased me off. *So I won't die of hunger*, I thought to myself as I paid Rafferty a five-pound deposit.

Then for weeks, O'Connor, mad with excitement over John Fitzgerald Kennedy's upcoming visit—as was the whole of Ireland—drove us all crazy with long speeches about the president of America: a Catholic, an Irishman, a war hero, and a blah-blah-blah-blah-blah. I, for one, distracted and excited about leaving Artane soon, and knowing nothing whatever of the man, paid little heed. As JFK's helicopter landed on the grass near his ancestral home in Dunganstown, County Wexford, all I could think was, *This is going to be my final blast on this old trombone that has taken me so far.* Then that handsome man started to speak and his words, filled with strains of hope and freedom, touched me like none before. It seemed he'd come all the way across the Atlantic Ocean to wish me well in my new life. His poise, his smiling eyes, his calm voice, held all the hope, sanity, and goodness I'd ever dreamed America would hold for me. The "Stars and Stripes" never sounded so grand as we played our hearts out for the man who somehow represented everything that's noble and decent about an insane world. I felt the same bittersweet emptiness I'd always felt on the bus back to Artane, after having my heart touched by someone outside of it.

Back in the orphanage, the brothers soon found me a cobbling job in Donnybrook and, at the last minute, because of Uncle Matty's refusal to take me in, a tiny, shared room in a terraced house near Arran Quay, by the Liffey. I was ready to go.

On my last night I said goodbye to the trombone section, Smasher and James Egan, and to my few remaining band friends. So many of the old sods had left in the past couple of years: Michael Farley, Fran Dunne, Andy McBride.

O'Connor, tough as ever, shook my hand very firmly. "You'll have a good life, Danny. You've got what it takes." Then, without a shred of irony, he added, "And don't go giving the school a bad name, ya hear?"

Now, dressed in my new flannel trousers I had the tailors make for me, I cross the playground with my tiny suitcase. I make my way to the admin office where, nearly eight years ago, Ma, her tiny shoes covered in cow dung, said goodbye for the last time. I've been in here many times over the years, but it hasn't changed a bit: still that same stuffy smell, the same tiled floor, and the same chairs Ma and that man sat in. This room has come to represent everything that is dreadful about Artane to me—more than the classrooms or the dorms or even the boot rooms. For the last time, I shake off the old feeling of suffocation I always get when I come here.

Martin Roe, the school clerk, greets me with a grin. He used to be in Artane himself, playing clarinet in the band. I've always marveled at how anyone would willingly choose to come back to this place. Wild horses!

"Okay, young Danny Ellis. Happy birthday to ya, lad. Let's get your papers sorted out and you can be on your way. Glad to see the back of us, eh?"

His good-natured grin disappears the moment he opens a huge, black ledger book. What is it about big ledger books that changes people who open them? This book is legendary among the lads. God's Own Diary. It contains the names of everyone in Artane, along with their parents and addresses.

"Let's see here. Now what was your mother's maiden name?"

"Marr. Frances Mary Marr." I'm using the Americanization of Maher that my grandparents had used. Always trying to be different, I throw it out glibly.

Roe makes a face. "Marr? Never heard of it. How do you spell that?"

"M-A-H-E-R," says I.

"Get away with ya!" he chafes. "That's not pronounced *Marr* at all."

"It is in America," I say cockily.

"Well, yer not in America now, me bucko. Your mother's maiden name is *Maher*—just like the twin brothers in the band, Michael and Timothy Maher."

Even before I know why, my mouth goes suddenly and totally dry. The coldest feeling creeps over me as the dawning realization catches up with my gut reaction. Staring at Roe in disbelief, I shout, "Jesus Christ! That's me brothers! They're alive! The Two Twins . . . Mikey and Timmy." The mention of my mother and the twins in the one mouthful did it!

"What in God's name are ya on about?" Roe is impatient.

"It's me brothers. They went away when I was six. I wasn't even sure if they were alive or dead." I'm dancing around with my hands on my head. "Jesus, Mary, and Joseph, they've been in the band with me for two years and I didn't know!" How could I have missed it?

"Stop cursing or I'll banjax ya!" Roe shouts. "Calm down, for God's sake, man. We'll see soon enough who the mother of the twins is." He goes rifling through that big black book. "Michael and Timothy Maher. . . . Now let's see here . . . here we go . . . Jesus Christ!" He covers his mouth with his hand.

"Frances Maher, 9 Green Street, Dublin City. Father unknown," he reads from the book.

The words are barely out of his mouth before I turn and hare it out of the office door. Down the steps, through the gate, across the churchyard, through the shelter, around by the handball alleys, down to the drinking fountains, up to the middle lamp. The lads, the screaming hundreds, surge about me like angry tides and it dawns on me: this is my last run around the playground. I remember my very first with my new friend, Rasher. I find my feet trying to make the horsey galloping sound: *kiddycup, kiddy-cup.* But I've been issued with ordinary shoes and they don't have the metal studs and heels. They make no sound. For a second it's almost a disappointment. I shake the feeling off. The Two Twins? Where are they?

Stop! Just look around carefully. Breathe! Take yer time.

Shielding my eyes from the July sun, I slowly move my head to search the playground. The angry sea of tweed takes on familiar shapes: the ball games, hurling, handball, and football. The games of toss the penny, marbles, and jack-stones. The wrestling. The games of chase, relieveee-aye-o, and cowboys. The lads playing hoop with the bicycle and car tires. The card games. The real fights and the desperate make ups. The playground symphony.

I'm suddenly calmer. That tattered tapestry, woven through every day of the last eight years, has become the warp and weft of my being. I've wrapped its protective cloak around me till I thought it *was* me. In that last long look around the playground, I feel my soul let it go forever. No regrets. No nostalgia. Nothing.

In my reverie, I've stopped looking for the Two Twins.

Then I see them. They're over by the shelter wall, kicking a cloth ball, together as always. My feet are frozen to the concrete playground. Fascinated, I watch them for a full five minutes.

I can't equate these tortured lads with the infants I loved and laughed with.

I can't believe I never caught on as I helped teach them to learn the music they so hated.

I can't feel what I think I should be feeling for my brothers.

But I can see them in that cot in Green Street; I'm mashing the cabbage into the spuds so they won't taste it. They hate cabbage. I hear Ma calling from the scullery, "Danny, I don't want you talking to anyone on the street anymore. They're all a bunch of gossips and they can get lost, the lot of them."

—⁂—

This concert is taking more out of me than I ever could have imagined: singing the songs, reliving the intimate details of my family and the orphanage in front of hundreds of people has left me totally drained. But I gather myself as we near the end, the story itself filling me with strength. The audience is on the edge of their seats as Duncan Wickel's fiddle plays me into the final strains of the final song. If I bend slightly beneath the lights, I can see half a dozen old friends from Artane in the audience as I sing:

I remember the storm when the twins were born
Cos my da had been gone for a year
He'd set sail for America's shore
Saving up to bring us there
But the birth of the boys tore the family apart
In a wind of scattering shame
But I was free from that irony
On the day I left Artane.

CHAPTER 36

Even without the heavy boots, my feet feel like lead as I walk over to the twins. What am I going to say? If I knew how I felt it might be easier. They frown when they see me. In two years, I've never seen either of them crack a smile.

"I'm your brother. You're the Two Twins," I blurt.

Michael looks up, totally nonplussed. Timothy ignores me, rolling the ball beneath his foot. He kicks it to Michael. Was I expecting them to feel something I'm not?

"You lads and I . . . we . . . we have the same mother, Frances Maher. We lived together for a while before you were sent away. To the nuns, I suppose. You were very small. I was six."

"You're my brother?" Michael asks casually.

"Well, half-brother, I suppose. I just found out at the office. In the book."

"What's a *half*-brother?" asks Timothy, making a face.

"Different fathers," says Michael. He kicks the ball to Timothy, who turns around, dribbling it.

"You know we're not allowed to play soccer, Timothy," Michael chides.

"Oh, it's okay. Just as long as we don't head the ball." Timothy continues dribbling the ball. Michael runs after him, stealing the ball with an expert tackle. I step after them to keep in earshot. They stop and look up at me, standing shoulder to shoulder. Their eyes hold no questions, no surprise, not even vague curiosity; it's as if Artane has stripped them of every shred of emotion, leaving nothing but distrust and a cold distance that none of us cares to cross. Totally at a loss, I turn around and look at the other boys running around on the playground. No inspiration there as lads pull at one another roughly. I scratch my head and realize the only thing I have to offer is in my right-hand trouser pocket. My hand reaches down to get it.

I turn around to face my brothers' blank stares. "Hey lads, I want you to have this." I hand Michael the large coin.

"Wow! It's a half-crown. Look, Timothy, it's a half-dollar." It's almost a smile.

Timothy shrugs. I wink. Michael winks. I shrug. Michael shrugs.

"Look, fellahs, I have to catch a bus. I'm to start cobbling in my new job at one o'clock." I hold out my hand. Michael shakes it. Timothy too.

"So long, lads."

"See ya," Michael says. Timothy shrugs.

I'm about to walk away when Timothy speaks up. "Where is your . . . I mean our mother now? Is she still alive?"

"I don't know."

The Two Twins look at each other.

"She disappeared when she dumped . . . when she put me in here. I never saw her again." I did for ten minutes. But that's . . . that's my story.

Timothy shrugs again, raising his shoulders almost up to his ears. Michael gives him a shove and they're wrestling now.

"Goodbye, lads."

No answer. They're back in their own world, belonging to each other. Alone now, I watch them move away in play, afraid and envious of the bond I'll never share. Then a tighter voice whispers, *a bond I don't need.*

With long, purposeful strides, I walk between the playing lads back to the office. Atop the stone steps to the office, I look back. The

Two Twins are examining my half-crown. I don't blame them. I'd be doing the same myself.

—⁂—

I walk down the avenue for the last time. My feelings are in turmoil. I'm free to do as I please. With the money for my trombone in my pocket, with Paddy Kierans' phone number chiseled inside my head, I know exactly what that'll be. But the Two Twins—it's too, too sad. *But I'm not sad. They don't need me and I don't need them.* Too many thoughts. I just don't know where to put it all. *Put it away. Put it all away.* I'm turning my back on my brothers. All my brothers. *But I can't help them.* No more than Rasher or Itchy or Tommy Bonner or a half-dozen other friends could help me as, one by one, they left me behind on the playground. *Stop thinking. Look at the sky. Go forward.* I feel it all fall away as I raise my shoulders and walk faster. The noise of the lads playing from behind me seems to say, *Go on, Dano. Step it out now, lad. Don't look back. Keep her going. You'll never walk alone.* Maybe that old Broadway song was right after all.

> *800 voices echo 'cross the grey playground*
> *Shouts of fights and God knows what*
> *I still can hear that sound*
> *But the memories now are bitter sweet*
> *I've dropped that heavy load*
> *And 800 voices cheer me on*
> *As I'm walking down the road.*

—⁂—

With the London concert behind us, we fly to Ireland. So many places I want to show Liz: Dingle, Glendalough, the Burren. We'll go to Artane School later this afternoon, but first I want to walk with her down by the River Liffey to Green Street, were I was born.

She takes my hand as we cross the Ha'penny Bridge to Lower Ormond Quay. Her hands are always warmer than mine, even in this chill. Look! There's that iron ladder where, half a century ago, I climbed down to fetch the *Steve Canyon* comic, nearly drowning. The Liffey man, God bless ya! Whatever your intentions were, I owe you my life. Looking over the wall at the river below, the swirling eddies seem to hold more than water. Memories have tides. Do tides have memories? Anna Liffey, you must.

Across the river on Essex Quay, a thick smoke, heavy and gray, rises from a grayer building. It seems loath to join the waiting sky and wraps itself around the brickwork of the chimney in languid reluctance. When I left Dublin in 1973, I vowed to put it all behind me. Forget the past, rise above it. If only it were that simple. We walk across the cobblestones of Smithfield Market. It's closed. Empty and quiet. But I can hear the shouts of the vendors and smell the vegetables and fruit. A softer voice echoes through the clamor: *A nice big head of cabbage first, son, and if they don't see ya, back later for a few spuds.*

—⁂—

As I walk down the long avenue, the familiar din of the lads on the playground behind me gradually merges into the traffic noise in front: my old life fading into the new. I've reached the gate. I walk through.

I'm out!

Not some sneaky escape, not some short visit to my uncle, not some Sunday walk with hundreds of lads in front and behind me. No! I'm free! Strangely, frighteningly free.

Bury that right now!

At the bus stop, four Donnycarney lads are clowning around. I'm standing back a bit, shyly, waiting for the bus. They start singing a Beatles song I've been hearing on Da's radio, "Love Me Do."

One of them, a fair-haired lad with freckles, turns to me and winks, singing almost into my face. *Come on, man, let's have ya!* My face goes red. His friends are clicking their fingers and dancing around me now in the high spirits of the July morning. I love this song, but I'm embarrassed. I wish the ground would open and swallow me whole. I stick my hands deep down in my pockets; *ah, there's the money for my trombone.* Christ, if only I had my horn with me now, I'd give these buckos a run for their money. The lads continue singing. The noise they're making is glorious. It starts to swell up inside me, like water in a balloon. The lads are almost at the harmonica solo . . . . I can't hold it back any more. The balloon bursts. Suddenly I let out a yelp and tear unbridled into that great riff.

Na-Na-Na
Na-Na Na-Na.

The look of surprise on the lads' faces lasts but a second and we're all at it now, clapping our hands.

Na-Na-Na
Na-Na Na-Na.

The song finishes as one by one we drop out.

"Massive! Brutal! Great stuff!" The boys are giving me the thumbs up and the red in my face is all over my body. We all shuffle about now, embarrassed in the sudden silence.

I look up. It's not going to rain, is it? No matter, here comes the bus.

The 42a bus creaks its way up the narrow—my goodness, how narrow—Malahide Road. Liz and I are seated upstairs in the front seat, looking out of the large window. I always sit upstairs on the front seat. Other buses look certain to crash into us, only to turn or stop at the last minute, inches from collision. My body braces itself. I'm aware that though the buses never hit us, I still carry the tension of the imagined impacts for too long. An old story.

The zigzag motion of the bus is exaggerated on the upper deck and I'm drifting off. There's an old familiar calm seeping up through the peaceful motion. I lay my head on Liz's shoulder and allow the deep tiredness of the last—well, let's not get carried away here— the last few weeks to take over. As my eyelids half close, thoughts stream by behind them as fast as the traffic, houses, and trees pass in front of them. Drifting in and out of the half world; asleep and awake, inner and outer, body and soul, past and present, all melt into one.

There he is now at the gate. Too thin, too tall, too tense, and, considering what lies ahead, far too cocky. He doesn't yet know that he needn't pretend to know everything. He doesn't yet know that he doesn't have to grab for everything, including his every breath. But he will. I'll help him.

He hunches his shoulders, trying to blend in with the shorter Donnycarney lads. They've just finished the last strains of the Beatles song.

The lads are clambering aboard the bus.

"Are ya coming or going or what?" one shouts to him.

But he's seen. He shakes his head. "No."

The bus drives off.

I walk over to him. "Well, if it isn't Black Daniel himself."

He doesn't miss a beat. "What took ya so long?"

"It's a long story. I'll tell you all about it on the way home."

"Wait a minute. Aren't you forgetting somebody?" He jerks his thumb over his shoulder.

Peeking through Artane's big iron gate, an eight-year-old boy is still waiting for his mother.

The noise of the Malahide Road traffic purrs away behind us as we walk over to the child. I bend down on one knee.

"Now, there's the best little man in the whole wide world," I say.

"Who the bloody hell are you?" he asks defiantly.

I look up at the sixteen-year-old. I look down at the boy.

"Well, you might say I'm the big man of the house."

EPILOGUE

As I walked free through that big iron gate for the last time, there wasn't a single shred of doubt or fear anywhere in my being. Like the Fool in the Tarot, with everything he owns crammed into a tiny backpack, I blundered happily into my life, oblivious of the pitfalls that surrounded me on all sides. As if watched over by some protective benevolence, I felt exhilarated, safe, and free. I knew only one thing for sure: I knew that no matter what, my music would provide for me.

What I didn't know was that I'd be battered for years by my own social ineptitude as I learned—very painfully—that the survival skills I'd picked up, the cheating, the lying, the lack of respect for authority, so effective and necessary on the Artane playground, wouldn't be tolerated on the "outside." What I didn't know was that deep down, I'd subconsciously resolved to have nothing whatever to do with my family. Perhaps I intuited that whatever fragile shreds of independence I'd garnered wouldn't survive the emotional storms that family could evoke. *I've learned all I need to know about rejection, thank you very much.* Ironically, it was the loving persistence of my sisters that would finally melt my heart—and Black Daniel's. We became lifelong friends, often marveling at the winds that blew us apart and back together again. We marvel also at the gift of gratitude we all share for the strength we've been forced to find. Not surprisingly, we all exhibit the same wry humor of those who've learned to make the best of things. We treasure what little time we can spend together—usually a once-a-year celebration, which is always full of the kind of laughter and inside jokes that can only spring from deep, shared pain—and triumph.

We never saw or heard from Ma again. As far as I can ascertain, neither did anyone else in her family. Old letters from her have surfaced, revealing her to be a sad woman with a very tenuous grip on reality. If once or twice I allowed a vague resentment toward her, it has long since evaporated in the compassion and understanding I've been forced to find for myself and others. Had her own family been present during her pregnancy with the twins, or had the prevailing culture been more enlightened, things might have gone very differently. Who knows? Over the years, I have found solace in the notion that those who cause us the most pain have come for that express reason. They teach us the hard lessons that can't be learnt any other way. In my experience, the shattering grace that tears us from loved ones can also reveal a timeless unity that remains unbroken. My deepest wish has always been that Ma started a new life in England and found happiness.

I met my father again when I visited New York with an Irish show band in 1969. At the time, he was still working for the Lackawanna Railroad in New Jersey. He never got over my mother: he carried her loss in his eyes and manner, allowing the sadness to saturate his life like the drink that couldn't drown it. Though ravaged by resentment and betrayal, he was a sweet, gentle man. But there was room only for sorrow in his heart, not for family. Sadly, the years apart—not to mention the ocean that separated us—was too great a void to cross and we had little to say to each other. There seemed no bridge between me, the wild teenager, full of the shallow excitement of life in a band, and the sad, broken stranger who couldn't bring himself to give or accept love. Our letters, which had always been extremely sporadic, finally stopped all together and we lost touch. He never returned to Ireland. He died in 2001. Although as an adult I couldn't reach him, I've always carried that last memory of him as he left Green Street for America, full of life and adventure. I can see and hear him now, his handsome face grinning as he comes smartly to attention and tips his hand to his hat in salute with a cheeky *See ya later, kiddo!*

With the help of trumpeter Paddy Kierans, within months of leaving Artane, I was making a good living on the richly eclectic Irish show-band circuit. From Dixieland to pop, from country music to reggae, I played in every dance hall in every little town in Ireland for ten years. I studied music and became a sought-out arranger, head-hunted from one band to another till eventually I was one of the best paid sidemen in Ireland. A dozen or so of Ireland's major acts recorded my songs, some of them reaching the charts.

Finally, in 1973, feeling a deep need to find what lay beneath the layers I'd wrapped around myself like Russian matryoshka dolls, I left my job as a bandleader in one of Ireland's top bands to pursue a mildly Bohemian lifestyle of meditation, musical experimentation, and volunteer work. I embarked upon a lifelong quest for healing, which has resulted in my *800 Voices* CD, concerts, and this book.

The last thing I ever wanted to do was return to Artane, even for a visit, so unfortunately I lost contact with the Two Twins. Although I never would have admitted it at the time, the line from my song, *"The birth of the boys tore the family apart,"* might have had some resonance. By the time I felt emotionally strong enough to make contact with them, the twins had disappeared. It wasn't until 2005 that I heard they had joined the Irish Army Band. Despite their having spent years rebelling against it, music, it seems, served them well too. I asked an old musician friend, who had contacts in the Army Band, if he would do some research for me and he found my brother Michael in Cork City. Given that I hadn't made any effort to contact him or Timothy in forty years, Michael was, understandably, a little cautious at first. But happily we've become friends at last, and I've learnt something of their story. The Two Twins had spent their whole lives moving from one institution to another: seven years with the nuns, eight in Artane, and forty years in the Army Band. They retired recently. Michael and I met in Ireland in 2010. We stay in touch by phone and email. I have yet to meet up with Timothy, but it is my hope that before too long I will meet him too.

For many years, as I fought to forge a new identity in society, I was somewhat less than enthusiastic about initiating any contact with old Artane friends. Then as music, and the love and kindness I received from others, rebuilt my soul, I slowly allowed some pangs of nostalgia to percolate to the surface. When the Internet emerged, with email and search engines, I gingerly began my hunt for the ragged rascals who ran around the Artane playground with me, not absolutely sure I wanted to find them. But I could find no sign of them anywhere online. It wasn't until April 2008 that the first tiny shoots of my past reached up to greet me. The material for my *800 Voices* CD had burst forth like a tsunami and I'd recorded it and put it up on my website. Then one morning I opened an email that said, in effect: "I wonder if you can help me, because I believe the Tommy Bonner you are singing about could well be my father. I was thinking about my dad and his early life, which he has never spoken of, and I put his name into Google. In minutes I was listening to you sing about Tommy Bonner. Fantastic shock! I would dearly like to know if he is the boy in your beautiful song."

Amazingly, it seems Tommy's family learnt more about his life in Artane from my song than he'd ever shared with them. Tommy phoned me the next day, flabbergasted by the lyrics and the startling revelation that, unknown to him, five decades ago his voice had been a weekly source of strength and inspiration to the boys of Artane. A modest lad, he was completely oblivious to the uplifting effect he'd had on us all. We've since become good friends and, goodness, what a blessing it's been for me to be able to give something back to him in that simple song. In the middle of a radio interview, on my trip to Ireland, the interviewer suddenly said excitedly, "Danny, we've just now managed to get Tommy Bonner on the phone line. How would you feel about singing that song for him in person?" Of course, I felt honored to sing for my old schoolmate, who'd inspired my search to find my own voice. He and almost his entire family were in the audience at my Union Chapel concert in London, as were a dozen or so old Artane sods, including my band pals Itchy Reynolds and Fran Dunne.

There's an amazing, almost time-warping magic to the fact that I couldn't find my Artane friends on the web till I unwittingly, with my songs, gave them an Internet presence. Then, one by one, they started to find me with their own online searches. In another mind-numbing burst of serendipity, my sister Katie made friends with a lady in a New Jersey healthfood store who turned out to have been in the same orphanage as her and Patricia, albeit much earlier. Months into their friendship, this lady revealed to Katie that she had a brother who had been in the Artane Boys Band. Katie rang me that night, saying, "Did you know a trombone player in Artane called Itchy Reynolds?" I called Itchy that night and we laughed together for the first time in nearly half a century. To this day, the reunion continues as more and more lads find my music online and contact me through email. "Hey, remember me? I'm the one who . . . ." Sadly, there's still no word of Rasher, but I keep searching.

Although in this book I've tried to convey something of the hardship, the neglect, and the wall-to-wall fear and dread endured by the lads of Artane Industrial School, I'm not sure to what extent I've succeeded. This is partly because I was in the band and we had a much easier time than the others. But it's also partly because I wanted to capture some of the fun and camaraderie, the mischief and astounding courage of the lads. The lengths we went to to recapture some grain of self-respect from the brothers, the constant conniving to stay one step ahead of them—and yes, our little daily triumphs—all had as big a part to play in this story as the brutality and abuse. I'm very proud of the lads I ran with; their heroism and resilience deserves as much—if not more—documenting as the criminal insanity of that institution. I believe, in the long run, innocence prevails over corruption, whatever form it takes, and that has been the main focus of this book. If readers wish to pursue a more detailed account of the everyday life of an Artane boy, I direct their attention to the Ryan Report, which paints a harrowingly accurate picture of Artane and other industrial schools.

After my Union Chapel concert in London, I took Liz up the Malahide Road to see Artane School. With the intimacy we've shared through twenty-one years of marriage, I knew she would be every bit as deeply impacted by Artane as I. But seeing the look on her face as I led her across the playground, past the chapel to the refectory, and finally up the iron stairs to the old dorms, it was as if, through her eyes, I was seeing Artane for the first time. An old hardness within me seemed to melt away in the waves of her compassion and I felt myself gather up the last shreds of my boy heart that still clung to those bleak, gray buildings. As her tears fell on the playground, I felt them reach deep down through the concrete to the century of hurt below and I knew I'd never need to return to this place again. In that moment I felt it all fall away from me forever: the loss, the loneliness, the desolation. I was finally free.

AUTHOR'S NOTE

Although this book is a personal, intimate account of my own childhood and not an attempt at history, I thought it might be helpful to give a brief overview of Artane School and its origins. For a more detailed account, visit www.childabusecommission.com/rpt/, the website for The Ryan Report, a study commissioned by the Irish government of abuse in Catholic institutions. This exhaustive and controversial report took nine years to complete, because of lack of cooperation from the religious Orders involved. Despite the damning evidence revealed by the Commission, much anger and frustration remains among institutionalized survivors as the report doesn't name any of the abusers and very few have been prosecuted. Because I wanted the story to unfold with the innocence of a child's perspective, as it happened to me personally, I was careful not to permit any post-Ryan Report "hindsight wisdom" to color it.

Artane Industrial School, established by the Irish Christian Brothers, opened on July 28, 1870, for the express purpose of caring for orphaned, neglected, and abandoned Catholic boys. The initial 56 acres grew to 350 by the 1940s, and by the beginning of the twentieth century, the three original lads had expanded to 825. By the time of its closure in 1969, approximately 15,500 boys had been "cared" for there.

Artane began as a grand and noble conception, and eventually devolved into one of the most abusive and brutal institutions in Ireland. The original mission—to care for poor and oppressed children—was soon compromised by the enormity of the task and the cold, self-serving pragmatism of the Congregation of the

Christian Brothers. With the collusion of Church and State, children could be sent by the courts to Artane and other similar institutions for all manner of petty offences: begging, nonattendance at school, thieving, and such. These institutions, of which Artane was the largest, were funded on a per capita basis; this seemed to encourage the Catholic Orders who ran them to "recruit" and cram in as many children as they could get away with. Hard-pressed parents, many living in utter poverty and unable to feed themselves, were encouraged to abandon their children to Artane and dozens of other institutions. Parents were convinced that their children would be better off with these "men of God," receiving, at the very least, the food and shelter they were unable to provide. (In my own and many other cases, there might have been some truth in that assertion, but the moral turpitude that this expedience encouraged ensured that parents turned a blind eye to reports of abuse. It's extraordinary to think how different things might have been had the funding been given directly to these destitute families rather than to the Catholic Orders.) These "homes" were characterized first by terror, then hunger, neglect, poor education, and cold, miserable conditions, and finally, emotional, physical, and sexual abuse. Artane became the most feared of all industrial schools and was proudly proclaimed by the Christian Brothers to be the most successful.

The impressive main building of Artane comprised five huge dormitories—each with up to 175 beds—a cinema, and the magnificent 325-feet Long Hall, which ran the entire length of the building. To one side of the Long Hall were various large rooms: a concert hall, a knitting room, band rooms, and some classrooms. Across the acre of concrete playground, to the northwest of the main building, were eleven more classrooms, fifty-two shower cubicles, and the laundry. Close by was the kitchen and the adjoining refectory, which could seat all 825 lads at once, as could the nearby chapel. Opposite the chapel was the brothers' kitchen and quarters, and the administration office. A huge outdoor shelter, with a tin roof and no walls, adjoined the playground. Come hail, rain, or snow, the boys played under this windy structure unless the weather was absolutely unbearable; then they were crammed like cattle in a long, narrow hall behind the eleven classrooms. To the north of the playground were the farms and the infirmary. To the west, behind the handball alleys, were the football and playing fields, where we ran in the summer. To the south were the trade shops, where boys over fourteen— traders—learned carpentry, tailoring, weaving, shoemaking, baking, tin-smithing, and painting. Self-sufficiency was a tenet of the industrial schools and Artane supplied much of its own food from the farm and poultry farm. Most of our rough-and-ready clothes and boots were made at the weavers, tailors, and shoemakers. The poor quality and shoddy workmanship (much like the general education offered by the brothers) was a testament to the lack of proper training given to the boys. Most lads, whatever their age, were put to work at chores of one kind or another. Some, like farmers, bakers, and traders who worked in the kitchen, spent most of their waking hours at their trades.

There were approximately twenty-five brothers in Artane, some of whom were too old or infirm to take an active part in the running of the school. Consequently, a small number of inexperienced and untrained brothers—who had received no instruction in childcare— were required to work for up to fourteen hours a day, seven days a week. The brothers, almost to a man, were tired and overworked. Some were deeply devout and some were genuinely driven by a desire to serve humanity, but many of them—including Brother O'Connor, the band director—had been pressganged into the Order by their parents. Obliged by their vows of obedience to carry out the instructions of their superiors without question, many brothers became disillusioned, spiteful, and criminally abusive, taking their frustrations out on the very children they'd sworn to protect and care for. Decades of complaints and litanies of abuse were ignored and suppressed by the Christian Brothers, the Church, and the State.

The Artane Boys Band was founded shortly after the school was established in 1872. In 1962, the school chaplain, Father Henry Moore, said in a report commissioned by then Archbishop of Dublin, Dr. J. C. McQuaid, "The band is the only worthwhile achievement of the school." Although Artane closed as an orphanage and industrial school in 1969, the band somehow remained intact, as it had begun recruiting members from outside Artane some time earlier. The old refectory was turned into a new band room and membership was expanded to include girls as well as boys. Because of this, the name was changed from the Artane Boys Band to the Artane Band. The band continues to play at major football matches and State occasions and to be loved by the people of Ireland. The band is still going strong to this day, a diamond forged in the fires of hardship and misfortune. When all else crumbles, music, like innocence itself, endures.

ACKNOWLEDGMENTS

This book sprung out of the songs on my CD, *800 Voices: My Life in an Irish Orphanage.*

It was during a David Wilcox concert that it first occurred to me that I was not being entirely honest in my own songwriting. The startlingly straightforward candor with which he sang of a contentious exchange with his father stopped me in my tracks. *My God,* I thought, *is it really okay to write of such things?* Still, it would be another five years before the child within me finally found a way to squeeze past my defenses. When that happened, it was my wife, Liz, who supplied the strength and encouragement for me to allow the process that David's song had started. I gingerly ran every line of every song past her, never sure that I should be entering those waters at all. The journey was to take us both through a series of changes that brought us closer than I ever could have thought possible. This book could not have been written without her loving support.

The following account of the wonderful chain of events that resulted in the publication of this book may serve to thank some of those involved in the process. It was David Wilcox's song "A Chain of Anger" that started it all, though at the time we didn't know each other personally. When I finished my album, *800 Voices,* I gave copies to some friends, including Asheville singer/songwriter Annie Lalley. Annie gave the CD to David Wilcox, who immediately contacted me. David then played it to his friend, singer/songwriter Beth Nielsen Chapman. When Beth contacted me to say how much she enjoyed the CD, I mentioned that I had started this book and she put me in contact with her friend Lynn Franklin, a New York literary agent.

ACKNOWLEDGMENTS — page 352

With Lynn's guidance and that of her editor, Liz Bukac, I finished the first ninety pages, which Lynn, through her British affiliate, Mary Clemmey, sent to Brenda Kimber, editorial director at Transworld. Brenda fell in love with the material, and with her and Lynn's constant encouragement and guidance I finished the manuscript.

My heartfelt gratitude goes out to those above and also to the following, for their love and support: my dear friend and co-music-publisher, Guy Fletcher, who, thirty years ago, was the first to encourage me to write of my orphanage experiences, and whose keen ear helped shape my writing; Bill Whelan, composer of *Riverdance*, for his encouragement and advice; Pat Egan, for his friendship and his belief in the material. Here, with this US release, I must also extend sincere gratitude to my American editor, Julie Matysik, of Skyhorse Publishing, and my American literary agent, Liza Fleissig.

I'm also grateful to those whose support buoyed me throughout the process: Alan O'Duffy, Jim Lockhart and Derek Mooney of RTÉ Radio, Janis Ian, Ian Booth, Peggy Seeger, Danny Doyle, Colm Wilkinson, Cahir O'Doherty, Noel Pearson, P. J. Curtis, Brendan Nolan, Marla and Joel Adams, Jim and Beth Magill, Doug and Darcy Orr, John Ellis, Stephen Barefoot, Timmy and Susanna Abel, William Paul Young, and lastly the Ex-Laxers—you know who you are.

A special mention must go to my daughter, Irene, who along with Liz read the manuscript almost as many times as I. Huge thanks for some stellar structural advice from my friend and neighbor, psychiatrist-turned author Michael Hopping, who also alerted me to the Wounded Child Therapy Technique, the alchemy of which, totally unknown to me, I was spontaneously employing as I dealt with my painful experiences during the writing process.

A very special thank you must go to Tommy Bonner and his family. Tommy supplied many of the day-to-day details of life at the orphanage that I'd forgotten. His photographic memory of events,

half a century later, is equaled by his humorous accounts of things
that were crushing for him at the time.

All lyrics herein written by Danny Ellis and printed by kind
permission of Commercial Arts Ltd, Licensing & Administration: 10
Heathfield Terrace, Chiswick, London W4 4JE, tel. 0208 987 4150.

Danny Ellis was born in the heart of Dublin, where he lived with his mother and siblings. He was left at the now notorious orphanage, the Artane Industrial School, where he lived for eight years until the age of sixteen. As a member of the Artane Boys Band, he learned to read music and played the trombone. He now tours as a singer/songwriter and teaches voice and songwriting workshops. His acclaimed album, *800 Voices*, is available online at dannyellismusic.com. He lives in the mountains of Asheville, North Carolina, with his wife, Liz.